A Century of Change in the Cotswolds 1888–1998

A remarkable document which charts the changes that have taken place throughout the 20th century in three Cotswold villages and one town: Hatherop, Coln St Aldwyns, Quenington and Fairford. Reuben Sims's memoires encompass a period from 1888, when his grandfather moved from Bibury to Hatherop, until his death in 1998. It is a social history spanning over 100 years and a testament to a way of life that no longer exists, written with a deep affection for his Cotswold roots and the people who lived and worked in the communities around him.

Ana Bianchi Evans has written *The Way We Were – A History of Coln St Aldwyns*, published in 2010 and *The Village Cartoonist*, illustrated by Aldwyn Francis Woodcock, published in 2012. She is an artist and writer and has lived in Coln St Aldwyns since 1985.

Hatherop villagers celebrate the Coronation of Edward VII in 1902

A Century of Change in the Cotswolds 1888–1998

The Life and Times of Reuben Sims in Hatherop, Coln St Aldwyns, Quenington and Fairford

Compiled and edited by
Ana Bianchi Evans

This book is dedicated to my two grandchildren, Santi and Maggie, and to the memory of Reuben Sims.

"Hatherop Church was Reuben Sims,
Reuben Sims was Hatherop Church."

Lee Bayliss

First published 2015

Coln St Aldwyns Publishing
25–26 Hatherop Road
Coln St Aldwyns
GL7 5AB
info@colnstaldwyns.com

Typesetting by Bookcraft Ltd, Stroud
Printed by Henry Ling Ltd, Dorchester

ISBN 978-0-9566991-2-1

Reuben Sims in Fairford Silver Band Uniform 1955

Foreword

I first came across Reuben Sims's diaries when I was doing some local history research. I was handed twelve exercise books of carefully hand-written text. Reuben was church warden at Hatherop for 43 years and his memoires start in the 1950s listing the odd village event. However, he soon developed a taste for writing and by the 1960s he started to record the people and events of his day as well as delving back in time to the late 19th century when his grandfather came from Bibury to live at Hatherop and work as Foreman Carpenter for the Bazley's Hatherop Estate in 1888. I soon realised that this was a remarkable document – a social history spanning over 100 years and a testament to a way of life that no longer exists. My memory of Reuben is limited to his last years when he could often be found sitting under the horse chestnut tree opposite the Coln Stores with Tom Lemon, their two dogs sitting faithfully at their feet, shooting the breeze as old friends do. Reuben, born in 1923, was a Cotswold man through and through, a dedicated church man, a talented musician in the Fairford Silver Band and church organ player, a man who had a strong sense of community, a member of the Royal Antediluvian Order of Buffaloes (the Buffs) and he was very decidedly an opinionated man. He left school aged 14 years and worked, first for East Gloucestershire Engineering in Fairford, then for the RAF at Fairford Aerodrome. By the time he died in 1998, the way of life that he had known as a boy had changed irrevocably and those changes are charted here with a deep affection for his Cotswold roots and the people who lived and worked in the communities around him.

Ana Bianchi Evans

Acknowledgements

Top on my list of people to thank are my fellow members of the Coln St Aldwyns Heritage Society: Terry Davidson, Jo Perkins and Nick Stroude who have kept me going on what has turned out to be a Herculean task. This book would not be in existence if it were not for two very special members of the Fairford History Society, who lovingly transcribed five of the twelve diaries in their free time – Alison Hobson and Valerie Higgs – no mean feat. Thanks also go to Lee Bayliss who originally mentioned the diaries to me and who has encouraged and supported me throughout this project. Frazer Hart who took me up the Hatherop Church tower and patiently unscrewed several photographs so that I could copy them for the book. Photographic help came from Christine Morley, Frazer and Ros Hart, Sally Worsley, Lucy Abel Smith, Adrian Goodman, Cathy Bazley, Henry Bennett, Nick and Helen Owen, Sue Vicary and Paula Lander. Lee Bayliss, Christine Morley, Flo and Steve Tarrant, Philip Bullimore, Cecil Barrett and Bill Keene have helped to identify many of the faces in the photographs.

A Century of Change in the Cotswolds
Timeline 1888–1998

(1885 William Sims, Reuben's father, born in Bibury)
1888 Reuben's grandfather, Reuben Sims Snr, becomes Foreman Carpenter on the Hatherop Estate
1889 Sims family move to Hatherop
County Councils created
1894 Parish Councils created
1901 Queen Victoria dies
1902 Coronation of Edward VII
1910 Sims family move from Sharringtons to the School House, Hatherop
1912 The sinking of the Titanic
1914 World War I begins
1917 Russian Revolution
1918 Reuben Sims Snr dies

Reuben Sims Snr

WILTS AND GLOUCESTERSHIRE STANDARD, SATURDAY, OCTOBER 13, 1928

SIR THOMAS BAZLEY'S COMING-OF-AGE.

Photo: W. Dennis Moss, Cirencester.

THE HOUSE PARTY AT HATHEROP CASTLE.

Left to right, standing :—Mr. G. Ritchie, Miss Rachel Bazley, Major Arthur Talbot-Ponsonby, Miss Bazley, Mr. Anthony Bazley, Miss Elizabeth Morrison, Miss H. Cadogan, Miss Jean Grant, Lady Margaret Douglas-Hamilton, Mrs. Talbot-Ponsonby, Sir Thomas Bazley, Bart., Baron F. Recum, Mr. Assheton, Miss Alathea Talbot-Ponsonby, Master C. Cadogan, Miss Dulcia Assheton, Mr. Findlay, Miss Joan Cholmondeley. Left to right, seated :—Mr. Benson, Major Hughes, Mrs. John Thorpe, Lieut.-Commander Cadogan, R.N., Mrs. Cadogan, Lady Leach, Miss Frances Bazley, Hon. Peter Bernard.

Sir Thomas Bazley's Coming of Age 1928

1922 William Sims marries Kate Upshall and they move to Netherton
1923 Reuben Sims is born
1927 Sims family move from Netherton to No 45, The Lodge, Hatherop
Charles Lindbergh flies solo across the Atlantic
1928 Edith Sims is born
Penicillin is discovered
Sir Thomas Bazley comes of age
1936 The abdication of Edward VIII
1937 Reuben starts work at East Gloucestershire Engineering, Fairford
Coronation of George VI
1939 World War II begins
1942 William Sims dies
1945 VE Day
1946 Hatherop Castle is leased to Owlscroft School (Cambridge) and becomes Hatherop Castle Girls School
1950 Edith Sims dies

1951 Hatherop wins the Bledisloe Cup for the Best Kept Village in Gloucestershire
Colour TV introduced
George VI dies
1952 Reuben Sims is elected as Hatherop Church Warden
1953 Hatherop Bus Shelter is opened
Gardener's Question Time in Coln Village Hall
Edmund Hillary conquers Everest
Coronation of Queen Elizabeth II

Gardener's Question Time with Frank Engelmann 1953. Back row from left: Sid Jacques, Mr Wicksie, John Winfield, Mr Timbrell, Pam Norris, Mr Norris, Vera Jacques, Tom Ford, Charlie Burge, Fred Trinder, Frank Beale, Jack Collett. Frank Engelmann is 2nd from left sitting.

1961 Quenington Brethren Chapel opened on Quenington Green
1962 The Last Train from Fairford
1963 The Big Freeze
President John Kennedy is assassinated
1964 Canon John Lowe preaches his last sermon at Coln
Reverend Geoffrey Mowat becomes Vicar
Beatlemania in America
1965 Start of the modernisation of Hatherop
Start of the Vietnam War
1967 Modernisation of the Sims family home
Reuben's mother, Kate Sims, dies
First heart transplant in South Africa
1969 Apollo 11 first space flight to land men on the moon
Concorde lands at Fairford
1970 Barrow Elm Cottages fire
Coln Village Hall sold
Coln St Aldwyns School closes

Reuben leaves Gloucestershire Engineering to work for the RAF at Fairford Aerodrome

1971 Decimal currency is introduced
Hatherop Post Office closes

1972 Dutch Elm Disease strikes
Hatherop Castle Girls School buys Hatherop Castle from the Bazley family
National Miners' Strike

1973 Three-day working week introduced

1974 Miners' Strike ends
President Richard Nixon resigns after the Watergate scandal

1977 Silver Jubilee celebrations
Reverend Derek Cowmeadow becomes vicar

1978 Quenington School closes
Birth of the first test tube baby

1979 Victorian Fair at Coln St Aldwyns
Margaret Thatcher becomes Britain's first woman Prime Minister

1980 Godwin Pumps Fire
John Lennon is assassinated

1981 Prince Charles marries Lady Diana Spencer

1982 Falklands Invasion
Birth of Prince William

1986 Nuclear disaster at Chernobyl

1987 Reuben retires and moves to 17 Golden Row, Hatherop

1988 The New Inn at Coln closes and the fight to save it begins
Pan Am 103 is bombed over Lockerbie

1989 Hatherop Church clock goes automatic
The Berlin Wall falls

1990 New Inn at Coln reopens
Nelson Mandela freed
John Major becomes Prime Minister
Invasion of Kuwait by Iraq troops

1991 Operation Desert Storm and the liberation of Kuwait by Allied Troops

1993 Reverend Derek Cowmeadow retires
Canon Tony Ross becomes vicar

1994 Channel Tunnel opens

1996 Earl Grey Pub in Quenington closes

1997 Death of Sir Thomas Bazley
Tony Blair becomes Prime Minister
Diana, Princess of Wales is killed in a car crash in Paris

1998 Reuben Sims dies

The Life and Times of Reuben Sims 1923–1998

People's Church Warden, St Nicholas Church, Hatherop for 43 years.

1951 – Bledisloe Cup for the Best Kept Village in Gloucestershire is presented to Hatherop Parish Council by Earl Bathurst.

The Bledisloe Cup Presentation for the Best Kept Village in Gloucestershire by Earl Bathurst to Hatherop Parish Council 1951. Back: Robert Browning, Sonia Hurst, John Lander, Jack Sainsbury, George Mustow, Mervyn Bayliss. Front: Sorrel Taylor, two lady judges, Lady Carmen Bazley, Earl Bathurst, Sir Thomas Bazley.

1953 – The bells were rung at 10am till 10.30am on Coronation Morning June 8th. Afterwards the ringers saw the Crowning Ceremony of Her Majesty Elizabeth II on the television sets of J Sainsbury, Vicar's Warden, and J Lander, sides-man.

Opening of the Hatherop Bus Shelter 1953. From left: Countess St Aldwyn, Earl St Aldwyn, Mervyn Bayliss, George Mustow, Dulcie Hartshorn, Sir Thomas Bazley, Robert Osmond, Col Gibbs, Mr and Mrs Jack Sainsbury, Robert Browning.

1953 cont. – The new Bus Shelter was opened to celebrate the Coronation.

Mrs Sims [*Reuben's mother*] and Reuben Sims have memorial stone erected to the memory of William Sims and his daughter, Edith Mabel Sims [*Reuben Sims's father and sister*].

February 16th 1954 – Annual Meeting [*of the Parochial Parish Council*] – The Vicar [*Rev John Lowe*] reported as a matter of interest, that a Golden Eagle had visited fields near Dean Farm. He watched it for 20 minutes.

1955 – At the death of the Hon Mrs Corbett, the root of the sycamore tree was pulled out by the estate workmen and the ground levelled near the spot on the south side where her ashes were buried.

April 13th 1956 – A private dance was held at Hatherop Castle for the coming out party of Susan Bazley. The castle was flood-lit and cast a reflection on the church tower making the weather-cock look like gold.

December 25th 1956 – Hatherop Church Rectory sold at the King's Head Cirencester for £3,400 [*sold to Gilbert and Margaret Barratt who lived there until 1979. Now owned by Frazer and Ros Hart*].

March 12th 1956 – A large cedar tree cut down in Coln St Aldwyns church yard – had been there one hundred years but was dangerous to the tower and was hiding the clock face. The trunk was 36ft long and 4ft 6ins in diameter. Cut down for the value of the cedar wood by antique dealer from Lechlade.

June 16th 1957 – Joseph Mills, a farm worker and tractor driver for 47 years on Glebe Farm, died suddenly this morning. He was in the employ of Mr J Sainsbury, the Vicar's Warden. He had a medal at the Three Counties Show on Tuesday 11th June for working 47 years on one farm. A valued man in the parish.

Oct 6th 1957 – Harvest Festival – R Sims has Asian flu and cannot attend. Russia has launched a satellite by rocket which is circling the earth. Some people say they have seen the light of it at night. USA is going to do the same shortly.

October 31st 1958 – William Puffitt was buried in the church yard. He was the last stone mason and craftsman of the old Cotswold class in the parish. He was 79 years old. The entrance drive stonework of Hatherop Castle is a memorial of his works in former years. His father was head scaffolder on the restoration of the church in 1854–55. When the tower was rebuilt, he said the corner walls were strengthened with cartloads of old saw blades.

December 1959 – Mr Scutton addressed a gathering of Deanery members and told them that a considerable amount of money must be paid in 1961. Members were very quiet and asked very few questions. Perhaps most were stunned as all our parishes have little money to spare. Collections in church are very poor – approx 6 pence per head and we are told by the MPs "that we never had it so good".

May 14th 1960 – R Sims wrote to Col Gibbs and resigned from the office of People's Warden. This was before the Harvest Festival. Col Gibbs replied, also the Rev Lowe, to the effect that I should continue in office. But the church mower is now by order of the council left for anyone to use at any time and none of the men councillors will do anything for the good of the church without payment. They would sooner stop away from the church meetings in case they are asked to do any little matter. The People's Warden does not agree with this and also there is the lack of interest here in church affairs so it is best another Warden is elected next Easter.

April 1st 1961 – New Gospel Chapel Hall [*on Quenington Green*] opened at 3 o'clock. Approx 200 people present including Rev J R Lowe. Building was built by Mr G Jobbins and Son, ground given by Mr P Mustow's son-in-law, Mr Meade, who has built a house nearby.

October 30th 1961 – USSR explodes a bomb in Arctic region – more than fifty megatons in spite of very strong world opinion.

March 21st 1962 – Memorial Service held at Hatherop Church for Mrs Ruth Evelyn Cadogan (1877–1962) who died on 14th March at Quenington Old Rectory. [*Ruth Evelyn Howard married Gardner Sebastian Bazley and had five children before he died in 1911: Elizabeth, Frances, Thomas (later Sir Thomas Bazley 3rd Bt), Rachel and Anthony who married Anne Hotham (later Lady Howard of Dean Farm). Ruth subsequently married Francis Charles Cadogan in 1913. They had two children: Henriette and Christopher*] A church full of people and large bunches of cut flowers, which were laid in the chancel during the service, were placed on her grave in the north east portion of the Gardner Bazley memorial in the church yard. She was cremated. Rev J R Lowe officiated at the memorial service. Muffled peal rung at 7.30pm that evening by Jim Shepherd, George Mustow, R Sims and J Westhall (tenor).

Mrs Ruth Cadogan in a family group after Frances Bazley's wedding to Richard Hughes in 1932. From left: Unknown woman, Henriette Cadogan (blurred), Rachel Bazley, Anthony Bazley, Ruth Cadogan, Ailanore Talbot Ponsonby (nee Howard – sister of Ruth Cadogan), Mrs Johnson (hidden), Mr Sieveking, Thomas Bazley, Christopher Cadogan, Mrs Hughes (behind), Mrs Sieveking, Mr Johnson, Lord Esme Howard. Front: Mishka the Samoyed.

February 20th 1962 – American spaceman went into orbit round the earth at a speed of 17,500 miles an hour. There is great rejoicing in the free world.

The Last Train from Fairford

June 16th 1962 – The last train went out of Fairford Station at 8.25pm – a crowded station of onlookers and those having a last ride – some in mourning with black suits and black top hats. Station closed for lack of support now as people travel more in their own cars. Also government policy to cut down non-paying branch lines and not caring about ordinary people who want to travel to the Radcliffe Hospital etc.

January 1st 1963 – Heavy fall of snow fills the Hatherop Road. Only farm tractors get through with food stuff for cattle. All waiting for snow plough.

January 2nd 1963 – Roadmen of Gloucestershire County Council clearing drifts by Fairford Lodge. Mr Taylor at Homeleaze Farm cannot get milk transported so is milking cows and pouring it down the drains. A great loss to all concerned. Mr J Sainsbury sent a tractor and trailer with his milk to Latton Creamery which was done under very difficult conditions. Rag Hill blocked, also the Hatherop/Fairford Road. No supplies of groceries or papers or coal through to village yet. Mr J Sainsbury went with a land rover via the Red Lion Inn at Poulton to Fairford and brought back 60 loaves of bread from Mr Radway the baker for his customers here. Lee Bayliss and JR Winfield came round with bread and milk. Mr J Lander went with his milk in a land rover to Burford across two fields and a small stream. A good drive in such conditions from Home Farm.

January 3rd 1963 – Snow plough came through from Fairford – a 9ft blade on a caterpillar tractor from Payman Plant Hire followed by a land rover and several workmen with shovels and the local Doctor Shaw walking to visit his sick patients. Snow from the drifts is heaped up 5 feet or more in places. Tradesmen with provisions will be able to come round now but a milk churn with milk is still in Mr Rixon's post office. [*By this time the sub-post mistress was Mrs Barbara Patheyjohns*]

January 23rd 1963 – The freeze still goes on. This night the coldest for one hundred years – 32 degrees of frost at Cockrup Farm. Ploughs still moving snow. Road to Fairford single track. Drifts on side of road up to 5 feet of frozen snow. No water at East Glos Engineering Works at Fairford. All frozen – shortage of paraffin for heating stoves and lots of burst pipes.

Kate Sims in the snow 1963 – view from The Lodge to Hatherop

January 25th 1963 – Sun breaks through and thaw has started – what a treat to feel the sun. No heat has been turned on in the church so God knows how much damage has been done.

February 1st 1963 – All radiators burst with frost in church. Taken out by Jim Day – a tragedy that the water was not drained. All radiators dumped outside along the west walls.

March 3rd 1963 – Heard a black-bird sing this morning. Everyone is very relieved by the thaw – never in human memory has it been so bitterly cold for so long a period.

May 1st 1963 – The parson at Coln St Aldwyns, with voluntary labour, lifted all the tombstones in the churchyard at the rear and side of the church and had trenches dug across the churchyard and placed all the stones in same. A lot of them are very old and names worn off by the weather. This was done because no-one would cut the grass round these stones by hand because a power mower could not be used. Now the stones are in line. Before the 1939–45 war the churchyard was mown by hand with a scythe by Mr William Jones for 15 shillings per week.

May 12th 1963 – Earl St Aldwyn has started making the Williamstrip cricket pitch larger and putting up new railings and posts.

November 24th 1963 – Canon Lowe preached on the fine qualities of President Kennedy of USA who was shot and killed on 22nd November. The assassin of President Kennedy has been shot and killed by another American.

January 26th 1964 – Canon Lowe preached his last sermon at Coln St Aldwyns church.

Induction of the Rev Geoffrey Mowat. From left: Mr Sainsbury, Mr Broderick, Earl St Aldwyn, Bishop Forbes Horam, Arthur "Curly" Mills, Reuben Sims.

May 3rd – Induction of Rev Mowat at Coln St Aldwyns church. A full church, refreshments were served in the Coln Village Hall.

November 14th 1965 – Modernisation of the cottages in Hatherop are being carried out – No 33 seems to have been the first since the outcry in the Daily Express about the forgotten village.

TO TENANTS IN HATHEROP PARISH

(A Forgotten Village?)

YOU may have seen a "story" in the DAILY EXPRESS recently (1st February) about Hatherop, a "forgotten village." Let me say at once that if Hatherop ***is*** forgotten, so are many other villages in the Cotswolds (and I believe elsewhere too). The problem of modernising cottages is very general and quite difficult. But I decided not to correct the "Express" because I think most people know that you cannot believe half of what it says — as with most newspapers, as long as they can make up a good story the complete truth does not matter to them. I did briefly answer another story in the BRISTOL EVENING POST, and even this paper changed what I wrote, to make it look as if I was anxious to press on with modernisation as a result of a report by the Rural District Council at Cirencester, and the resulting publicity. Actually, this is not so. Before the reporters came to Hatherop in search of a story, I had already decided that improvements must be speeded up, somehow, in case we have more winters like the present one.

Very few tenants have actually ***asked*** for any modernisation, but in the bitter weather it is important, especially for older people and invalids, to have more comfortable living conditions. I therefore wrote to the R.D.C. in Cirencester on 22nd January last, asking if they could build some special houses (bungalow type) for old people. (The Council had suggested the usual two-storey houses but the rents would have been over £2 per week and so this would not have been of much use to Hatherop). I am glad to say that the Council has now agreed to build six old people's houses in or overlooking Hatherop Park, when planning permission can be obtained from the authorities. These could be lived in either by Old Age Pensioners, also widows, bachelors, spinsters, or by married couples with no children.

This proposal will be discussed further at a Parish Meeting which anyone living in Hatherop will be invited to attend, probably during the first half of March.

One of the difficulties has been to spare Estate staff to do the improvements. Ever since the War there has been a long list of needed repairs to cottages, farm buildings, walls and so on, but in the last few years we have been catching up with this and last Autumn, for the first time, we could say we were keeping up with the necessary repairs. But we still could not be sure of finding time to do more than one or perhaps two cottages each year. We have therefore decided to employ building contractors as well. This means having two cottages empty at the same time, as not many cottages can be modernised satisfactorily without moving the tenants somewhere else while the work is being done. So this building of "old people's bungalows" will be a great help to us. Also, we have satisfied ourselves that old age pensioners will be able to afford the rents.

We have one remaining difficulty and that is drainage. The old village drain, laid in 1907, was not intended for sewage and it is not likely that it could cope with sewage for the whole village without any trouble. We have for years been expecting main drainage to be laid by the Council (it should really have been done at the same time as the mains water, or before). We now hear that it is not due for another five years or more and we obviously cannot wait so long. So we will go ahead as best we can. But we must warn tenants, before baths and W.C.s are installed, that they may have to be asked not to use soapless washing powders. We, and many other owners of property, have found that these powders clog up any drainage system and make much more frequent emptying necessary.

We would also point out that none of the Hatherop cottages has been let at an economic rent for very many years, and when these are brought up to the required standard there must inevitably be an increase in rent for all tenants concerned.

If you have any questions about this scheme you could ask them at the Parish Council Meeting, to part of which, all Parishioners or tenants will be admitted.

Hatherop Estate Office,
22nd February, 1963

THOMAS S. BAZLEY

Hatherop Estate letter to tenants

1966 – An elm tree 8ft in diameter and 66 ft long was felled in Hatherop School near the Kissing Gate. It took two men, two days with chain saws to cut through the base of the tree.

March 29th 1967 – Mabel Kate Sims and her son Reuben William Sims move out of The Lodge No 45 Hatherop so that modernisation can take place. Mother very worried after being at Lodge for 40 years. Have arrived at the left-hand cottage belonging to Mr Mustow of Coln St Aldwyns who owns Court Farm behind the Earl Grey Public House. Mother has been brought here by the blacksmith, Mr Bartlett, in his van. Mrs Woodcock of Coln made the beds. Mother cried bitterly.

September 1967 – The Lodge was finished the first week of September. I have been to feed my fowls there every day on my Vespa scooter. Mother is not very well still. We both go to the Harvest Festival at Quenington church, beautifully decorated. We also go to the Chapel Supper at Quenington Institute.

October 15th 1967 – Mother not well – pain in chest but we go to the Chapel Harvest Festival with Mrs Jack Tarrant. Mum sings with a lovely sweet voice. I go to Doctor Stephens at Lechlade who comes out on Tuesday 17th October. Says Mum's heart is bad. I get a lot of tablets for her from the Fairford Chemist. Pay the rent of £1 5s per week to Mr Mustow for Mum on Wednesday 18th October.

October 19th 1967 – Give Mum her dinner. She passes away between half past one and half past three in the afternoon. I am fetched from work. Dr Veale of Fairford comes out and said she passed away without pain. Mother is buried at Hatherop church on October 25th by Parker, Slade and Smith. The cortege travelled to Barrow Elm turn and went past the Lodge. A great many friends came and we had Mum's favourite hymn "The Day Thou Gavest Lord is Ended". Our family graves will be levelled now. I have had 60 odd letters. The Rev Mowat officiated at the service. He was a great help to me.

November 17th 1967 – Loveday and Loveday move my furniture back to The Lodge, Hatherop. The Rayburn stove heats the rooms well. I have had it going for three days and nights. The bathroom and electric light is very nice – no more emptying the bucket lavatory. Old lavatory by the store house pulled down. My mother lived here for 40 years and was happy and proud of this house with only one cold tap and a brown shallow sink in the store house. How lovely it would have been to have brought Mum here again but the Lord decreed otherwise. I have signed the agreement for the tenancy which comes to me by law after my mother.

My grandfather Reuben Sims came to Hatherop from Bibury in 1888. He walked backwards and forwards for six months while the house in the centre of the village next to the school, standing on its own ground, was built. He was foreman carpenter. He died in 1918. My father William Sims was born at Bibury in 1885. He married my mother, Kate Upshall, in 1922. She came from Sturminster Newton, Dorset. My father was the

William Sims 1941

Kate Sims 1965

first to volunteer for service in the First World War and saw a lot of heavy trench warfare. He was wounded badly in the legs and right arm and suffered a lot after it. He started work on half a crown per week and had three pound per week when he died in February 1942.

My mother was left earning thirty shillings per week and my sister earned nothing as she was ill with Muscular Dystrophy and died aged 22yrs in February 1950. My mother had a widow's pension of 10 shillings per week for 15 years and paid a stamp of 3s up to 6s out of this for 9 years to qualify for her full retirement pension at sixty which she had for 9 years and which rose from £2 to £4 per week at her death. She had a very hard life but was very happy and contented although so little money to manage with.

January 2nd 1968 – R Sims played the Last Post at Harry Winstone's funeral at Fairford church. Harry Winstone was 87 years old and was a founder member of Fairford Band in 1903.

January 9th 1968 – Heavy fall of snow in night – 12 inches in churchyard. The pantry of The Lodge has been included in the kitchen now and is nice and warm with the Rayburn. Don't know whether Mum would have liked such a big room. New front room grate does not seem as hot as our old register cast iron grate with green tiles at side and lovely stone mantle shelf which was broken up.

January 13th 1968 – Thawing today. Turned out a lot of old letters belonging to my mother from airborne troops, who were stationed here in the park at the bottom of the garden in the 1939–45 war, thanking her for her kindness to them at different times. Made me sad again. From Mum's Autograph Book 1918:

What is love that all the world should talk about it?
What is love that neither you nor I could live without it?
Love is a tyrant and a slave, a torment and a treasure.
Having it you know no peace, lacking it no pleasure.
Would we shun it if we could? Ah! I almost doubt it.
I would rather fear the pain than live without it. RBR

Do not know the writer, perhaps a servant girl friend at Hatherop Castle.

March 7th 1968 – I think of my family all at rest today. My father was a good man who worked all his life on Hatherop Estate as a carpenter like all his family before him. From John Sims, born 1760 – died 1835, who made the oak bureau about the year 1800. My father died in the front room at Hatherop Lodge No 45. He was in bed downstairs for some while. It was very cold with snow on the ground then in 1942 when he passed over at 7 o'clock one morning on 2nd January. Mum looked after my father wonderfully well. My sister grew steadily worse with her kind of polio and we used to wheel her in a wheelchair to Fairford and round the Moors and Eastleach. She passed over in the front room also in bed by the rear window like my father only so peaceful on 20th February 1950. My mother cared for her most wonderful as she could not stand upright on her own but could just manage to feed herself. She was very fair with golden hair and laughing eyes.

Edie Sims 1945

I used to carry her upstairs to bed until it was too much for me and Mum. We used to come down to her in the night if she called. She was very intelligent and bore her affliction well. She used to go to Quenington Chapel, the old one on the Fairford Road corner until she could not manage it and I used to ride her there for a while on my cycle rear carrier. She like listening to the cricket on the wireless. If she were alive today of course we would have had television now the Lodge has electric light. I often think of my mother who was so jolly and bright and worked so very hard for us all. She took various little jobs of housework that became available to help out after my sister died. In the war for a time she went on the telephone exchange at Coln Post Office for Mrs Atkinson and came home at 6 o'clock in the morning. My mother was very honest and outspoken when anything was wrong. Some people in this village did not like her for that – they never knew what a struggle my mother had to keep going. Today the younger generation do not really know what hard times are with family allowances and government grants for children etc. The Labour government have done much for the ordinary people of this land. When I started work at Fairford at the East Glos Engineers in 1937, I rode to work on a push-bike which my father bought me from Bert Aston in Fairford for £5 2s 6d. It was a lot of money for my father to pay. Neither I, nor my friends, ever dreamed of owning a car, perhaps a second hand motorcycle. Today young lads of 18 buy second hand cars to drive to work and drive around at night and pay about £300 for them and think nothing of it.

April 8th 1968 – Jim Shepherd died in the council bungalows this morning. His wife and he moved from No 8 to the second bungalow going into Hatherop. He was sexton and bell captain for many years. He was a good man who did a lot for our parish church. He buried my father and my sister Edith. He could chime three bells well with foot and hand.

April 11th 1968 – Jim Shepherd buried today. About 50 people present. The British Legion brought the Standard and the Union Jack was on the coffin. Jim was 74 years old and he used to mow Hatherop churchyard with a scythe twice a year for about £12. He also wound the clock and stoked the coke boiler for about 30 years.

April 27th 1968 – Janet Shakespeare, my cornet partner in Fairford Silver Band, married Mr Peter Smith of Quenington in Fairford church.

June 2nd 1968 – Think of my mother, Kate Sims, today, how wonderful she was. She could make a shirt, dress a hare or rabbit or pluck and dress poultry, clean steel grates and fire fenders till they glittered. At one time, in domestic service, she told me she cleaned 14 steel grates before breakfast when short-handed and the Hunt Balls were in season.

January 11th 1969 – My birthday – I am 46 years old. I had a GEC television set installed on 12th December – rent and buy for 11s per week from Currys, Cirencester.

Christine Patheyjohn's wedding to Robert Morley. From left: Mr and Mrs Morley, Brian Morley, Robert Morley, Christine Patheyjohns, Mr and Mrs John "Pat" Patheyjohns, Sue Patheyjohns.

February 1st 1969 – Wedding of Christine Patheyjohns to Mr Bob Morley of Fairford.

March 2nd 1969 – Concorde maiden flight at Toulouse – flew for 25 mins. Good landing witnessed on television today.

March 13th 1969 – Mr J Sainbury retired as Vicar's Warden after 22 years service. I am sorry he has retired he was a good man who gave of his time and money for the good of our Parish Church. He always gave lovely sheaves of corn to our Harvest Festivals. His wife also repaired the pew kneelers and countless things for our church.

April 9th 1969 – Concorde airplane lands at Fairford from Filton.

May 21st 1969 – Mrs Westall, wife of the late Mr Westall – cowman at Glebe Farm – is buried by the chapel with her family. She lived in the old people's bungalows since coming out of Golden Row. A roadway for garages is being made in the centre of the village through gardens and path to Golden Row – a good mess. A well was found in front of Ernest Sharps house near the road and was filled in.

July 21st 1969 – Stayed up all night in kitchen at Lodge and watched the men land on the moon on my GEC television. It was good and marvellous – went to bed at 4.45am – looked out of the window facing Eastleach Road and it was broad daylight.

Earl St Aldwyn and Herbert May opening the clubhouse extension.

July 13th 1969 – New extension at Williamstrip Cricket ground opened by the Earl St Aldwyn. The club members did most of the work themselves.

September 6th 1969 – Sir Thomas Bazley gave all tenants a lunch at Hatherop Castle. His son came of age at 4 o'clock. The tenant farmers went in to tea also. The tenants gave his son, Sebastian, a wrist watch and the tenants from Eastleach, a silver-backed hairbrush. George Mustow presented the watch for the Hatherop tenants.

October 19th 1969 – I visit my aunt Beatie Humphries, my father's sister, and my aunt Minnie Sims, my father's brother's wife, often at Down Ampney. My aunt Beatie told me a tale about Sarah Griffin who was 92 years old when she died in 1904. My aunt used to read the bible to her. She told me how, when Parson Davies visited Sarah and gave her some money, Sarah said "I hope you have the highest seat in Heaven". Times were hard for the working class in those days. Social Security has altered all that. My aunt has two china dogs which were given to her by Sarah Griffin who was blind.

November 15th 1969 – ATV first night in colour. Mine is black and white.

Christmas Day 1969 – I have had the flu for three days, been very ill here, have seen no-one except Mr Roger Newman who brought my cockerel which I take out with me to the Iles family at Lechlade. He has taken it to Lechlade for me. I have done no shopping and drink Oxos. My firm have pushed 100 cigarettes through my letterbox and £5 10s which is my wages for the last few days. They did not knock or enquire how I am but such is the way of a capitalist world today. Everyone seems to be striving for this or that, mortgage on houses, cars, modern equipment, travel but cannot find the peace of God.

Boxing Day 1969 – Had a visit from my old workmate Bert Ayers of Poulton and Mrs George Mustow of Hatherop who brought my Christmas Fare, and Mr J Iles from Lechlade. Later I shall visit all of them. This Lodge is lovely and warm and an inside toilet is a great advantage. In the old days one had to go outside with an old coat on and a candle whatever the weather. Yes, this modern living is sheer heaven.

28th December 1969 – Heard this morning by letter that Rose Upshall, my Mum's eldest brother's wife, had died on 26th December 1969 and will be cremated like her husband Walter on 2nd January 1970. I loved Aunt Rose, we wrote nice letters to each other since my Mum passed over. She was 69 years. Walked to Coln St Aldwyns for shopping. Came back across the Grandage – saw the tennis courts which were all the go in the 50s. It is strange how these things flourish then fade away.

March 15th 1970 – Commander Cadogan died at the Old Rectory, Quenington.

March 21st 1970 – A muffled peal was rung with changes called by William Godwin. The church was full of people for Commander Cadogan's funeral. A brother of Mr Bennett played the organ. Rev Robert Hughes, son of author Richard Hughes and step-grandson of Commander Cadogan, preached a good sermon. Commander Cadogan was a fine naval officer who did everything first class. He was one of the old school who lived in the old days of power and supreme authority. He did much good on church and school committees, had great wit and was the employer of my father for some while. I remember when I was a boy, how he wore his naval uniform with cockade and sword when reading the lesson at the Armistice Service after the First World War. His ashes were interred in the Gardner Bazley grave this evening.

March 26th 1970 – My last day at East Glos Engineering Works as welder, fitter and blacksmith. I felt it greatly after 33 years starting in April 1937.

Shook hands with my employer John Arnold who wished me well at my new job at the Air Ministry at Fairford Drome.

March 29th Easter Sunday 1970 – Communion at Hatherop Church 8 o'clock. 14 people present. We have the new form of service 1967. I do not like it. A lot of the old fine prayers, the flower of the 1662 book, are missing. I will not change to this new version. I remember many times at the festivals, going with my mother across the park to the 7 o'clock services – how lovely the mornings and those lovely old prayers which took away my wicked ways.

May 3rd 1970 – The houses on Golden Row are still being modernised. An archway has been made through the centre to provide access to the rear. The garages are finished – rent 12s 6d per week. Young Mr Moulden and his wife are building a bungalow on the bank overlooking the river and in the distance Lea Field Farm at Quenington. A challenge for any man.

July 1970 – Coln St Aldwyns School closed this summer term for lack of young pupils. A good building where I went to school till I was 8 years old after the schools were changed for age groups. A great pity it is closed.

August 25th 1970 – Evening – the two cottages at Barrow Elm which have been empty two years, caught fire and the roofs are totally destroyed. Two good houses built in 1876. I believe sold recently.

October 19th 1970 – Three years ago today my mother passed over. Her memory and love is ever green with me.

October 31st 1970 – Have heard that Coln Village Hall has been sold by Earl St Aldwyn with the little church property house in front of it. The PCC have no say in the sale of church properties nor do they receive any money for the church out of same. The church cottage was very old and needed repair – it had one cold tap outside. A widow lived there [*Mrs Spreadborough*]. The rector would spend no money on the property. The widow moved out and now she lives in the old people's bungalows. I believe the garage, at the back of the house, which belonged to the church and where the rector kept his car, is also sold. Previous to that I believe it was stables. No figure for the house sale has been stated.

The Coln Village Hall was a barn, some say it was a tithe barn years ago. It had a very high ceiling with electric lights hanging down. Some high trestles formed a stage under the high window facing the church. The walls were panelled with boards stained brown approx 4ft high. Rope swings hung from the ceiling at the lower end for keep fit classes which were held before the war. The old joiner Mr Bert Cuss told me he laid the beech wood block floor in a herringbone fashion in the year 1920. A large coke burning stove was in the far left hand corner on entering the building. The entrance inside the barn porch was enclosed with two wood panel doors. The gent's toilet was on the left, outside of these doors, and the ladies toilet and powder room was reached by turning right inside the main doors and continuing to the far end past the stage and entering a door on the right hand wall corner. Before the 1939–45 war the stove was discontinued and classic radiators placed round the hall, heated by a boiler at the back of the hall approached by a door on the opposite side of the hall curtained off and a flight of stairs outside. The walls above the panelling were white-washed and around which were hung various stuffed animal heads of deer and buffalo, some shot by Lady Susan Hicks Beach I believe, on her tours to Africa about 1906 and some given by Mr Craven. The ceiling of board and rafters was high and took away the smoke and fumes when the hall was full of people. About eight pan shaped globes hung on wires from the ceiling and gave good electric light. Round the walls were long trestle stools for people to sit on for dancing nights and chairs were stacked in the lobby outside. In the hallway refreshments were served on trestle tables at half time at the dances. There was a large fish in a glass case over a curtained doorway opposite side to the hall entrance (must have been used to stoke boiler). Meetings of all kinds were held there – sports club dinners, socials and whist drives. Mrs Blackwell at the New Inn used to clean the hall.

Mrs Blackwell at the New Inn 1930.

The Coln Independent Co-op used to hold its Annual Meeting there and pay out the dividend money before the local Estates Rent Days. Before the 1939 War the dividend was half a crown in the pound. If you took in lodgers as my Mum used to do, you came away with £5. This was a big thing. During the war successive managers came and went. The dividend dropped to 3 pence in the pound and then nothing. Lots of people had not paid bills, never did. The reserve fund of £15,000 gone. The Bibury Branch paid its way but at a general meeting the Earl St Aldwyn said he would provide a private shop. As the lease from him was nearly run out except for two years, a sale was held and the shop closed down. Lots of stuff was dumped at Ready Token dump. A great business of coal round, bread, groceries, fish, meat – also a clothes department finished through bad management. The shareholders were paid out the full value of their shares at the end I believe.

At the Coronation of George VI in 1937, the stonework to the entrance to the Hall was improved. Also a party night was held there. But in those days of which I speak the villages were very much apart and on that party night food was brought from two villages, Hatherop and Coln. Quenington had their own at Godwins Works. To have the food and drink, villagers from the three villages were asked "were they from Hatherop or Coln". This state of affairs no longer exists thank God.

Previous to the party at the Hall for the Coronation of George VI, sports were held on the Williamstrip Cricket Pitch for all. The Rev Lowe flung a lot of rotten eggs in the air, I was one of the young lads who caught one and had the mess and smell over my grey suit. My Mum took part in the wheelbarrow and thread-the-needle race – great fun had by all. The Essex Regiment was stationed at Williamstrip House in 1941. The Home Guard was formed in 1940 and the sergeants used to train us on Sunday Mornings. Later, the Pioneer Corps were there at Williamstrip and a special unit at Hatherop Castle. The public were kept away from there. Machinery used to be blown up in the park quarry.

Dances were held twice and sometimes three times a week. Charge 1s 6d – the elite ones 2s 6d. The money was for the Red Cross or supposed to be. But who cared – the band or Mr Victor Cox's radiogram was on the stage. Mrs Gaiger had a band and her son played sax, she played the piano. Those who played in the band in the war years were Mr Charlie Gaiger on the piano, Ken Gaiger on the saxophone, Bert Cuss of Fairford on the trumpet, Billie Greyhurst the violin, Stanley McMarnest on the drums. What pleasure they gave to us all. The girls came from everywhere. Everyone was in uniform – even us who were civilians went in Home Guard uniform. The girl's dresses, by the way, were below the knee and not like the Sixties – hardly a skirt at all. The room was packed with people, a lot came in after the pubs were shut and crowded round the floor. The soap powder was sprinkled on the floor, we got plastered but danced the Palais-Glide, the Hokey-Cokey, the Quick Step, the St Bernard's Waltz and we all had a good time. The room hummed to the sound of the band and people. Sometimes there was a spot prize, a few cigarettes or something small, or a snowball dance. An interval was held and a few sandwiches and tea provided from somewhere although we were all on rations. They were all gay nights – you see there was no other entertainment around.

When the Americans came about 1943 most of the coloureds came to the dances and enjoyed dancing with the white girls. I expect a lot of those fine men were killed on D Day or after. We had some fancy dress dances and used to dance the old year out and the new in. In 1944 the Hall was decorated by the army with coloured parachutes hanging from the walls for a dance and Land Girls from the Manor were there as well. I danced a lot with Rose Day and Gwen Bailey in those days.

Dancing in the Village Hall c.1950. From left: Gilbert Burge, unknown lady, John 'Pat' Patheyjohns, Bill Cole, Harold Burge.

Another time, a tent was placed like a canopy over the entrance to the Hall to give more room and a few trestles to sit on at the sides of same. Plenty of beer about and at one time, the top end by the stage, saturated with it. The dances used to end and we all walked home – no transport then. Boy Oh Boy, what nights they were. One New Year night when the bells were first allowed to be rung at midnight, we all went outside during the dance to hear them ring. Yes, the old Hall saw some gay nights in those days.

When the pillars were put in after the war, round about the 1950 mark, a new floor put in half way up the walls and a flight of stairs was fixed to get to the floor above, with a new stage fixed at the other end of the Hall. The old heating was smashed with the frost in 1947 and it was heated first by paraffin stoves, then a coke stove downstairs and then electric heating. Good fitting doors were added and a kind of porch. Downstairs was a kitchen and a serving hatch for eating purposes, but it never caught on. Old people had a job to climb the stairs and the place was dark with the windows just half above the floor. It was low in head room and you danced in a smoky atmosphere. The stuffed heads were thrown out. No, the old atmosphere of the Hall had gone forever, nobody wanted it any more.

December 8th–15th 1970 – Electricity power cuts by power workers in support of a pay claim. Lots of people all with electricity and heating in a fix – great inconvenience. All the paraffin stoves in Fairford and Cirencester sold, also mantles for Aladdin lamps and every candle sold from the shops which were got in for Christmas. Rationed to 2 candles each – in London they were sold at £1 each. I sold Mum's double burner lamp for 30 shillings – regret it now. All the candles of Hatherop Church have been distributed to people. A lot went to light Hatherop Castle.

December 25th 1970 – The strike over – Miss K Brindle, our treasurer, had enough candles to fill the candlesticks for Midnight Communion on Christmas Eve. A very cold night but warm in church with 70 people for the service by the Rev Mowat. We sang carols with Mr Morris from Coneygar on the organ. Previously in the week, we went to the old people's bungalows at 6.30pm to sing carols; by car to Mrs Pelly's at the Little House; then to Dean Farm to Lady Howard, then to Williamstrip House and finished up at Mr Hart's house, Glebe Farm, Hatherop. We were quite bright as we had hot punch at Dean Farm and gin at Williamstrip House, lots of hot punch and hot dogs at Mr Hart's house – a great finish to a great night of singing carols.

February 8th 1971 – Mr Edgar Jack Sainsbury, who retired from the Glebe Farm to Homeleaze Farm, died today, he was 60 years old. He was Vicar's Warden of Hatherop Parish for 20 years and we have lost a good friend of the parish. I had some wonderful times with him when he was in office. His outstanding success was his sequestration of this parish after the departure of Canon Lowe.

February 15th 1971 – D Day for decimal currency. Miss Brindle our treasurer finds it rather strange with our accounts but I think it will be a lot better as time goes by when our old penny is withdrawn. To think that years ago my father used to give my sister a penny to go along the street to No 33, where Miss Smith lived with her mother and had the shop and post office, to spend on sweets. Half a penny would buy a sherbet or liquorice.

July 9th 1971 – I have bought a black Labrador dog from Mr Donald Browning, Hatherop. A big, fine dog – twelve months old. Gives me so much company and pleasure – will carry my papers and letters. The best welcome I have had home since dear Mum died, God bless her.

July 26th 1971 – Special Parish Council meeting in the School because of the Post Office being closed, at the old Reading Room that was, after Mrs Amer has given up. A well attended meeting of parishioners. Sir Thomas Bazley in chair. The council members afraid to speak. It was all decided before hand by the Post Office – that was quite clear. Three Post Office men there. Pensions to be got from Coln or Quenington. I fought hard, also Dr Moorhead of Hatherop School. She questioned the Post Office officials. But it will close. Our Parish Council is a poor 'yes man' bunch – we must replace them.

August 2nd 1971 – I have heard that Canon Lowe died today. A fine, tall man, 71 years old. The best man in this countryside with knowledge on birds and wildlife. He was vicar here for 30 years and could mix with all classes. He served these 3 parishes with never a holiday. The vicarage at Coln was full of birds, owls, pheasants etc. He was a real country parson. A man you could have a good row with yet soon forget it and bore no ill will.

Canon John Rashleigh Lowe.

September 7th 1971 – I take Scramble my dog for a run night and morning in Green Island as the park is full of cattle. This dog is the joy of my life. He bounds along at a good gallop and is a fine sight. I noticed this morning a new garage built in Coln Vicarage grounds. No-one has heard about this. It must have been out of the sale of the church cottage where Mrs Spreadborough lived.

October 9th 1971 – A thanksgiving service held at Coln Church at 3pm for Canon Lowe. All the notable locals were there. Mrs Lowe and her two sons and daughter-in-law were in the front pew near the pulpit. Earl St Aldwyn acted as usher, also Baden Powell. Mrs Langley from Quenington stood at the door with Earl St Aldwyn. Very few young people present.

October 21st 1971 – Met Lil Ford tonight who told me her mother had died. Mr Fred Ford was a great friend of my father. They were great shots in the old Williamstrip Rifle Club in the days before the 1914–18 war and often talked about their time in that war.

November 27th 1971 – Ted Hartshorn's daughter was married.

February 16th 1972 – The miners have been out on strike for 6 weeks. Power cuts have now taken place this week at different times. Miners want wages higher by £8. Tory government thought they could hold their wages down or break the strike like they did the Postman's strike. But the miners are very determined and power stations have about a fortnight of coal left. Paraffin lamps in Peyman's shop, Fairford are £16. All candles and heaters sold out. Great havoc in industry.

February 27th 1972 – Power cut from 6–9pm. I am writing by my Aladdin Lamp. Lots of people have thrown away their old oil lamps. Miners should start work tomorrow. Pickets have been withdrawn from the coal dumps. They have got rises of about £6 per week recommended by Lord Wilberforce who held a quick enquiry. Lots of trouble fighting with police at coal dumps. This strike has nearly brought the nation to a standstill. Luckily I had a ton of Welsh nuts last summer.

March 10th 1972 – I bought a Reliant three-wheel van in which I travel to Fairford Airbase each day. Have sold my scooter for £18. Wish I had bought this van before with all the wet rides I had to Fairford for years, especially the 1947 and 1963 winters, but I did not have the money in those days.

March 31st 1972 – My old mate Bob Hutchings called with his wife this evening in a good sports car. Reminded me of the old days when his father was keeper at Williamstrip and I went up the Williamstrip Road to their house every Sunday afternoon and we had a lovely tea.

Keeper and Mrs Hutchings.

April 1972 – There is some feeling by the new people living here to close two of our churches and use just one for the three parishes. The young people with families like the 10am service and the Norman church of Quenington is preferred. But R Sims would never agree to the closing of the fine Norman church at Coln or the Hatherop parish church where we have had such fine services and where he and his people before him served the church with all their strength of spirit and such material wealth as they could give.

June 14th 1972 – The three Parish Councils met in Hatherop School to discuss whether the Family Services at 10am should all be held at Quenington. Some talk about closing churches but complete denial of same. A lot of retired rich ladies from Quenington, very few council members from Coln, more men there from Hatherop. Meeting ended with no decision. Not enough working men and women on these councils and concern at lack of interest by young people.

September 1st 1972 – 5 large elm trees cut down in Hatherop Park – dried off with Elm Beetle – a great shame. More of them are affected. Some of them are 400 years old. Have found out that the Church Commissioners sold the Glebe Cottage by Coln Vicarage and the money was put to improve the Vicarage and what was left was placed in the benefice of

Coln Parish to increase the parson's stipend. What is so distressing is that the church authorities do not say how much money was acquired and I doubt if many people here know about the sale. A problem will arise because Coln School is closed and the school teacher is still in the school house. A sale may be made but only a copy of the deeds can be found.

October 22nd 1972 – 20 elm trees to be felled in Hatherop Park with Dutch Elm disease.

December 4th 1972 – Ernest Sharps died and was cremated at Cheltenham after a service on 9th December. He was 78 years old and the last of the old estate workmen who hauled the coal with horses from Fairford Station and later drove the estate lorry for some years. I look back on this year – Mr and Mrs Gaiger are dead at Quenington. They were a fine couple who always led the dances at Coln and were at all the great whist drives at Coln, Kempsford and Fairford. Mr Gaiger was a fine singer of comic songs and his wife played the piano. He was captain of the cricket club for many years when I played too. Those were the days of fine village life before the television came, now everyone stays indoors round the box.

Christmas Day 1972 – Go to Coln midnight communion. A good congregation – sing a lot of carols. Wish Mrs Woodcock a Happy Christmas at the old people's bungalows after the service and also Mrs Bartlett, the blacksmith's wife. Mr Hart visited me today. Brought me a lovely bottle of sherry, God bless him. Went to Lechlade for my Chistmas dinner with Mr John Iles and family as we have done for some years in my mother's time.

December 28th 1972 – Minnie Sims, my Uncle Jim's wife, died at Coney Hill Hospital. We bury her at Poulton Church on Tuesday 2nd January. She was a good woman, very devoted to my Uncle Jim, who was one of the finest wood workers in the west of England. I would say better than my father. She cleaned and polished everything and was a perfect wife to Jim.

January 2nd 1973 – We buried Aunt Minnie today. She was 82 years old – as you grow older your friends die away. The following generation do not know you. Ciss Adams, her sister's child, has had all the arrangements to do. I stay with her and her husband and rest of the family for tea. Some of the Sims furniture has come to me, also the warming pan that was used in my father's time.

February 6th 1973 – We bury Mr Percy Mustow today. He was the same age as my father – 88 years, born in 1885. He was a good farmer and a loyal supporter of Quenington Chapel. There were a lot of people present and we sung two hymns. He was taken to Coln burial ground.

April 4th 1973 – The old elm trees are still being sawn down, the trunks taken away and the rest burnt. A great shame to see these fine trees 6 feet in diameter at the base disappear.

April 14th 1973 – Mrs Flo Stephens, nee Griffin, was found dead in her house, the first in Pudding Row, this morning by Mr Hartshorn delivering the papers. She did not look well the night before as I visited her every Friday night for over 6 years with our eggs. She was 71 years old and had suffered a lot with her legs and had shingles this last 6 months. Her husband, Ernest Stephens, is at a hospital in Gloucester to give her a rest for a while. Her father, Ted Griffin, was a great church goer, choir-man and bell ringer when I was a boy. The Griffins have been in that house for 300 years I have been told.

July 19th 1973 – Jesse Blackwell died and is buried behind the old Coln Laundry in the new ground. He was one of the last of the old time butlers and was at all the big engagement parties etc. He worked at Hatherop Castle and Williamstrip House when my mother was in service there. A slight man, very quick, very smart and a witty laugh. Also very generous. He did endless meals for the St Aldwyn family.

Jesse Blackwell (sitting left) with George Winfield and Countess St Aldwyn.

September 30th 1973 – Went to the Quenington Harvest Festival in my Reliant three-wheel van. The Rev Keble took the service and preached about people having better houses and more wealth than any previous century had given but they were forgetting the Almighty which is so very true. The many times my mother and I have walked to Quenington Church, others also. None had much money but the church was packed with people and all sung well.

October 25th 1973 – Mr Charles Mustow, brother of Percy, has been dead and buried now about three weeks.

He was a fine man, 92 years old, tall and quiet spoken. He devoted his life to Quenington Chapel. In his teens he was a bell ringer at Coln Church but, like his brother Percy, found his inspiration in Quenington Chapel. I helped carry his son, David who went to school with me and had TB, to rest in the fifties.

The Mustow family – From left: Charles, Dons, Norman, Emily (nee Smith), Diane, Jess, Psyche wife of Clem.

Mr Harold Godwin was cremated after a service at Quenington Chapel today. He was the employer of the Godwin Pumps manufacturers. A tall, powerfully built man who made a fortune in business and kept a lot of local men employed in regular work.

Harold Godwin.

December 25th 1973 – Midnight communion at Hatherop Church was a glorious occasion owing to the fuel crisis – only two lights were used in the chapel. All the candlesticks were used and created a fine scene with the glow of the oak pews and 80 people singing carols. The organ played beautifully by Mr Morris of Coneygars. The majesty, wonder and joy of public worship were fulfilled.

March 11th 1974 – Miners go back to work today. Electricity was on later at 10.30pm for the election which was brought about by the miners who could not agree with Mr Heath's wage offer. The whole country would soon have been brought to a halt. The new minority Labour Government has given in to the miners – they have got nearly all they asked for.

March 23rd 1974 – Castle School and some local singers are singing parts of Handel's Messiah in Hatherop Church at 6pm. I do not approve of the unscrewing of the old candle holders on the parson's desks and planks and staging across same for the singers. This is a favourite practise of Hatherop Castle School. The Rev Mowat leans over backwards to suit them but forgets the village people who have not much time for him. We have a dull lot of clergy in the East Cotswolds except the Rev Keble who is always round his church and parish of Fairford. That's a good man, but on reflection, they all have good qualities.

April 6th 1974 – Sally Mowat is married at Coln Church – a fine bride in white as she came out from the vicarage and was married by her father. We rang the bells well, afterwards a reception at Hatherop Castle. We all drank enough champagne and came home at 4 o'clock. I noticed the lovely stained glass window had been taken out of the church end of the old school and new windows being put in the front side to make it into a dwelling house. I was not pleased to see this done to the old school which I went to until I was 7 years old. Now in the Standard, part of the school is offered for sale freehold for £7,500.

May 22nd 1974 – Ewart Lander is buried in Hatherop churchyard – a lot of people present. He was 75 years old – a tall man, a good farmer and a good singer.

Ewart and John Lander delivering milk.

June 29th 1974 – A good PCC at Farmer Hart's Glebe Farm. Coffee and sherry afterwards. R Sims told them it was time a Sunday School was started – there has not been one for about 30 years.

October 13th 1974 – Yesterday helped carry Mr Holloway to his grave. A good cattleman in Mr Sainsbury's time. Hatherop Sunday School was started in September in Hatherop School on Sunday mornings.

April 2nd 1975 – The Sunday School which I asked the Rev Mowat to start has 25 young children who have scripture in the Church of England day school run with two parents, Mrs Gibbs and Mrs R King. Hope it will prosper.

May 10th 1975 – The young school master and his wife and spastic child have left the school house to live in Cirencester and travel to and fro. Our school managers cannot find a good Church of England school master to support this school and church. What a difference with Mr P Garner, our school old school master – a very fine man indeed. The school masters today only want money.

May 14th 1975 – Harry Herbert was cremated today after a service in Coln Church. A good man, a great trade unionist who did much for his fellow workers at Godwin's Works in the old days when wages were very low and the work hard. A large congregation and good singing of the hymns. He was carried by the local cricketers.

June 6th 1975 – A memorial service held at Quenington for Mr William Cole. Church full of people – we shall all miss Bill, a short, round-faced man who loved a good joke and was good at accounts. He played the organ superbly well – a pillar of our church.

June 7th 1975 – Wedding of Jane Lander [*to Leslie Musty*] of Netherton Home Farm. We rung the bells with Mr George Mustow. A very pretty wedding. Photos were taken by the de Mauley doorway.

January 3rd 1976 – A great gale which raged last night blew some trees down – one mighty cedar tree at Macaroni Farm at the front of the farm house. The transformer in the field, The Piece, was hit by a tree and all the lights in the village were put out. Out came my paraffin lamp. Those with deep freeze units were worried about produce but the current came on again on Sunday. This storm did great damage to many trees around this area. It was best to stay indoors, it was the worst storm I have known. It blew off the cross on chancel end of the church, blew down an evergreen oak in Hatherop Castle grounds and brought down about eighteen feet of the west wall of the churchyard.

Charles and Annie Barnett.

May 3rd 1976 – Mrs Annie Barnett, a great friend of my family was cremated and her ashes buried in her husband's grave, Mr Charles Barnett.

She had left Hatherop to live with her sister at Chippenham for the past six years. What wonderful times my family enjoyed with them through the years from my boyhood onwards. I shall never forget. They were both good people and real Church members. The trees in the Park are still being felled and burnt having the Dutch Elm disease.

June 14th 1976 – Service to bury ashes of Mrs N Rixon, a good congregation wife of Charles Rixon (Bubbles). Service for George Chater in Quenington Church, he is buried in the cemetery on 22nd June. He was 95 years old, crippled with a leg injury. For years he used to live opposite the church lychgate with his wife, then moved to the top of Snake Drive, Quenington and has lived away for the last 10 years or so in a home for aged persons. He used to be secretary for the local pig club when we had a row of potatoes planted for us in the local farmer's fields.

Saturday 26th June 1976 – The Elm Disease is attacking the three elm trees at the bottom of my garden – they are about 2' 6" in diameter and there seems no end to this disease. The children of the future will never know what it was like to see a giant tree 6' in diameter spreading out its branches giving beauty and majesty to the landscape and towering up sixty feet or so.

Tuesday 29th June 1976 – Had three teeth out today with Mr Ashton of Fairford – my cornet playing days are now over as I am having a full set of false teeth. But what fun I have had playing that cornet for Fairford Town Band.

Fairford Silver Band 1957 – Reuben Sims centre with cornet.

Monday 12th July 1976 – Mrs Harry Maunders visited me at 5.30pm and told me the sad news that Miss Kathleen Brindle "Bridget" had passed away at lunch time at Newquay Hospital. I'm very sad, as she was such a wonderful worker and treasurer for Hatherop Church. She was a good school teacher of the old style, kept order and was respected, did wonderful work for the girl guides, seen to all monies, gave generously to Hatherop Church, seen to all the missionary boxes, bought and put up all the candles and Christmas lights on the Christmas Tree by the war memorial, cleaned the church, ran the Fete Draw, sold more tickets than anyone else, decorated the church with flowers, loved all nature, a good singer in the choir all her life, a fast walker and did all the jobs at Hatherop Church no one else would do. God Bless Her. Decided her grave shall be by her Mum and Dad, who were also good church people.

Kath Brindle.

Friday 16th July 1976 – I have taken a day of my holidays and am getting ready for Bridget's funeral – am giving flowers from my garden, she loved flowers. Funeral at 2.30pm. Picked up by Mr Sly in car, to castle entrance, take flowers up the stairs to church, people were arriving and taking seats. Church decorated well. Run out of burial service books, nearly all the seats taken up. Miss Jackson played the organ. Two hymns "Abide With Me" and "For the Beauty of the Earth". The ringers under Mr George Mustow rung a muffled peal. I went up and gave a hand with a ring round. Thanked the Rev Mowat for his service, came home, a busy day but did my best for Bridget Brindle.

August 7th 1976 – All this week hauliers from Crewe have been sawing down more elm trees, burning up the branches in fires as big as a cottage and taking away the trunks on low loaders – a tragic and pathetic sight. Charles Barnett told me his father and others used to rest under the trees for shade in the last century during the heat of the day when they mowed it with scythes and continue work when it cooled in the evening.

August 24th 1976 – Everything is hot and dry – a great danger from fires. But farmers still light their stubble. You really can never tell a farmer anything. The Labour Governments have really put them on feather beds. Bless 'em. Have just bought a second hand colour television to sooth my sorrows.

Sunday 12th September 1976 – The Rev Mowat announced at Evensong at Hatherop Church that he would be taking up a post in Malaya for two years to answer a call from our Bishop John for a priest. This is quite a shock to us.

Sept 30th 1976 – The elm tree on the village green has been sawn down and taken away. There will be no elms left in this part of the Cotswolds.

Oct 21st 1976 – 6.30pm – Went to Coln Vicarage for a combined meeting of the Church Wardens and Treasurers of the three parishes to meet our new Bishop John Yates from Yorkshire. After a talk to us all about our Rector taking up a new living in Malaya he said we shall be having another Rector but could not promise the Angel Gabriel. We had sherry and a fork supper very nice. Bishop John Yates is average build with black hair, young looking, aged 44 years. He should do well here in Gloucestershire. Our clergy are better than they used to be years ago, not to say they were not good men in our father's day but a lot of the old class position situation has disappeared. It is good we meet on more friendly and informal terms.

Nov 5th 1976 – We buried Miss Day of Dean Farm – an old lady of 93 years. The Day family have been at Dean Farm for many years. She is survived by two brothers, having come home to look after her aged parents before the Second World War.

Nov 8th 1976 – Miss Alice Griffin was buried at the east end of the churchyard. She was 87 years old. She is buried where she wished to be by her parents and sisters. Her mother did washing and so did Alice who was a gay talker and I loved to talk to her. Her brother Ted was a choirman and bell ringer when I was a boy and used to say "I hope you boys will sing like sky-larks this morning".

Dec 4th 1976 – At eleven o'clock I drove to Manor Farm House, Coln St Aldwyn to Mrs Brazier who held a introductory meeting of a clergyman for the parishes after the Rev Mowat leaves at Christmas for Malaya. This clergyman was a cleric at Cambridge University and writes books. Whether he will get the post here I don't know. But he has a wife who has been a nurse and she seemed to go down well with Mrs Brazier and the ladies present including Lady Howard of Dean Farm.

Sunday 19th Dec 1976 – A combined service of carols at 6 o'clock at Quenington Church. After the Service, Earl St Aldwyn led the churchwardens of all three parishes to the chancel where we stood and the Earl gave an address on the service of the Rev Mowat to the parishes. Then he walked to the Vicar's desk and presented to the Rev Mowat, who stood there with his wife, a cheque for £339 which had been collected as a going away present from the parishioners. The Rev Mowat was very pleased and suitably replied, catching hold of his wife's arm to comfort her at this moment. I gave him a little travelling clock I had bought from Mr Powell's shop at Fairford and told him to place it in his vestry in Malaya.

Christmas Day 25th December 1976 – 2am – I write this after walking home from church where we had our Midnight Communion by candle light. This was the last service taken by the Rev Geoffrey Mowat. There were one hundred and four people present. He shook me by the hand and thanked me in the vestry for my help during his twelve years with us and I wished him well in his new post in Malaya. He is a good man.

Saturday 1st January 1977 – I have entered the Hatherop Church tower in the Gloucester and Bristol area competition for the best kept tower.

Tuesday 11th Jan 1977 – We bury Mrs Alice Sharps, wife of Ernest Sharps the estate lorry driver. Mrs Sharps was a good supporter of Chapel and Church. After the service I helped carry her coffin shoulder high to the Church entrance gates in the street where she was taken by hearse to be cremated at Cheltenham.

Friday 14th Jan 1977 – Mr Akers came to see me to say his mother, Mrs Annie Akers, had died and would I see about the grave. Mr Murray the Reverend from Ablington officiated at the burial service of Anne Akers on Wednesday, Jan 19th at 2 o'clock. There were a lot of people there. Annie was a large lady like her mother – jolly and loved her family. She had a lot of chest trouble but bore her troubles well. I remember her father Harry Sharps when I was a boy who used to play the accordion at night at the back of the cottage where they lived in the centre of the village where there used to be three cottages, now two, in front of Golden Row. At 3 o'clock I stood with Mr and Mrs George Mustow and Mr and Mrs George Twining at the burial of Mrs Alice Sharp's ashes near her husband's grave. Yes, our Cotswold people, brought up before the Welfare State, with their independence and thrift are slowly crossing to the other side. I trust the trumpets sound for all of them.

Sunday 23rd Jan 1977 – I go to Evensong at Coln St Aldwyns church. After the service I went to Mrs Woodcock's home in the old peoples bungalows. She likes me to talk to her after Evensong. She is 84 years old. She nursed me when I was a fortnight old. She told me that the front door of the old Manor House at Coln was the doorway to the dairy when John Barton lived there and the door was a wire netting one. The first Earl St Aldwyn had the house renovated and it was well kept when my mother worked there as a housemaid. Of course it was a very strict Victorian atmosphere then and quite a lot of class distinction. The curtsy went out with the 1914 war.

February 6th 1977 – Mr Harold Wheeler and his wife told me today they were leaving the School House where they have lived for some years and are going to live at Siddington. The Wheeler family were in this Lodge when it was built and used to stay up at night to open the gate for the coach from the last train at Fairford and of course no washing must be shown on Wash Days.

February 13th 1977 – I journey to the Church for Communion at 8am. My labrador dog sits in the chancel while I pull the bell. Mr Murray from Ablington prepares for the service. The clock strikes eight o'clock – no one came. I apologise to the Rev Murray and go to Glebe Farm, ring the bell, Farmer Hart came to the door in his dressing gown. I wish him good morning and give him a good rocket on no-one at the church for prayer to Almighty God. Told him I'll finish with the work of warden. The castle school find it inconvenient to come to our Evensong at 6 o'clock on Sundays and want a Parson for their own service of Morning Prayer. Everyone has to bend the knee to Hatherop Girl's School. But I'm not doing it. I have given all my efforts for the good of the Parish of Hatherop. They must fit into that pattern. I am not pleased this morning.

Feb 17th 1977 – Visit Dr Moorhead in the evening at Hatherop Girl's School to find out about the Castle Girls' services. She was very nice and charming. Said she would hold the services without heat as they had already paid £30 for the heat at Christmas. Of course I melted before such charm and told her she could have the heat and the church would stand the cost. She explained it interfered with the running of the school to come to Evensong. Of course Reuben sympathised. I came away in a good frame of mind.

Sunday 24th April 1977 – Am going with Mrs Bartlett, the blacksmith's wife, to Princess Margaret Hospital at Swindon to see my Aunt Beatie Humphries who will be moved tomorrow to Cony Hill, Gloucester old people's home. She has been at Swindon after a fall since Christmas.

Friday 29th April 1977 – Drove to Williamstrip House at 12 noon to meet a prospective parson from Cowley, Oxford. He seemed sincere, a little old, wife rather precise and formal – may have to interview more.

May 28th 1977 – At 3 o'clock a Confirmation Service was held at Hatherop Church. 12 girls were confirmed by the Bishop of Tewkesbury. Juliet and Katy Van Oss were among the fourteen girls confirmed. I remember drawing the water for their baptism in the font jug from the kitchen taps at Hatherop Castle on a fine sunny day such as it is today.

Monday Evening 6th June 1977 – A large bonfire was lit in Painter's Field, Quenington, to celebrate the Silver Jubilee of our Queen Elizabeth II. The Brownies and Guides sang songs to a guitar. About 500 people there. Reuben Sims got out his flags and trimmings from her Majesty's Coronation and also flags from the Coronation of George VI and put up a picture of the Queen on the front wall of the Lodge facing the road. Plastic carrier bags had to be bought which had on them the Union Flag on both sides as flags could not be bought at any price. Then they were glued on strings and hung up. I wrote on a silver covered piece of wood "God Bless Her". How my mother would have revelled in this kind of thing. She won the Pound for the best decorated house at the Coronation 25 years ago.

Tuesday 7th June 1977 – We rung the bells at 1.30pm then went to Hatherop Castle where the fancy dress parades, comic football tug of war, side shows etc all got under way. John Winfield, Jim Day and Baden Powell were the chief organisers. Plenty of teas were available in the school rooms. At the Fete it was announced that Reuben Sims had won £5 for the best decorated house in the three villages. There were some good entries: Mrs Sue Mackenzie at the top of the hill; Mrs Robert Morley at Golden Row; the Worsleys at the Firs by Pudding Lane; also Mrs Don [*Freda*] Collett at Quenington by the cemetery and John Winfield, bottom Lodge at Coln. Mrs Sorrel Taylor, of No 1 The Piece, had the prize for the senior citizen's best decorated window. At night a dance with fancy dress was held in the Castle school room by the old garages and stables. A very large crowd danced till 1am. There was a fancy dress parade and Reuben Sims, dressed up as a Jubilee painter, had second prize – a crown. A great night with a disco-band thumping out the tune and a bar where beer flowed freely. One free pint on entry. Gosh, were we all tired but very happy – it was a fine Jubilee.

Jubilee Dance at Hatherop Castle. 'Painter' - Reuben Sims 2nd place; 'Posh Lady' – Baden Powell; 'Old Man' was the winner of the competition.

Tuesday 28th June 1977 – Held Church Wardens meeting at Glebe Farm, Hatherop. Farmer Hart and Reuben Sims; Brigadeer Shepherd, Quenington; Mrs Langley, Quenington; Baden Powell, Coln; Earl St Aldwyn, away as usual. His class are nice to have around when certain things are done or discussed, but to depend on them for regular active church work, I'm afraid they have a race to go to, a shoot or holiday. Still the

Lord moves in a mysterious way. Should have been an hour's meeting – lasted from 7pm till 10pm. Had a job to decide where to have induction, Quenington wanted it there, I had a heated argument with them that it should be Coln as the Vicarage is there. Mrs Langley and Reuben Sims where quite heated with one another. Reuben Sims was the only person there that was born and bred here. It was decided Quenington Church would be too small and for eats afterwards could be the School or Institute. Coln – well the Church will take all but the School is sold to Mr Powell. The Earl sold off the Village Hall which is filled with junk and lies idle. Hatherop has the Castle School class rooms and the village school. The village workmen's club was not mentioned – they are having more extensions and block work, toilets and it is always in use. There is always money for booze. Mrs Langley said people do not like the large pillars in Hatherop Church because they cannot see what goes on. At Quenington they have a lot of wealthy people who run the church there just for themselves. They sit tight. I would have liked to have extended the hand of friendship to the Chapel near the Green and perhaps have used it for eats after the service but for Mrs Langley this was quite out of the question. We are very narrow still in our church life and the Chapel people are very devoted – they will not be drowned by my stuffy Church of England ways. In the end if Coln cannot find a place for eats afterwards we will have the induction at Hatherop and the meeting favoured the Castle School class rooms for eats. I would have preferred the village school.

July 6th 1977 – We have been examined by the Association Panel of Judges for the best kept tower competition in the Gloucester & Bristol Diocese. I am told by Mr William Godwin we have reached the finals and our tower will be judged again by another panel of judges. Every night I go across the park and visit the tower – one hour's work a night is enough then one does not get tired. One gets used to crawling under the bells and sweeping up the dust with a dust pan and brush. We have £200 in the bell-fund, so with the agreement of Mr George Mustow, our Captain, I have got Mr Barnes of Fairford to put an extra light on the cross beam in the bell tower and a chandelier of three lights in the ringing chamber and alter the hanging bulb in front of the clock to a fixed position on boards by steps in clock room. Mr M Bayliss has made up the worn step leading into ringing chamber. Of course in our fathers' and grandfathers' time, men went up our tower with their hob nail boots and perhaps gaiters. There were very few soft bottom shoes with work folk.

Sept 9th 1977 – 7.30pm at Coln Church – a full church witnessed the appointment of Rev Derek Cowmeadow to this United Benefice of CHQ. The clergy robed in the Vicarage, the Church Wardens prepared for the procession in Mr Powell's rooms which were part of our lovely old Church School. The clergy and church-wardens, in front of the Bishop of Gloucester, walked up the church path and into the church by the main door. The Bishop gave the address on the qualities and duties of the Parish Priest. After the hymn had been sung, the bell under the tower pulled and the blessing, we all went out and had refreshment in the Manor close by through the church door in the churchyard wall. The Manor has been bought by a business firm who have spent a lot of money repairing it as it had fallen into very bad disrepair. The rooms were crowded with people. Earl St Aldwyn spoke at the end of the room and said how his grandmother had lived there and how new people had come into our villages to live with us Cotswold folk and were helping in all kind of ways to run local events etc. All the cars were parked in the field next to the Manor – some difference to our people's time when they all walked or rode cycles to these events.

October 9th 1977 – Aunt Beatie is now settled in Paternoster House, Cirencester – her memory is not as good as it used to be but at 87 years? Go to Harvest Thanksgiving at Quenington Church at 6 o'clock – the first Harvest Festival taken by our new parson, the Rev Derek Cowmeadow. I remember the times my dear mother and me walked to the service at Quenington Harvest and raced back home before it got dark as my sister sat alone in the front room. What a blight on my sister's life that polio was and she bore it so well.

October 12th 1977 – A Hatherop PCC meeting was held at the house of Mr and Mrs Voaden in Hatherop. A lovely old Cotswold house with large rooms, it faces the Park gates. The Rev Cowmeadow was in the chair and the meeting made history as far as I was concerned as Lord Teynham [*Hatherop Estate land agent*] and Lady Howard were there. I have never known a meeting in an ordinary man's house before where the members of the establishment have been present. A very lively meeting – they always are at Hatherop. It started at 7.30pm and finished at 10pm. Tried to push Lord Teynham's car as the battery was flat but no start, so he had to leave it in the Park gateway that night.

Sunday 18th Dec 1977 – At 6pm a concert by Fairford Silver Band in the chancel of Coln St Aldwyn Church. A full church of people. Earl St Aldwyn, his wife and son with his lady friend where there in the family pew. They came in late – a bad example for a church-warden. But the St Aldwyn family are taking more interest in their local church affairs and this is a good thing.

Jan 8th 1978 – Sunday Evensong at Coln Church 6pm. Plough Sunday – the first time in living memory a service of this sort has been held in the parishes. An old horse plough was placed in the chancel, painted blue and black front wheels. The two church wardens, Earl St Aldwyn and Baden Powell, with their staves standing by the side of the plough and the Cockrup Farm Manager holding the plough handles for the Rev Cowmeadow, to bless the plough. It was a wonderful sight and a new experience for us all.

Sunday 29th Jan 1978 – The Sunday School that we started three years ago at Hatherop School has closed because of lack of support from pupils. We started with twenty-two young children but gradually the support has dwindled down to about four pupils. Mrs Roger King and Mrs Gibbs have done well to keep it going but unless you have support from the parents in church work you cannot expect the children to follow on. There is plenty of money spent on children today. The Sunday School did not lack teacher talent or help when needed. I gave two religious books as prizes last Christmas. The Sunday School will open again next week at Hatherop Castle Girl's School so perhaps it will revive again.

Sunday 19th Feb 1978 – Stack a load of logs in shed for Miss Judith Stride-Darnley who lives in a house in Coln Street.

Thursday 2nd March 1978 – Mr Bert Cuss the joiner at Quenington died today. He was 90 years old last Feb 13th. A man of very great skill with wood and was one of the finest craftsmen of our time. He did a lot of repair work voluntarily for Quenington Church, particularly in the time of Mrs Money who did so much for Quenington Church and churchyard.

Bert Cuss (on left).

He gave of his skill and time to repair the two roll top tombs on the south side of Quenington Church free of charge when Swinford of Filkins had the job to repair them when it was found out that they were very fine tombs. He loved making stairs and he also did a great deal for Mr Harold Godwin the pump maker. He had a fine singing voice and loved the old hymns and psalms.

Sunday 5th March 1978 – Drove to Cirencester in the afternoon to see my Aunt Beatie. She remembers her grandmother who my grandfather brought to Hatherop from Arlington when he moved in 1889. How she lived upstairs. My father William was her favourite, she gave him sweets and once came down the stairs and stopped my grandfather spanking my father when he was a boy. She said my father was a real Sims. She, my grandmother, did not show the same affection for Aunt Beatie, Aunt Nellie and my Uncle Jim. My grandfather had her buried with her husband under the yew trees on the north side of Bibury Church.

Monday 6th March 1978 – 2pm – went to the funeral at Quenington Church of Bert Cuss, the 90 year old joiner. What a clever man he was, he fixed the oak draught stopping on the outside of the vestry door in the time of Mrs Money. When she called a London firm in to price the work and they wanted £70. Bert done it for love. Yes, those old Victorians we are fast losing were grand independent people. No welfare state for them to fall back on. It comes to my mind other work Bert Cuss did. A set of stairs in Japanese Oak made and fixed in Bob Soule's house at Southrop. These stairs were made in the garden at the back of Yew Tree Cottage. The lecturn in Quenington Church was lowered making it so much better to read from. Yes we shall miss this old joiner who till about twelve months ago, could be seen out with his terrier dog, a man of average height and build, wearing a cap. He had a bald head, always his white apron, top quality breeches, long brown stockings and highly polished brown shoes. The Good Lord will give him everlasting life.

March 19th 1978 – The announcement by the Education Authority that Quenington School is to be closed and Hatherop remain open has caused a lot of comments from Quenington people in the Standard Paper. They have fought hard to keep their school open but to my mind Hatherop School is situated much better and is a far better school all round.

Easter Sunday 26th March 1978 – A good congregation at Hatherop Church at the 11am service. Church pretty with flowers. £16 odd for Parson's gift but nowadays it has to go to the fund and gets divided between all clergy. People do not like this method – it was so lovely for the Church Warden to present the Easter Collection to the Incumbent. Lots of these new ideas take some of the joy from our Services.

Maurice Moulden died this night. He was buried on Wednesday the 29th March at 2.30pm. When I was a boy, I went to Coln School at the same time as his daughter Joan and his son Eric who was lost over Germany in a bomber raid in the last War. They used to walk to school from the bottom cottages at Barrow Elm when Maurice worked on the Homeleaze Farm. In later years he lived in the house by the river at the bottom of Coln Hill opposite the stoney-path and the bridge, later he moved to Netherton to one of the cottages at the top of the hill going down to the river. I was born in the adjoining cottage. Then he moved up to Hatherop, where Mr and Mrs Sharps had lived. This cottage is opposite the house where my grandfather lived as Estate Foreman in the last century. My grandfather and my grandmother died in the School House. The one which now has a bow window in. The window was put in while I was at Hatherop School in the early thirties and I remember seeing the workmen sawing the freestone out at the back of the school on a bench with cross-cut saws and water.

Mr George Mustow informed me that during this last week or so, two pairs of men came at different times and inspected Hatherop Church Tower for the best kept tower in the Bristol and Gloucester Ringing Association area. The competition has been keen and in the final are Hatherop Church and Frampton Mansel Church. After a thorough inspection these judges cannot make up their minds as to which is the best tower so a lady came out to inspect Hatherop Tower named Miss Bliss who is a past Chairman of the Association and who has a great knowledge of bells. Mr Mustow said she made a thorough inspection and put her overalls on and went down into the bell-frame and looked at the staple pins in the bells. I presume to see if they were greased – which they were. Miss Bliss did not disclose her verdict but went on her way.

Monday Evening April 3rd 1978 – At 9.30pm Mr and Mrs William Godwin knocked on the back door of this Lodge and told me that Hatherop Tower had won the Competition and brought me the model of a ringing tower which we keep for twelve months and a certificate which will be framed and hung in the belfry. On this night great was the joy of Reuben Sims. I gave Mr and Mrs Godwin two tots each of rum and cake and had one myself. After four years work at the tower ringing room, clock room and belfry we had won. George Mustow now has the trophy which I took to him the next lunch time in his sitting room and is very proud of it.

George Mustow with the winning Tower Trophy.

Sunday 9th April 1978 – I went to Mr George Mustow's house, collected the trophy and carried it across the park to the church and placed it on a coffin stool in front of the litany desk by the lectern. We had great hymns of praise. The Rev Cowmeadow called R Sims and Mr G Mustow out into the Chancel and also the Church Wardens of Coln, Earl St Aldwyn and Sir Alexander Able Smith of Quenington. They both congratulated us on our win and the Rev Cowmeadow spoke of our achievement in such a large Diocese and ours so small a Parish. We had a full band of ringers and rung for half an hour. This was the happiest day of my life. I wanted that Trophy for the Parish of Hatherop.

20th April 1978 – I picked up Mr George Jones of Coln St Aldwyns and drove to Bibury for a Funeral Service at 2pm – the burial of Jim Griffin. George and me represented the St Aldwyn Lodge No 6723 RAOB [*The Royal Antediluvian Order of Buffaloes is a non-political and non-religious Philanthropic Organization which inspires its members to commit to a peaceful and meaningful way of life.*] Jim was 65 years old. A quiet, stocky man – son of Ted Griffin the bell ringer, whose family had lived in the roadside cottage in Pudding Lane for 400 years. When I was a boy he lived in the cottage with his father and step-mother near the village tap, next to cottage No 33. This cottage Sir Thomas Bazley has just sold to a Castle school teacher. Jim worked for Mr Arly Barton at the farm. I believe he helped in the hunter stables. He married and had his own cottage in Bibury Square for some years. A good cricketer for Williamstrip and Bibury. A hard hitter with the bat and wonderful wicket keeper who stood close behind the stumps no matter how fast the bowling. A likeable man and very willing to do a good turn – he came back from Dunkirk in the last war by the grace of God. He had not been a regular supporter of the Buffs for some years as he was troubled with asthma.

April 23rd 1978 – After Evensong at Hatherop Church, the ringers went to Glebe Farm by kind invitation of Mr and Mrs Hart, together with their son James, and drank a toast to the success of our tower in the competition. Afterwards we all went outside on the lawn on the south side of the house and had our photograph taken by Mrs Hart.

April 30th 1978 – Still a lot of feeling about closing one of the two schools that remain open – Hatherop or Quenington. Hatherop is by far the best building and with modern electric heating and a good food kitchen. Lots of money has been spent on Hatherop School since I went there with the vault and a bucket toilet system. Toward the end of my schooling at 14 years, a modern toilet for both boys and girls was installed but it has been improved since. A letter in the Standard Paper by Mr Ken Mustow of Quenington saying that there were no pubs, only a club at Hatherop, and that most of the people were pensioners, has upset a lot of parents of Hatherop children. Also a letter from Mr Peter Cook, a Hatherop School Manager from Quenington, a self sure man who has a lot to say and does very little, stating figures and facts about why Hatherop School should be closed – a man who changed his mind. Mr Jim Day of Quenington went with a delegation from Quenington to London, after the Education Authority had decided Quenington School should close, and got the decision reversed. Lots of backbiting about ladies who want the schools kept open to preserve their jobs. Lady Clarke, Councillor, changed her mind and said Hatherop should close. In all great bitterness has sprung up when there is no need.

May 6th 1978 – Go with Mr Bert Ayers of Poulton to Princess Margaret Hospital, Swindon and see Mr Ray Cuss. Ray had a major throat operation two years ago and still is a very sick man. Talks with a voice box. We two did all the talking as Ray cannot speak much. How old age and sickness retards one. Ray was never ill. Smoked twenty Players cigarettes every day. He was fifteen stone and one of the cleverest men Fairford ever produced. He could repair your car, fix electric light, do your plumbing, a good turner, could black-smith, do woodwork, repair your watch or clock. If Ray could not do it then it was unrepairable.

May 18th 1978 – Gilbert Burge told me the news that Ray Cuss had passed over into the hand of Almighty God this morning at 6.30am. He has reached the other side and the trumpets have sounded!

Saturday 20th May 1978 – The Sub Committee of Gloucester Education committee have come out in favour of closing the fine school of Hatherop and keeping the second class school of Quenington open. At first the Education Committee decided Quenington School should close. Lady Clarke changed her mind. Mr Jim Day went to London with a protest party against closing Quenington School. Peter Cook (the fussy a-lot-to-say man) and Ken Mustow (the new Gentry of Quenington) wrote in the Standard. They have played a prominent part in getting Quenington School up to the standard required by the Parish Council etc. They have more children at Quenington on the council estate. Hatherop School has had thousands of pounds spent on it and is vastly superior in every way but it looks as though it will close. Great bitterness has sprung up between people at Coln, Hatherop and Quenington. At a secret ballot of parents at Quenington School "Hatherop School to be Kept Open" was upheld by an overwhelming majority. The latest Standard Newspaper report says Hatherop will close. The waste of money by the local Authorities is really astounding to the ordinary lay man. The battle goes on.

Sunday 28th May 1978 – A good 11.30am Matins at Coln. Judith Stride-Darnley played the organ. Judith is a sweet girl.

June 3rd 1978 – Had dinner with Judith Stride-Darnley and her Mum at Coln St Aldwyn. This was held out in the garden at 7.30pm a lovely warm evening. We drank my elder flower wine.

June 11th 1978 – Judith has been in bed with a heavy cold – took her some fruit and honey. Went to Fairford yesterday and got her bread and vegetables.

Saturday 17th June 1978 – A coach load of ringers and visitors from Basingstoke visit and ring at Hatherop Church from 3pm till 4pm. Reuben Sims took his great grandfather's round table across the Park and brought the model tower and certificate down from the bell tower and placed it on the table at the entrance of the chancel for all to see. After the visitors had gone George Mustow, Mrs Mustow and Reuben Sims took the tower model and certificate to Sir Thomas Bazley's house at the Folly where we were shown round the garden by Sir Thomas Bazley and had a lovely tea with Lady Bazley and her family – only Martin was missing, he was detained at Cambridge. We left the model and certificate with Sir Thomas to show to his son Martin when he arrived. What a pity only Sir Thomas Bazley comes to Hatherop Church – this is on rare occasions – and sits in the Family Pew.

Sunday 18th June 1978 – The battle to save Hatherop School from closure goes on. At the last Council Meeting (according to the Wilts & Glos paper) Quenington had not submitted who was going to stand the cost of putting new toilets at Quenington School. Also the new kitchen to be built, as the children now have their meals with food cooked on cookers in the wooden Reading Room.

Wednesday 5th July 1978 – Notice boards are put up at the bridge at the bottom of Hatherop Hill saying the Grandage is for sale. I am rather sad to see so much property sold but during this last eleven years the Bazley Family have sold off an awful lot of property and land. I have my rent fixed now for three years at £10 per week, the rates are £2 per week. A far cry from the days when I was a boy here and my dad had this property for 1s 6d per week.

Saturday 15th July 1978 – I journey to Lechlade and pick up two photos at Peter Reason's shop. Prints I bought from the Evening Advertizer Paper. One photo I hung today in the Ringing Room of Hatherop Church, the other I am going to give to Mr George Mustow, our Ringing Captain. I hope he will be pleased with it and it will remind him of the award of winning the Best Kept Tower in the Gloucester and Bristol Diocese for 1977 – the proudest day in the life of Reuben Sims.

Saturday 22nd July 1978 – I travel to Fairford Church for the 2 o'clock wedding of Sharon Cuss to Ian Jones. Sharon joined the Fairford Silver Band when a schoolgirl and played the cornet. She played beside me on many band engagements and was a fine girl. A good service in the church where she and I played the Last Post etc for funerals and Armistice. Although the Armistice Calls used to be blown outside, they are now blown inside because the men of the Wars are older, do not do the marching or like waiting about on a cold November Morning. After the service we made our way with cars to the Commodore Club at the Welford gravel pits and had plenty to eat and drink I came away about six o'clock but the party was going on with dancing at nine o'clock. How well people are dressed today. But I fancy we were more content and happy than some of our people today.

Aug 4th 1978 It stated in the Wilts & Glos Standard paper that Hatherop School would close. Had a talk with Mr John Lander about the closing of Hatherop School. Told him the School Managers should have sacked Mr Cook, the Hatherop School Manager, who is doing his very best to close the school. He told me they could not sack him. I fail to see why not.

Friday 18th Aug 1978 – At 11am we held a Memorial Service in honour of Mr Denis Taylor, who till he retired, was the farmer at Homeleaze Farm. The Almighty called him on Tuesday – he was 77 years of age. A very nice, kindly man who lived on his own in Hatherop opposite the church lych gate. Miss Stride-Darnley played the organ. A lot of people were there. Mr Taylor's family, his two sons and daughter. His old friends at the Working Men's Club, including Mr Charles Rixon, his son Cyril and his wife, George Mustow and Charlie Mills. Mrs Joan Browning, Mrs Maunders, Mr Tarrant, Mr Sharps, Mr Terry Hartshorn and many others, including Mrs Moulding whose husband worked at Homeleaze farm for many years.

Oct 6th 1978 – A Barn Dance held in the Terapin Room at Hatherop Castle School was a great success. The tickets were £1 which included a Plough Man's lunch first of all. Cheese, beetroot, bread rolls, butter, raw carrot and pickles. Then the caller started the dances people were shy at first – very few had done any barn dances but soon everyone was on the floor and a great time was had by old and young. There was no trouble – the fights which go on today are at disco dances. The band consisted of an accordion, a violin and drums. The dance finished at 12.30am with the Okey-Kokey Dance. The Rev Cowmeadow and his wife organized the dance with no money to start it with but the cheese was given I am told at a cost of £30. The bar was run by Mr John Winfield of Coln St Aldwyns, a good friend of mine and always willing to lend a hand at any parish event. I am told the dance ended with a profit of around £80. We must have more of these dances. They are not designed to make money but to have a good time.

October 20th 1978 – went to Quenington Chapel at 2.30pm for burial service of Mr Harold Tugwell of the Limes, Quenington. A very nice quiet man, who gave so much time to his chapel. A large congregation, including the Rev Cowmeadow.

Monday 23rd October – Burial Service in Fairford Church at 2 o'clock for Canon Keble. A full church and all the local clergy present. A good sermon from the Dean of Gloucester. Canon Keble was a good man, and highly educated, always a pleasure to be with and a good sense of humour.

Dance Committee at Hatherop Castle c 1950s. Back standing from left: Sid Jacques, Reuben Sims, Annie Barnett, Mervyn Bayliss (behind), Charlie Barnett, Mrs Ford (with glasses), next to her is Fanny Mustow, Cliff Swallow, Jesse Blackwell, 2 unknowns, Vic Cox, John Lander, Jack Sainsbury, unknown woman, George Burge. Kneeling: George Mustow, Margaret Loving, Mrs Silman, Mrs Sainsbury, Dickie Cole (sitting), unknown woman, Sybil Lander (in white), Kath Brindle, Arthur "Curly" Mills.

A play on the history of Fairford by local talent ran for a week the previous week, a full house each night. They raised about £1,000 for Fairford Hospital. A cast of local talent totalling about ninety persons.

November 4th 1978 – Terry Hartshorn was married in Hatherop Church at 2.30pm. A large congregation at the wedding, the bride looking charming, the organ played and we rung the bells for half an hour under Mr G Mustow – treble, Chris Harrison, R Sims, Fred Harding, Mick Adams, and John Westall – tenor. We all went to the reception at the Working Men's Club where all was jolly and gay.

November 6th 1978 – Bert Ayers of Bell Lane, Poulton passed over in Cirencester Hospital having been admitted the previous day with severe chest pains. His health has not been too good the last two years. He was 71 years old. When I was apprenticed by my father William Sims at the East Glos Engineering Company which was owned by Mr Reuben Briggs, I was told to work with Bert Ayers. Bert showed me how to "shut" metal together in the forge and to blow the bellows. Also to make scroll tops for pokers and knobs on window catches and to "shut" lengths of knife back steel on mower knives. Sometimes in a thin crop season when the crop was too thin to hold the knives steady we used to repair a dozen knives a week. I also worked with Bert repairing the woodwork and iron-work on carts and wagons and bonded wheels in the summer on the bonding platform heating the bonds in a large wood fire in the yard towards the back doors, or gate as it is today. We also worked on pumps and water wheels and pipe-work. We made fire tongs for the forge fire and lots of field gate fittings. Bert was the main welder at the works then beside Mr Briggs. In 1940 when Bert and us all used to cycle to work with our gas masks, we made the iron work to hold wheels which were fastened to two telegraph poles with barbed wire attached which were swung across the road at each end of Fairford to hold up the German invader should they have come. Before he was married, Bert cycled from Ampney St Peter to Fairford and back very working day. Later Bert cycled from Poulton from his home built by Yells of Fairford. A quiet man was Bert, a fine craftsman and a good church man. He was buried at Ampney St Peter church on 10th November.

Sunday 19th Nov 1978 – The Rev Cowmeadow announced that Mr Charles Bartlett had died today and the funeral service would be at 12.30 on Thursday 23rd Nov. Charlie Bartlett took the blacksmith's shop on after Mr Walter Dunn retired at 50 years old. The date I believe is 1937 will confirm it later. His wife used to use the sledge hammer for him then and did all the striking. He was a very clever blacksmith and made much iron work and shod all the horses on the local farms. Charlie was a very hard worker. The war made him into a special constable and he was a very smart figure patrolling round at night in the last war. He did all his forge work with the hammer and shut bars together in the forge. When I went to the Buffalo Lodge at Coln New Inn from 1949 and during the 1950s, his forge could be seen glowing at eight o'clock at night. When my mother would not leave this Lodge till all the furniture had been moved to Quenington when this house was to be modernised, Gladys Woodcock came up to help and told me to fetch Blacksmith Bartlett with his van and take my mother to Quenington. I went down on my scooter and asked him – he was working at the vice and soon dropped his tools and drove the van to this Lodge. We got my mother to put her coat on and she got in the van and he soon had my dear mother down to Quenington. That was the way my wonderful mother, who worked so hard for us all, left this house she loved so well. Mr Bartlett was so willing to do what he could to help us. A wonderful man, the Almighty will give him eternal life.

Mr Bartlett with the Pig Cup prize at Conygar Farm.

Sunday 7th Jan 1979 – There is a threatened oil tanker strike – lots of workers want more money, great unrest. Repair a ball valve for Judith Stride-Darnley, our organist who lives at Coln St Aldwyns.

Sunday 14th Jan 1979 – The lorry drivers' strike and now the rail strike is very serious for our country.

January 23rd 1979 – Open the back door of this Lodge at 6am find two inches of snow. Half of the new Farmors School is closed. The caretaker neglected to keep the heat on so frost has burst a lot of pipe work. The caretaker should be sacked. Cirencester School I am told has also froze up.

Saturday 3rd Feb 1979 – It is the anniversary of my father's death in 1942. Today I drive Judith to Fossebridge garage to collect her new car. I follow her home via Ablington. Now she can drive to her job at Cheltenham and take her Mum around. Since Christmas, on most nights, I drove to Northleach to pick her up off the bus from Cheltenham.

Sunday 11th Feb 1979 – At Evensong at 6pm at Hatherop, the Rev Cowmeadow said Gladys Woodcock had died and would be cremated after a service in Coln Church on Friday. Gladys was a great Cotswold character, outspoken, very true and loyal to her church. She nursed me till I was six months old and was a great friend of my mother.

February 16th 1979 – Gladys Woodcock, our dear friend of 86 years, was cremated after a service in Coln St Aldwyns. Viscount Quenington read the lesson, a large congregation, and we sung some good hymns. Peter Hicks Beach had a poem he composed I copy it down here.

> *Everyone here knows all about Gladys*
> *Of that exceptional neighbour, character, storyteller*
> *To whom life was a gift each day*
> *A practical soul no flowers at her funeral*
> *"It'll be too late then" she said*
> *"I'd rather have them when I can enjoy them*
> *No use to me on my death bed"*
> *"I don't want to be buried beneath a grave*
> *For someone to weed and tend*
> *I'll be no fuss and bother when I'm no longer*
> *And my life has come to an end"*
> *We're just lucky we had her amongst us so long*
> *Each treasures his favourite story*
> *She died as she said that she always wanted to do*
> *"Sudden death and sudden glory."*

Gladys went into the old people's bungalows at Coln [*Memorial Cottages*], built out of the stones from the side buildings at Williamstrip House in 1947 and she is the last of the first occupiers. She planted the garden privet hedge there and also the lovely rose bushes. Her maiden name was Tombs. She told me how my grandfather Reuben Sims walked down from Hatherop one winter's night to see her mother just before she died. One of the statements of Gladys Woodcock "I never turn anyone away from the door who comes for money, no matter how small my contribution."

Gladys Woodcock.

March 11th 1979 – I drive to Fairford Cottage Hospital and take a small bunch of yellow aconites from this Lodge to Mrs Baker, my friend John Winfield's mother, who is very ill there. She was asleep. John and his wife were by her bedside. Saw Mr Hedges and his wife in the hospital, they were fine considering their ages. Mr Hedges told me he is 97 years old on 23rd March 1979. Of average height, his brain very active he remembers our night school days, when we all cycled to Fairford Farmers School next to the Church from 7 o'clock to 9 o'clock for study on maths, book-keeping, woodwork or engineering drawing. I sat and passed the UEI exam for English in 1941 and I have still retained the certificate and the note he wrote me after I passed and told him so, he was very pleased. He told me the old workhouse known as the House of Industry was pulled down and the hospital built on the site. The stone from the old work-house built the primary school at Fairford in 1870.

March 13th 1979 – Saw John Winfield at the new Buffs Lodge opening at the New Inn at Coln – learnt his mother had woken after I had left the hospital and smiled when she saw my aconites. She passed over later that night. John Winfield and Bill Godwin the bell ringer came and visited me every night while my mother lay dead upstairs. I have never forgotten their kindness to me.

March 16th 1979 – Jim Hawkins of Quenington has died. He was the baker for Mr Lewis at Quenington Bakery and the shop on Mawley Road. Some years ago while lighting the bakery oven with paraffin to start the fire, it blew back and burnt one of his hands badly. Jim Hawkins was a nice friendly man who worked at Godwins later until he retired. His wife died not long ago, he devoted his life to her, she was a lady who was never well – the doctors could do nothing for her. Baker Lewis always had good bread and delivered to Dean Farm and Fairford with a van.

Baker Lewis in Quenington. From left: Albert Bartlett, Baker Lewis, Bert Bartlett, Mr Lawrence, Mr Hughes.

March 26th 1979 – I see on the television news Points West, a report about the bitter battle between Hatherop and Quenington over the closure of one of the schools. They say that the Rev Cowmeadow has resigned as Chairman of the School Managers.

March 27th 1979 – Mr Robinson called in the afternoon. Told him I am going to have a phone put in. He said whatever the cost as I am on my own, it was the right thing to do. Mr Cyril Sly, the undertaker from Northleach, called. He said Mrs Pollard of Dean Farm had died and was there room to bury her by her husband? I said "I was not sure, lots of burials had taken place in that area. Mr W Smith of 18 Hatherop, Sid Day and John Bedwell. It would be best by Arthur Day by the west wall."

March 30th 1979 – I am not well with flu. Have a red rash on my face which smarts and stings. Have little sleep. Judith called at night bless her heart. Will bring me bread and orange juice tomorrow. Mr Eddie

Hunt my workmate called, what a wonderful man he is. He said I should change to a Fairford doctor who is nearer and will come out to me.

March 31st 1979 – Had another sleepless night. Judith brought my shopping and grape and orange juice. Eddie brought rock cakes and pies from his wife. They cheer me up. How nice to have such friends. Farmer Hart has been and brought me 6 eggs. Another sleepless night. I sit in the chair by the Rayburn Stove all night with Scramble my black Labrador dog. How faithful he is, humans should be the same.

April 2nd 1979 – I am feeling better, cannot shave top lip. Have a red rash which is very sore on face. Drive to Lechlade in three-wheeler with Scramble in the back. See doctor who gives me pills for rash. Drop in a note of thanks to Mr Eddie Hunt of Quenington and Judith Stride-Darnley. Pay shopping bill at Coln shop. Talk to Mr Sandy Moaby about the flu, come home. How nice it is to be around again thank God. Listen to Mrs Thatcher on the box in an election speech.

April 3rd 1979 – The Rev Peter Murray of Ablington came to see me this morning. He said he did not mind the flu although I have been home a fortnight now. I lived because Mr Eddie Hunt my workmate called and Judith Stride-Darnley our organist who came and tapped the window, brought my bread from Fairford and orange and grape juice, how good she has been to me during this time. Brother Roger King called at night at 6 o'clock and said he was sorry he had not called before he did not know till today I had been home for over two weeks and he would tell the Lodge how poorly

Buffs at the Lodge Room in the New Inn, 1960. From left: Jack Gaiger, J Howard, Reuben Sims, T Pearson.

I had been. I told him not to worry as it was me who was wrong. I had neglected the Buffalo Order and was out of compliance therefore no benefit could be obtained. I realise I have neglected attending the St Aldwyn Lodge and lost the friendship of the Brothers. My dear mother always kept me up together with the Order, as she was so very proud of me in the Coln St Aldwyns Lodge. I gave Bro Roger some money and will attend more regular in the future and make a new start.

April 26th 1979 – At a PCC meeting at Hatherop School, Farmer Hart resigned as Church Warden. Mrs Jennie Voaden was proposed. Hatherop's first lady Warden.

May 3rd 1979 – Polling day for General Elections and Council Elections at the same time. I went to Judith Stride-Darnley's house at Coln St Aldwyns at 11.30pm and we listened to the results. The gains were made by the Conservative Party. I came away at 2am. I noticed those in council houses had gone to bed. The owner-occupier houses were all lit up and people must have been watching the results. I came home and watched the results till 4am.

May 4th 1979 – Mrs Thatcher is the First Woman Prime Minister. The Conservatives have won by a working majority. I thought this would happen. We have had a long hard winter with lots of strikes with schools closed, lorry drivers strikes, the dead unburied and a shortage of bread etc. The people were fed up with it. The Labour Government has done a great deal for people but was not strong enough against the trade unions who formed the Labour movement. We should have five years competitive industry. Trust it will pull us through.

May 18th 1979 – The end of a two year battle about whose school should close. Much bitterness has been engendered among our people over this matter. But trust time and Almighty God will heal the self inflicted wounds. I am sad that Quenington School is to close, it is another link broken in village life. As the case now stands, Hatherop School is situated far better to serve the needs of the children.

June 9th and 10th 1997 – *The Victorian Fair at Coln St Aldwyns* – A slight rain started the day on Saturday but the Almighty sent the sunshine for two solid days and great was the joy at Coln St Aldwyns. A traction engine was placed across the Church and Manor Roads, a fair organ was there. Stalls selling everything from fudge to plants. Nearly every one turned out in Victorian dress, ladies and children and men. Farm workers in smocks, a soldier, policeman, a shepherd and his sheep. John Winfield as a blacksmith; Dennis Bartlett as a butcher; Earl St Aldwyn as the local squire, also his wife in a lovely floral dress. The Rev Cowmeadow in his

The Victorian Fair – (top) Jennie Voaden, Clifford Moss, Reverend Cowmeadow, Countess St Aldwyn, Earl St Aldwyn; (bottom) Judith Stride Darling, Reverend Cowmeadow, Mrs Cowmeadow, Reuben Sims.

19th century clerical dress, his wife in a lovely long blue outfit. Reuben Sims as a school master. Judith Stride-Darnley wore a Victorian dress given to my mother when the Smith family left Hatherop. A film company took shots from the Church Tower and on the Vicarage Lawn where the ladies played croquet and the children danced the maypole. The Sunday evening ended with a service outside the Sanctuary end of the Church and the sermon and music were provided by the Salvation Army. Two very hot days, every one tired but very happy.

June 24th 1979 – I journey to Barnsley and visit Mr David Verey at his home and give him my old carpenter's book 1812 – the property of John Sims my ancestor born 1760–1835. Also my miliameter used by my grandfather Reuben Sims late in the last century. I told Mr Verey it is to be placed in his Mill at Arlington forever as a record of my family. He told me he will make me a Patron of the Mill.

July 21st 1979 – George Mustow and Reuben Sims chime the Coln Bells before and after the wedding of Mr and Mrs Bennett's daughter at Coln Church. The Fairford Band played at the reception and could be heard at the Hatherop Lodge.

August 2nd 1979 – Bill Grayhurst of Quenington was buried. He was for many years a blacksmith at Godwins. He was a good violin player and used to play a lot with Mrs Gaiger's band during the war years in Coln Village Hall. What wonderful nights of music and dancing they were when there was nothing else going on. His wife Mrs Greyhurst only passed over about five months ago. She sung for years in Quenington Church Choir with a wonderful strong voice.

August 12th 1979 – Eight people at the 8am service taken by the Rev Cowmeadow in the de Mauley Chapel. Made me feel so much better as really I am a wicked man. I moan about all the riches people have and do not put in to the Lord's House. I moan about the pubs and clubs and non attendance at the Lord's House. I am greedy and want everything. I am inclined to be hasty tempered and walk out of Church Meetings if things do not go my way or I cannot get things moving. In short I am a horrible man but trust the Lord will forgive me and give me everlasting life among my family who were so dear to me.

My late employer Mrs Vera Ruth Arnold passed away and I had time off from work at RAF Fairford to go to her funeral service at Quenington Chapel. The Chapel was full of people as she was a fine business woman and knew a lot of people being the daughter of Mr Harold Godwin the pump manufacturer. Yes, she was the power at Godwin's and also at East Glos Engineering where I worked so long.

September 6th 1979 – The burial service of John Westall was held at 11 o'clock – a large congregation in Hatherop Church. The Rev Cowmeadow officiated. Reuben Sims spoke a few words on his life. John was buried in a double grave by the de Mauley door. There was no room to bury him by his son who was drowned in the improvised swimming pool made out of an old gravel pit in the Grandage at the bottom of Quenington Hill in 1947.

October 14th 1979 – Had the phone installed in August cost £53 – have not had bill yet. The phone is a real boon to me.

October 21st 1979 – I think today of my family, my mother died on the 19th Oct 1967. How time flies. My Dad, a God fearing man, badly wounded in France in the trench warfare of the first war, suffered all his life. His three medals are in the front room, also his discharge emblem. I am told he and Fred Fox, the footman, were the first in the village to volunteer. He went to France in 1915 in Kitchener's Army. He was in the army 3 years and 165 days. The young Doctor Bloxome was good to him through the years, and my mother was wonderful, a real dynamo for work and cared for us all. Of course no money when my dad was ill. £1 National Insurance, 10 shillings the Conservative Club and 10 shillings War Pension. My Dad was a good woodworker like all of my family since John Sims of Bibury whose woodwork book I have given to Arlington Mill. After 1942 when my father died my mother kept our

Reuben Sims, Kate Sims, Edith Sims, William Sims 1937.

home going – she earned 10 shillings per week, my sister nothing as she had muscular dystrophy and grew steadily worse from the age of eleven till she died at twenty two years. The journeys to Fairford to catch the train in the morning to get to Oxford – my mother pushed her down in a wheel chair to the station, then from Oxford to the Radcliff Hospital. At night I met the train at Fairford at 5.30pm. Mother rode her cycle home to get the tea on. I had ridden her bike down in the mornings and I pushed my sister home. We had tea about quarter to seven in the evenings and it was lovely.

October 27th 1979 – Have heard that Mrs Shepherd, 88 years old, has been taken from the old people's bungalows and is now at Stratton St Margaret Hospital. She is a lovely quiet person, a Wheeler born in this Lodge. Her daughter Lily and I played together when we lived side by side at Netherton. Lily is now Mrs Reeves and lives at Coln and has some fine sons.

November 4th 1979 – A good Evensong. George Mustow, Tom Lemon, Jennie Voaden and Reuben Sims in the choir. The men's surplices look nice being washed and starched by the Burford Laundry at Fairford and the loops sewn on. The younger generation know nothing about washing and starching clothes and I cannot get anyone to do the job. The cost was £5.20p. In the days of my mother and when I was a boy in the choir, Mrs Barnett at the Castle Laundry used to wash them – it seemed the natural thing to do. Today all family people are out at work, to provide funds for their own personal pleasures in spite of the family allowance at £4 per child. I have been given two history handwritings of the Parishes of Coln and Hathrop and a great deal of information they reveal. The books I write about were the property of Miss Kathleen Brindle given to me by Mr Robinson of Barn Cottage from Mrs Nora Sainsbury who was the wife of the late John Sainsbury of Glebe Farm Hatherop. The writing looks very much like Miss Brindle's, I must find out.

December 2nd 1979 – Evensong at Hatherop – the school are doing their plays and they have taken down the brass candlesticks etc. I am very unpopular with Hatherop Castle School because I do not like the church pulled about. The school does very much for the old age people here and a lot of people have good jobs through the school. To the Rev Cowmeadow I am known as the rascal. Doctor Moorehead at the school hates me I think.

December 5th 1979 – Church meeting at the School. Seven members present. Lady Howard and Reuben Sims are the two oldest members. Discussion on the Church being used for plays by the Castle School. I am afraid like all the clergy from the time of Canon Lowe, the Rev Mowat and our present Rector, the Rev Cowmeadow, the Castle School is a great attraction for them. Nothing came out of the discussion, only that the School should meet the Church Wardens about what they are going to take out of the Church in the way of fixtures etc.

Sunday 9th December 1979 – The Arch Deacon of Cheltenham the Rev Eric Evans preached the sermon in Hatherop Church at the Feast of Saint Nicholas being invited by Reuben Sims. Afterwards the Arch Deacon, together with Mrs Jennie Voaden and my lifelong friends Mr and Mrs John Iles from Lechlade were given supper at the Lodge by Reuben Sims. This is history in the village of Hatherop. Never before has an Arch Deacon been entertained at a bachelor working man's home. Always these occasions are ended with the visiting preacher either going straight home or entertained by the incumbent or people in good circumstances. The weather was very rough and cold with heavy rain during the service but afterwards in the Lodge front room, with the fire going, sherry, ham, potatoes, tomatoes, apple tart, cheese and biscuits, all was fine. Gave the Arch Deacon three cabbages, some swedes and a bottle of wheat wine, he gave me a bottle of sherry. I cleaned and polished for two days, am very tired now.

January 22nd 1980 – Thoughout the awful weather in 1979, January, February and early March, I left the Fairford camp where I work every day and came home, made a flask of coffee and some sandwiches and went to Northleach Market Place and picked up Judith Stride-Darnley off the coach from Cheltenham where she teaches at a school and brought her back to her mother at No 15 Coln Street. We used to stop and have coffee along the road or sometimes in the Market Place. In early February we bought a Wolseley car for her with the money I loaned her – nine hundred pounds. She has had great pleasure from it driving her mother around all that year. She also took her boyfriends around unbeknown to me. Our love did not develop – mine grew but she found another man and she gradually drew away from me. This December and January have been two of my saddest months since my mother died when I found out my dear Judith had a boy friend. I would have married Judith Stride-Darnley if it were possible. But the Almighty intervened. I must get better and find an older girl who will look after me.

Feb 2nd 1980 – At this time I have had fourteen pounds back of the nine hundred pounds I loaned Judith Stride-Darnley in January 1979.

February 25th 1980 – Judith Stride-Darnley gave up playing the organ in Coln and Hatherop Churches on Feb 10th. We shall all miss her good playing. Reuben Sims has the Church harmonium at the Lodge to practise on and will play some of the hymns this summer God willing.

March 9th 1980 – Reuben Sims played the organ in Hatherop Church for the Evensong at 6pm. Some mistakes but on the whole the congregation thought a good effort. The sudden notice given by Miss Judith Stride-Darnley to finish the organ playing in Hatherop and Coln Church has made problems for our Vicar but we are getting by and I am getting better at playing.

April 1980 – The April magazine complemented Reuben Sims for volunteering to play the Church organ at Hatherop for Evensong. The fees over the last year Miss J Stride-Darnley had were £65. As Church Warden I do it free and love it. I shall never forget the cold night in January 1979 when Judith could not raise the £600 needed for the car after I had given her £300 and how after being interviewed by a finance company found they were so committed with debts that she could not have the money, she hugged up so close to me and later I drew out the money from the Cheltenham and Gloucester Building Society. What a big con it all was. Judith the educated school teacher with the soft cultured voice turned round against me and deceived me. I never believed it possible.

April 19th 1980 – Have a phone call from Mrs Stride-Darnley saying Judith was ill from German Measles and she could not get to Lechlade where the chemist was open to get her prescription made up. What was I to say or do? As a Church man and a belief in Jesus Christ I said I would take her to Lechlade. I got in my van drove to Coln and picked up Judith's mother, took her to Fairford where the chemist we found was shut, drove on to Lechlade and got the prescription. Bought some grapes for Judith 75p and drove Mrs Stride-Darnley back to Coln.

April 21st 1980 – Drove Mr Harry Gardiner to Coln and we split some logs for Judith's fire. She was sitting in her room downstairs rather thin and drawn. Her mother does not like me much because of my affection and does her utmost to keep me away from her. But she need not worry now. The agony I have suffered since December has gone due to prayer to Almighty God. Judith will be my friend but I will not marry her now.

May 17th–18th 1980 – Coming across the park after the communion service at Hatherop Church saw a large black cloud of smoke over the top of Quenington. Thought it was a bonfire with tyres and how strange to light a fire when everything is tinder dry. Found out later that evening when talking to my neighbour Mr Jack Barnfield and Mr Norman Tarrant's daughter rode by on her cycle. She said had been to Quenington where she saw Godwin's Works Fitter and Machine Shops all afire. Mr Phillip Bullimore was waiting for one of his racing pigeons to land when the paint shop blew up at 3.17pm. The fire spread within

The Fire at Godwin Pumps.

minutes throughout the factory. The local families were evacuated for a while in case the oil tanks blew up. I drove round Sunday morning at 1pm and it was all out. Ten fire engines there. They pumped water from the river at the bottom of the hill. The sheds and machines all black with fire. The firemen saved a large fuel tank outside the top shed facing old man Godwin's house from catching fire and saved the large oil engine inside at the end of the bottom shop. But all the machines are black with fire which they say started in the paint shop. The tin roof fell in and twisted metal hanging around. A great tragedy for all who work there.

June 8th 1980 – I take the Stride-Darnleys their bread from Baker Radway on Mondays and Fridays because the road is closed in Coln. The main sewer trench is being dug in the centre of the road, a major job. A good number of years the sewage has been coming out into the meadow by the river and a fearful smell for the residents at the bottom of Coln.

July 12th 1980 – Had a visit from Judith and her mother. Their electric kettle has gone wrong. I have a spare one at work and will bring it home on Monday for them. Judith is a very attractive girl.

July 27th 1980 – Walked with my dog to Coln Church for communion at 8am and met the Williams family from USA, the descendents of Nobel Williams, a farm worker here who played the violin and rang the bells. It is said that Nobel had to leave Cockrup Farm because he played 'Pop Goes the Weasel' on the chiming ropes. I played some hymn tunes on the bells which the visitors recorded in the tape recorder and also played the organ which their forebears had played. Another of the Williams family came, a man in his seventies I would think, and he played the organ also. We all had a good time together and I hope the Williams family going back to the states will have enjoyed their visit.

August 23rd 1980 – Drove to Quenington Chapel for the funeral service of Mr Barry Burge at 11 o'clock. Barry was 79 years old. A good man, hard working and worked for Yells, the builders of Fairford, for many years. Saw Ethel Barry's sister who worked with my Mum at Hatherop Castle and who was a great friend of Mum's. Barry had a heart attack after coming up the hill at Quenington for some work he was doing at Quenington Court. He and his wife were wonderful dancers and we all had such gay times in the war years.

Nov 5th 1980 Bonfire Night – The roughest, coldest night for fireworks I ever remember. Kept inside the Lodge with a good fire in the Rayburn Stove. Remember when I was a boy in the thirties when my Mum and Dad brought a bag of fireworks.We made a bonfire in the garden and Mum made a guy which was fastened to a stake – my Dad lit the fireworks. Rockets were 2p, also Catherine Wheels which we fixed to the line posts. Mr and Mrs Barnett from the Bothey at the top of Hatherop Hill came along and after the fire had burnt down and the fireworks used up we went indoors for some supper. What happy nights they were.

November 8th 1980 – After a phone call to Paternoster House on Friday night I visit my dear old Aunt Beatie of 92 years. She is lying in bed in a small room, lovely and warm. Her end is not far away on this earth. Watch the Remembrance display at the Albert Hall on the television in the evening. I remember when I was a boy in the early thirties how we all listened to the wireless on that night together with Mr and Mrs Charlie Barnett. The Last Post, the poppies falling. Now I can see it all in colour. I am glad it still survives. I remember my father and all the suffering of his wounds in the trench warfare in France with the Gloucester and Devonshire Regiments. How my Mum looked after him so well and how proud she was to give him his medals to put on his waistcoat for the Armistice Parade at Hatherop Church. He said he "would have worked in this country for nothing just to live and sleep in a good bed" rather than stand in water logged trenches and all in the shelling slaughter. Shrapnel is with his remains in Hatherop churchyard and it was never taken out of his right elbow because he might have lost the use of his arm, whereas he could still use a plane and saw but could not straighten his arm right out as normal. That is why he could not do a lot of ringing.

November 9th 1980 – Rung Paternoster House at 9.30am they told me my Aunt Beatie had passed away at 8.30am. God Bless her.

November 13th 1980 – Journey to Down Ampney at 1.15pm for my Aunt Beatrice's funeral. Reuben Sims was the only mourner following my Aunt Beatrice Humphries from the lych gate to the Church. Mrs Grace Telling, her son and his wife Mr and Mrs G Telling, Ciss and Reg Adams, George Wright and others following at the porch. Afterwards we went back in to the Vestry where Mr Slade read out the will which left George Telling £30. Paid him and he signed the receipt. I thanked the people for coming and drove home. My Aunt was 91 years old.

November 14th 1980 – Went to a Victorian Evening Concert at Hatherop Castle price £1.50. Jennie Voaden sung well, Dr Henderson, Tim Morris and wife, John Read all played the piano. John Chudleigh sang songs. He has a good tenor voice "Just a Song at Twilight". Tim Morris's wife played the piano well (I expect that is why he married her). Jennie Voaden sung "Mother, Take the Wheel Away" "Home Sweet Home" "Tales of Araby" but the three ladies excelled themselves at the end with Rule Britannia, a fine rendering. This show was held in the ornate drawing room. Many such concerts were held there in my grandfather's time.

I forgot to say the maid came in at the start and switched on the lights and curtsied to Dr Henderson. From my Aunt's day and later, all the working class curtsied to their betters. The men said Sir and doffed their caps or bowler hats if they were like my grandfather. I can remember when a small boy going to Coln School and a lady curtsying to another lady, her superior, outside Coln Stores on the road up to the Manor. I never forgot it. The last war and the welfare state stopped all that. The majesty of Hatherop Castle rooms and the oak panelling shows the wealth and privilege of our leisure classes and our people had good secure jobs provided they did not kick over the traces. My mother thought the world of it as she worked and lived in and my father worked inside when repairs were required. Then he came home and put his best black shoes on and they both chatted at tea about what was going on.

December 18th 1980 – At night take a Christmas present from Mr William Dunn of Kempsford, nephew of Walter Dunn who was the blacksmith at the bottom of Hatherop Hill before the war when I was a boy, to Nurse Wearing, she is over 80 years old, at the Nurse's Cottage. Hatherop School all lit up like a factory. A parents meeting, lots of big cars parked around the village green. In spite of the recession family allowance has gone up to £4.75 per week. Old age pensions have gone up to about £40 per married couple per week.

December 27th 1980 – Rev Derek Cowmeadow's daughter was married to Mr Fred Bayliss of Quenington, son of Sydney Bayliss, at Coln Church. Reception at Hatherop Castle with 100 guests.

January 1st 1981 New Years Day – Saw no one today. It is now a national holiday. We used to work on as usual a few years back, just wish each other a Happy New Year and on to work. Times change. Not always for the better.

Mervyn Bayliss winding the Hatherop Church clock by hand.

January 11th 1981 – Mr Bayliss wants to give up winding the clock, no ringers, no one to cut the church yard, no young people in choir or congregation. John Read is looking up the history of three villages according to the Doomsday book. Two mills entered. They are still there only not used. We used to get our meal for our chickens from the mill by the main road in Coln. It was worked by Mr Mustow. The other mill worked a saw for cutting logs.

January 19th 1981 – Mr Dennis Bartlett told me that the old beech tree opposite the lodge at the bottom of Hatherop Hill, where the bombs dropped down behind the wall and went into a long line across the Williamstrip Park in 1940, has a disease and may have to be felled. I remember when the bombs whistled down that night how frightened we were. I got under the bedclothes. I was sleeping in the small bedroom facing the Park. My Dad and I went to the Park with many others on the

Sunday afternoon and looked at the craters. Blacksmith Bartlett made a shovel out of a tail fin. My Dad said the airplanes would not be anything to worry about as he had often fired a Lewis gun at them in France in the 1914 war. But times have advanced so much in 20 years. Lots of people picked up the jagged pieces of bomb metal. Mr Charlie Gaiger was talking to my Dad about the bomb craters south east of the cricket pitch and said he had seen far bigger holes with the shells in France, my father agreed. But later on the bombs were much bigger as both sides developed them. As I cycled to Fairford to work, the straight stretch of road by the far hill turn was stacked with piles of bomb about 5 feet long and about 9 inches in diameter. The Americans had arrived then and used to unload and load them onto lorries. Big, powerful lorries driven by coloured drivers who were great favourites with the children because of the sweets they had got and with our local ladies because of sex.

I sat for the English exam at Fairford night school and had to write about a fire extinguisher. I've still got the diploma. Cycling home at night I often saw the Ack Ack bursts in the sky over the Bristol area. Bob Hutchins – keeper's son at Williamstrip, George Mustow, John Westall, Reuben Sims were in the Home Guard. After Dunkirk we were in the LDV Local Defence Volunteers. We used to go the Castle and stay up

The Combined Home Guard at the Severells 1944.

on the Tower with shot guns which fired BB shot which were 5/8 inch ball bearings. Two men at a time went up at dawn and about 9pm in the evening looking for German paratroops. Fred Ford was with me one night and we had a Gibbs Elephant Gun with five cartridges. We did not know how to load it so we asked my father how to load it. Glad we never saw any enemy. Red warnings came through on the phone to Col Gibbs at Church Mead as used to be. Col Gibbs renamed it The Severalls.

When Capt Sturt took over the Hatherop Home Guard he made us a fine body of men. Parades every Sunday morning at 10.30am marching up and down the street with Sgt Ledbetter of the Essex Regiment who was stationed in Williamstrip House. Some queer things were written in the report books kept for every night's events. Usually it was "quiet night nothing to report" one entry in the Hatherop book said "quiet night nothing to report but Mustow and Buster mad all night". Mustow was Jesse Mustow now a farmer at Perrott's Brook, Cirencester. Buster was Mr Buster Sharps of Coln, a forester now retired. Where the old book has gone no one knows. We had lots of night exercises across Williamstrip Park and across the Grandage attacking Quenington. Sunday morning they invaded from Fairford and Quenington and also from Southerop, Hatherop and Quenington. After 1942 the invasion threat eased, men were called up more but I was exempt being in an agricultural engineer's job. I went for a medical and passed at Oxford. I remember my Dad, who was lying in bed in the front room when I came back, said to my Mum that he was pleased I had passed the medical but hoped they would not take me while he was ill. My Dad died on Feb 3rd 1942 and all the Estate workers, including Mr Browning the foreman, came and saw him in his coffin. It was very cold and frosty. The men pick-axed a way out from this Lodge and 8 men carried him shoulder high along the road, through the Park gate and across the Park as was his wish. Now I am a bachelor of 58 years old and spend many lonely hours here at this Lodge which was such a happy place of laughter with all the lodgers when I was a boy. But I am proud I looked after my Mum and my crippled sister till their end in this world. I thank Almighty God for that.

January 21st 1981 – Visit from Mr William Godwin the ringing master of the Cirencester branch of bell ringers. A fine man dedicated to bell ringing. He said how the association were aware that the fine peal of bells at Coln St Aldwyns are now neglected. The Coln Church members are sitting on their money and doing nothing to get the bells and tower peal right.

It is very strange how things work out. In the early fifties Mr Bliss manager of Coln Co-op stores told my mother he had some powder that you could soak clothes in and they would come out clean. She did not believe him. But she tried some and found he was right. The powder was Persil. Then the washing machine, then the spin dryer, then the television, then the deep freeze, and the refrigerators, then coloured television sets and tape recorders and cassette players. The hut was put in the Park for billiards and games, then drink and ladies could go in. Now an extension to the club is being built and it is open every night and youths of 16 years old are waiting at the door for it to open. Ladies with families drawing £4.75 each per week per child are out at work. The church clock needs a winder, the churchyard needs a worker, the bells need ringers, the pews need a congregation but "my wages are not thy wages" said the Lord.

Sunday 22nd March 1981 – Holy Eucharist at Hatherop Church 8am. Present – only Rev Cowmeadow, Reuben Sims and Scramble the black Labrador dog. R Sims sat in the choir stall right hand side of the organ. The heating pipes run under the seat there. Scramble laid out in the aisle on the red carpet. My villagers were all in bed, blinds drawn, as I walked through the village.

March 28th 1981 – The Grandage has been railed off in sections with timber fencing and I believe it is being sold again. There were no fences there when the Bazley family owned it. It was only when the Dingle family rented it for cattle grazing that signs were put up on the gates to tell you to keep to the tracks from Netherton to the Iron Bridge at the bottom of Hatherop Hill. Such is human nature.

Easter Sunday 19th April 1981 – Have cut out the photo of Harold and Gladys Wheeler which was in the Standard this week. Their Golden Wedding Anniversary. Harold was born at this Lodge. There is a well known photograph of Harold driving a binder with three horses. Gladys's maiden name was Herbert from Quenington. When I went to school one of her brothers, Fred, died. He was a pupil at Hatherop School in the days of our Headmaster, Mr Percy Garner. A fine schoolmaster – used the cane. 'The mailed fist in the velvet glove.' Harold loved sport and used the cart horses on Glebe Farm, big fine horses that pulled the carts and ploughs and the binder that cut and tied the sheaves of corn. Gladys was a fine energetic girl who cleaned the brass in Hatherop Church. A fine dancer – we all had great fun in Coln village hall during the blackout days of World War II and we also danced in a large canvas hanger which housed the air drop baskets for the airborne landings at Arnhem. Dancing to a radio-

'Golden' Easter for Siddington couple

MRS. GLADYS WHEELER met her husband Harold at the age of 12 when he used to pull her hair at school! On April 18, they will be celebrating their golden wedding anniversary.

Mr. and Mrs. Wheeler of 54 Elizabeth Way, Siddington, were married at St. Nicholas' Church, Quenington, on Easter Saturday 1931, in snow!

They started 'courting' at Gladys's eldest brother's 21st birthday party and have never looked back since then. 'It doesn't seem like 50 years" says Harold "It's because we've always worked together and had no secrets."

Harold was born at Hatherop Lodge (then known locally as 'Wheeler's Lodge') earlier the home of his grandfather, and left school at 14 to work with the horses at Glebe Farm, Hatherop.

The couple lived at Hatherop for 40 years and remember cycling from there to Cricklade or Cirencester for dances. Returning at 2.30 a.m. by oil-lamp made no difference to Harold's 5.30 a.m. start with the horses! "Late for work twice in those days and you got your cards," he says.

He worked there for 41 years, and heavy horses were still used on the farm until 18 years ago, when he left to work for the council. Mr. Wheeler, who is 72 next month, retired in 1964, but has never lost his interest in horses and is still a racing enthusiast. He's also a keen gardener and football fan.

Gladys ('Jim' to her husband) is 69, and she retired when he did. She too left school at 14 to work in Powell's clock and watch shop in Fairford. She returned to work there after they were married, to stay a total of 27 years, with a break while she worked in the house at Glebe Farm.

Gladys made their anniversary cake herself, and the couple have been celebrating with friends and family at home throughout the week.

MR. HAROLD WHEELER and his wife Gladys, who live at Queen Elizabeth R.D. Siddington, and are due to celebrate their golden wedding anniversary on April 18th, Easter Saturday.

gram on a floor which was made up of concrete slabs covered over with large green tarpaulin sheets on VE night. This was in Hatherop Park opposite No 1 Bungalow.

Tuesday 21st April 1981 – At 12.15pm a service was held in St Swithin's Church, Quenington in memory of John Arnold my second employer at East Glos Engineering, Fairford. "The Boss" was placed in the chancel with flowers on the wood coffin and on the floor of the chancel. Old Godwin workers were there including Mr and Mrs Jim Newman, Fred and Mrs Harding, the two Cole brothers from Lechlade and Eric and Derek Cole who did so

Harold Wheeler.

much for Quenington Church in years gone by. Rose Bailey, Day before she was married, and her sister Ellen Townsend were there. The Boss was very clever with the slide rule and we always had plenty of iron and parts to repair agricultural machines with. Yes, I enjoyed my life in the agricultural machinery repair business – hard work but very interesting. Had a chat with my old school teacher John Arnold's sister Mrs Kinch. A wonderful teacher and how we all loved her.

May 23rd 1981 – Played my new organ which I have had this week on trial, my other small organ I have let go to Stroud Music Centre for the full money I paid for it. Should have some good winter evenings' music. The Landlord's agent wants to put the rent at the Lodge up to £17 per week, I think it is too much. But there we are. The family allowance has gone up so someone gains from my tax as a single man.

June 14th 1981 – Mr Herbert Hedges died in Fairford Hospital. He was Headmaster at Farmors School in the High Street. He was 99 years old. A man of average height, he believed in discipline and used the cane but was quiet spoken and a very polite and friendly man. He was admired by us all. I went to Fairford School for about a month after I did not completely pass the grammar school exam. My father bought a new cycle for me from Burt Aston's shop for £5 and half a crown for the carrier – no discount. My father worked for Mrs Cadogan, she was a manager of Hatherop School and took great interest in it, so my father had me brought back to Hatherop School under Mr Garner who also was a fine Schoolmaster. But when I left Hatherop School in April 1937, I went to the Fairford Evening Institute, known as night school, under Mr Hedges. Of course it was different from ordinary school – we were more free and were going to work for wages 5/– per week. We had good trips to the GWR at Swindon, the Gas Works and also Morris Motors at Oxford. But order and respect was the order of the day. We called him Sir and he addressed us by our Christian names and was always interested in how we were getting on. The night school fee was 5/– per term. I remember sitting for the English Exam in his study room at the top of the stone stairs in what is now the Youth Centre and Library. I wrote the exam about fire fighting equipment and have still got the pass paper of which my mother was so proud. I sat for the Maths Exam but did not pass. When I started work I went to Mr Hedge's house and had piano lesson by his daughter Jan on the school piano upstairs in Fairford School 2/6 for 35 minutes. When my father died in February in 1942 we could not afford more lessons but I am very happy that I learnt what I could at the piano in those days.

July 6th 1981 – A funeral service for Mrs Ruby Gibbs at Hatherop Church. She was one of the last Victorian ladies upright, honest and true. A fine Lady. For many years, with her husband Col Gibbs, she sat in the front pew facing the Rector's seat. Always interested in Hatherop church. Lady Howard and Lady Worsley did the flower decorations.

July 16th 1981 – A meeting at Glebe Farm to discuss about uniting the three church councils into one council. Farmer Hart provided two large bottles of white wine – very nice. Jennie Voaden and Reuben Sims were the only Cotswold born people there. Such are the changing times here. Representatives of all the three parishes were there. Quenington were concerned about a central control of finance, wanting to keep monies separate.

July 20th 1981 – A joint meeting of all three PCCs at Williamstrip House chaired by Earl St Aldwyn with information from the Arch Deacon Eric Evans. The meeting voted that we should be one council, some protests about finance from the Quenington member but the vote was carried that we go back to our own PCC meetings to vote the whole thing valid. Most of our top people want a joint council.

July 29th 1981 – Prince Charles Wedding to Lady Diana Spencer – I rise early and put up my flags and trimmings on the old Lodge, like my mother did for George VI's Coronation. Farmer Hart pulls up with his Land Rover about eight o'clock – he thought I had left it late for trimming up. But for the last three weeks at odd times at night I have been making up boards and pasting on my pictures. Last evening my great friend Mr Eddie Hunt came and fixed my flag and bracket on the sewage vent pipe. My TV set is not working so I went to Quenington School where a colour set was in the room. Lots of elderly ladies watching it, including Nurse Wearing of Hatherop and Mrs King who told me it was her late husband's birthday today. Mrs Violet Moulden did a wonderful job in providing a good salad lunch and a good sweet and a glass of sherry. I came away about two o'clock. A wonderful wedding in St Paul's Cathedral and lovely music. Lots of people are looking at my decorations – I finished them about 10.30am having started at 7am. Nothing worthwhile is done without effort.

Aug 4th 1981 – My decorations on this Lodge are still hanging fine. The street decorations by the school put up by Farmer Hart, and his own on Glebe Farm wall, were stolen on last Saturday night sometime after the Club had turned out. Such is the mentality of some people full of drink.

Aug 6th 1981 – Heavy rain in the night, the ground needed it. Arise at 6am take down my decorations. Three and a half hours to put them up, half an hour to take it down. The little plastic flags came off the sticks in the wet and the large picture I had of Her Majesty Queen Elizabeth II, Prince Charles and Lady Diana Spencer had slipped off the board. Lots of people have taken photos and it has given great pleasure to our people. I'm very pleased.

Aug 9th 1981 – My flags are all spread out in my front room and the hall to dry. Later I will take them off the sticks and store them in the old tin trunk upstairs. It's a long time ago in 1935 – the Silver Jubilee of King George V – when my mother made a flag with her hand-sewing machine. At the Coronation of George VI Mum really went to town with flags like all the other people in the village. How Mr Fred Ford laughed when he came along to see my Dad while the decorations were being put up – we were all happy. At VE Day Mum and I put stakes in the garden round the curved wall and hung what crepe paper we could find along with the flags. But this time I had to put everything high up on the house wall – people steal so much today yet, with the Welfare State, have so much. The engagement of Michael Hicks Beach, Viscount Quenington, has been announced so we shall have another great day God willing.

Sept 2nd 1981 – Mr Mervyn Bayliss called in the evening and told me I had wound up the chimes too hard, bumped the weight up to the beam, the wire rope had slipped off the pulley and jammed in the casing. I went to the tower, climbed the ladder and looked down into the weight box. Sure enough that is what I had done. Saw Mr Bayliss again at his house and we decided it was an engineer's job to jack up the weight and put back the rope on pulley.

Sept 4th 1981 – Saw Mr Chris Kinch at my old firm East Glos Engineers who will come and look at the job. I used too much strength and not enough brain.

Sept 9th 1981 – Cut some asters and walked to church at 1.30pm for Mrs Hartshorn's funeral. We carried Mrs Ted Hartshorn shoulder high to the grave at the west end of churchyard near the Castle where she had worked so many years.

September 10th 1981 – Meet the Sly brothers with the coffin of Dr Moorhead's old nanny, Mrs Gale. Wheel her to the church and place her in the chancel on trestles. The Hatherop Castle Girl's School will play a large part at this funeral I expect.

Sept 11th 1981 – I walk to the church for the burial of Mrs Gale, aged 80 years. Dr Moorhead and her daughter were there and all the school girls from Hatherop Castle school. A new school organist played the organ rather loud. The organ is powerful, perhaps he wanted to make a good impression the first time.

Sunday 13th Sept 1981 – Holy Eucharist at Hatherop church at 8am. At end of service I was told by Mr Pearson to leave my dog, Scramble, at home as he spoilt the service for everyone. The season time is not quite over and Scramble yelps. I took him outside and tied him to the boot-scraper by the door but he still yelped. Went to see Mr Pearson after breakfast and we both got hot under the collar – he sent me off. I wished him good morning.

Sept 23rd 1981 – PCC meeting at the village school. Lady Howard was late – collided with her car into one of Farmer Hart's tractors with outspread tine harrows. Got on well with Mr Pearson so all is well but will leave Scramble at home.

Wednesday 30th and Thursday 31st October 1981 – On these two evenings Mr Lee Bayliss and his father Mr M Bayliss lifted the jammed weight of Hatherop Church clock and freed the wire rope jammed in the pulley and re-hung the weight. Lee is very much used to heights and sat on the weight rope beam when I went up the ladder to have a look at what they had done. Saved the church a good repair bill and put right the damage Reuben Sims had done by winding the weight up too high.

Oct 8th 1981 – R Sims is having a photo taken of the 1941 photograph of Hatherop Home Guard taken at the site of the Old Rectory, Church

Hatherop Home Guard 1941 Back: Robert Hutchings, B Allen Middle: Harry Day, Bill Ash, J Westall, Cyril Rixon, Algy Bartlett, Harold Wheeler, J Hutchings Front: W Osman, George Mustow, Desmond Westall (on ground), Captain Sturt, Reuben Sims.

Mead now called The Severalls. The photo of Hatherop Section will be fixed in Hatherop ringing Tower as a lot of the men have passed over with the years. Capt Sturt took on the command of Hatherop section. He was a retired Cavalry man and a very good officer – he made Hatherop Home Guard a fine section. In private life he was an insurance agent and lived in Carey Cottage, Back Street, Quenington. He is now dead. How the old first war officers loved being in uniform again. The ARP room was at The Severalls by the back door. After 1941 no more camera films were available. From 1942 the build-up to get back on the continent was the sole aim and to beat the Germans. We want no more wars.

Saturday 31st October 1981 – Went to the opening of the new community centre at the old Quenington School. Lots of youngsters enjoyed the games of eating dough nuts on strings and the bobbing apple in buckets of water. Letter from Earl St Aldwyn was read out wishing the centre success and thanks to Mr Waring, who laid on the recording wiring, Mr John Moaby and Mr Jim Day for work they had done. Lots of refreshments brought round by Mrs Hart and her daughter. Mr Hart and Lady Worsley were also present. A folk group with Mr Ian Summerland, singer and guitar playing. The new role of the Quenington School had begun.

Sunday 22nd November 1981 – Visit of Frank Smith's daughter Kathleen from Cardiff, with her new husband Bill. Kathleen told me how when she was a young girl, she came from Cardiff by train with her mother to Cirencester Station and came out to Hatherop from Cirencester in Mr Lander's cart. They stopped at various cottages on the way with cotton and elastic and all sorts of goods people had ordered. Bits of paper were pinned on the gates for him to call.

November 21st 1981 – Pulled up the bells for Mr Michael Rixon's wedding at 2 o'clock. The church was full of people, lots of cars in the Castle forecourt. A maroon Roll Royce had white ribbons on by the Castle archway. At 2.30pm we ran the bells for thirty five minutes. A Hatherop man married in Hatherop Church, a fine affair. The reception I believe is being held at the Palmer Hall, Fairford.

The bell ringing team for Michael Rixon's wedding day. From left: Chris Harrison, Fred Harding, Reuben Sims, George Mustow (Captain) Mike Adams, John (Nipper) Reeves.

Sunday 13th Dec 1981 – Trees and the Irish yews all white and laden down with snow. Very pretty – the wonder and the power of Almighty God. Invited out to lunch by Mr Robinson and Mrs Bland but declined – must look after my dog and my birds. Cotswold people do not travel far in this weather. Electricity goes off. Fetch out our old paraffin lamp and two candlesticks with candles. Thank the Good Lord I have this Rayburn Stove going, keeps this house warm. In the days of my mother, before modernisation, we lived in the small front room, but very cold in the bedrooms. You did not hang about getting in or out of bed.

Dec 24th 1981 – Christmas Eve Service at Coln Church at 11.30pm. Service conducted by the Rev Derek Cowmeadow and layman Mr John Chudleigh. About eighty communicants including Lord and Lady St Aldwyn, their son Michael with his fiancé – a young lady from Brazil, and Peter Hicks Beach. The old church was decorated beautifully. Tall chrysanthemums stood each side of the altar, white and bronze. We sung the Christmas hymns and a long line of communicants stretched up the aisle. We wish each other a Happy Christmas and go home.

Jan 8th 1982 – Strong east wind with snow has blocked Hatherop/Fairford Road. Try to get to work with three-wheel van. I had to stop at the top of Hatherop Road before Barrow Elm. Snow blowing across road from Green Islands. Met a service truck coming towards me. We both were stuck. Farmer Hart's snow plough with Mr Gordon Legg came up and gradually got through. From the Fairford end came Lord St Aldwyn's Range Rover with Mrs Dorothy Wood on board. He put a rope onto the truck and pulled the truck clear. I backed my three-wheeler back some distance, managed to turn round and, with some pushing from some more men in a large car, got back to the Lodge. Farmer Hart is driving around firstly in a Land Rover and now on a tractor – a very busy man.

Jan 9th 1982 – Have plenty of food in store and sausages etc. in deep freezer. All traffic is stopped except for Farmer Hart's tractors going down the Eastleach Road. At one o'clock saw Mr Cyril Rixon who had walked to Home Farm to get some milk. He came in and I gave him a glass of my wheat wine and also the recipe for same. Our people made wine nine gallons at a time. Kept the cold weather out.

Jan 11th 1982 – Walk to Coln Stores with a knapsack on my back and a good stick to walk with. Walking back through Hatherop met the Coln Post Mistress who was taking the pensions to the old folk. She does this twice a week.

Jan 14th 1982 – A very cold, frosty morning. Talk to Mrs Lee Bayliss [*Kate*] who has got to take her child home from Hatherop School as the electric heating has broken down. With the old coke boiler there was never any trouble, simple and effective. She tells me how she stands about at 8 o'clock in the morning with her other child waiting for the Mini Bus to take the child to Fairford School. The Mini Bus is usually late and they all get so cold. Such is the way of modern school teaching methods.

Feb 4th 1982 – A memorial Service for Harold Wheeler in Hatherop Church and his ashes interred in his family grave by east window. Harold came from an old Cotswold family. A nice quiet man was Harold, a carter at Glebe Farm for years. He was about the last to use a horse binder and we used to have lovely sheaves of corn standing each side of the Parson's pews and at the altar in Hatherop Church – wheat and barley. We gave full honours to Harold, a good church man and did a lot in the churchyard at various times like his brother in law Jim Shepherd had done before him. Harold and his wife were a jolly couple, we missed them when they moved to Siddington to retire.

Good Friday 9th April 1982 – R Sims had a quiet day at home, rather tired. The Falklands dispute is very serious – hope the matter can be resolved without fighting. We have had enough war. But our people must be protected from invaders.

April 24th 1982 – Viscount Quenington had a blessing of his civil marriage to Gilda Maria Saavedra, a Brazilian lady, at Coln Church. The reception was at Williamstrip House at 3.30pm. The civil marriage was at Cirencester yesterday. Mrs Jennie Voaden sung Ava Maria at the service at Coln. Tom Lemon said the church was full of people with a Fairford Choir. Tim Morris at the organ. Eric Evans, Arch Deacon and the Bishop of Gloucester were there. I went to the reception with Mr Robinson and his daughter. The large marquee stretched all along the east side of Williamstrip House. Some say 1,500 people present and a thousand bottles of champagne drunk. The cake, made by Mrs Lemon, was three-tier and stood on a table. We were introduced by an MC in a red coat and white shirt, lots of morning dress and ladies in fine hats. Shook hands with the bride and groom and wished them well. Tables were round the tent where people could sit. The main centre poles were lit with two electric lights on each pole and a basket of flowers each side of the pole near the lights. Lots of waitresses with eats and bottles to top up the glasses. Heard the speech of the best man and the Viscount's reply. The side awnings were lowered a little as the tent got hotter. A television

Viscount Quenington and Miss Gilda Saavedra on their wedding day.

camera was at the entrance to the tent as we all came in. A West Indian steel band played at the northern far end of the tent. A fine reception, a lovely couple and a fine day.

May 1st 1982 – Announced on TV that the Falkland Island airfield at Port Stanley has been bombed by our aircraft. It has taken three weeks for our task force to get to the Falklands since the invasion by the Argentine troops. An unnecessary invasion.

May 8th 1982 – Our navy torpedoed the Argentine battle-ship with an air missile or rather hit it and it burnt out. A very sad affair but a matter of principle.

Friday 28th May 1982 – Watch the Pope's visit to England. The first visit ever. Heavy fighting in the Falklands, will be glad when it is over, losses on both sides.

Saturday 29th May 1982 – The Pope is getting a good welcome. I'm very pleased. The welfare state has took so much religion out of our people or rather their need of Almighty God.

Jock Reeves (on right).

Whit Sunday 30th May 1982 – Have had a visit from my friend Mr Tony Nash of Fairford who was on his way to see Mrs Jock Reeves. Tony told me the sad news – Jock aged 58 years died yesterday. I went to school with him – he served in the RAF and played a lot of cricket for Williamstrip. A nice quiet chap was Jock.

Tuesday 1st June 1982 – Goose Green has fallen to the Paras. Hope Port Stanley will be taken and our people relieved of the Argentine invader. Armed aggression must not pay.

June 9th 1982 – I have tried during my thirty years as Church Warden to do the best I can for the House of God in my small parish of Hatherop in whose ground the remains of my grandparents and my family all lie. One has lots of complaints, lack of people doing things you would like to see done. Mistakes I have made. The churchyard I levelled with Mr Charles Rixon. The frame for the Hatherop Ringers photo of 1981 was the mirror frame that my grandfather used for shaving. At night we shaved with a candle stood on top of the frame, unheard of today. My grandfather made good picture frames, also my father. The value of money was so different, my grandfather never earned or got £2 per week. £3 per week had first come in while my father was ill in 1942. Today I receive £100 per week and £150 is not uncommon. People have more things today, house purchase on mortgage, a car, TV, some on continental holidays. Teachers have another rise of £8.50p, a new age of property owning in this village, brings a new kind of society to the Cotswolds.

June 14th 1982 – White flags out at Port Stanley. The Argentines have given in. 11,000 troops surrender at Port Stanley, our country staged a wonderful force from eight thousand miles away and we are all relieved.

June 21st 1982 – Service for Albert Moaby in Coln Church at 2pm. Albert Moaby was 81 years, volunteered for the Second World War and served in the Orkneys. He is survived by his wife who is an invalid. George Mustow visited me at 4 o'clock and said he would like me to contact ringers in case the Royal Birth took place. At 9 o'clock the TV gave the news – a boy. So we shall be up the Tower Tuesday night at 7 o'clock. The Lord giveth and the Lord taketh away.

June 22nd 1982 – Tuesday night at 7 o'clock G Mustow, Chris Harrison, Mike Adams, John Reeves, Fred Harding, R Sims and the Rev Derek Cowmeadow rang Hatherop church bells for one hour in honour of the royal birth of a boy to the Prince and Princess of Wales.

July 3rd 1982 – A phone call from Mrs William Godwin of Northholme Road, Cirencester, to say her husband William Godwin is seriously ill in Memorial Hospital, Cirencester and would I let the Cirencester Buff Lodge he attended know. I'm very sad at the news. Brother Bill Godwin is a fine man and a good churchman and a wonderful bell ringer. A wonderful Buffalo when he was here at the St Aldwyns Lodge.

Sunday 4th July 1982 – Drove to Cirencester in the afternoon, parked my three-wheel van in the Forum car park and walked to the hospital. Do not know the way well enough to drive round there with this modern road system. Found Bill Godwin, bell ringer and Buffalo, asleep in the private ward off the main men's surgical ward. His wife holding his hand – the hand that had pulled so many ropes for peals in so many towers in this land and had learnt so many people young and old to ring. His eldest daughter was there and a son in law who came in. Bill is under sedation. He did not wake while I was there. Said good-bye to his wife and family and came away. I knew it would be my last look at Bill in this world.

Monday 5th July 1982 – Heard this evening that Bill Godwin had passed over that morning. Bill Godwin was a peal or method ringer who will be very much missed around here.

Sunday 26th September 1982 – Journey to Coln St Aldwyns in my three-wheel van to pick up Mr Tom Lemon and drove to Eastleach Church for their Harvest Festival at 11am. Small, opened-up bags of corn were in the porch, also two sheaves of corn each side of the old Norman doorway. Apples, fruit of all kinds, also flowers in the plain glass windows. What a fine old church it is. I think of my Uncle Jim Sims buried in Poulton churchyard who in 1906 worked on the new roof timbers on the church working for Bowley of Lechlade. They were putting them up piece by piece till Mr Bowley came and he said "come on put the roof trusses up whole not piece by piece". One man got drunk. The policeman came later and Mr Bowley said take them all and lock them up. This tale was told by my uncle Jim who was there.

October 27th 1982 – Go to the funeral service of Mrs Dorothy Bayliss in Quenington Church at 2 o'clock. A good congregation and a large gathering from the Bayliss family – Sid, Sam and Percy. Mrs Bayliss was a very jolly person and attended both Church and Chapel. She was ninety years old.

November 2nd 1982 – Notice a swelling on my dog Scramble's jaw. Take dog in three-wheel van to Mr Baxter's surgery at Lechlade in the evening. Dog examined by vet who said Scramble will die in a fortnight – he has a growth on his jaw. I am very shocked. Bring Scramble home, go to Buffs at Coln Forge, talk about Scramble. Decide in kindness to Scramble, who is fourteen years old that I will have him pass to happy hunting grounds. A fine big black dog with a fine head and jaws and big fine paws and fearless – price £3.

November 3rd 1982 – Drive Scramble to Lechlade after he had been along to Mr and Mrs Charlie Mills and had his morning bone which he always carried home. The saddest day in the life of Reuben Sims since he lost his mother in 1967. Mr Baxter put Scramble to sleep. His soul is now with his creator. Drove Scramble home, buried him at the Lodge where he walked across the road to Mrs Mills for bones. I have great grief. Scramble would jump and rush up Hatherop Tower stairs and sit in the ringing room while we rung the bells. He would lie in chancel of church while I played the organ on a Saturday evening. He would lie at the end of the nave by the Norman door in Coln Church at 8am Holy Eucharist. He would carry a pigeon when shot and was a wonderful house dog. No one will ever know what friendship he gave so freely to me. Of course you have worries and responsibility with a dog. Often I fell foul of our new rich visitors over Scramble. But it did not worry me. I'm a Cotswold man, born and bred here and have seen many changes in the last fifteen years. Not all for the good.

Sunday 14th Nov 1982 – Remembrance Service in Quenington Church. Rev Robson took the service. Mrs Lucy Thomas with her medals of the Second World War carried the Legion Wreath up the nave of the Church to Canon Robson in the Sanctuary who placed it on the altar table. Earl St Aldwyn read the names of the fallen of the three parishes in two world wars. We sung "O Valiant Hearts". Tom Lemon and R Sims sat in choir stalls the pulpit side. The local guides the other side. Their singing was not too bright. The church was not quite full, not so many ex-service men at these services as there used to be. Men used to wear navy blue suits, black ties and bowler hats. The last war has been over for thirty seven years, but lots of smaller wars. Now it is brown suits and light coloured ties for a lot of people.

Nov 20th 1982 – I have a yew post and a plaque put up at Scramble's grave. I am in contact with the RSPCA of Cirencester about another labrador dog. I must have a dog here – it is so quiet without one

Tuesday 7th Dec 1982 – Chatting amongst ourselves at Buffs at Coln Forge and talking to Mr Roger King, I found out the records of Hatherop Football Club from 1903 to 1951 were lost in a fire. One has to remember we had six years of war when sport stopped. The young as their age group came up went off to war, or in reserved jobs. Travel was curtailed, blackouts and ration books, some of the older men who kept the books of various things passed on and in one way or another lots of records were lost. No photos in 1942. I remember the Home Guard Physical Training group which I was in, giving a display on Coln Manor lawn. Coln Village Hall sounded with music and dancing three times a week. No civvy clothes in sight on the men after 1942. Most of the dances held were in support of the Red Cross. It is quite open to conjecture whether all the monies went that way. But who cared in such austere times. The older men had a night out at the local pubs after mid week Home Guard lectures, or night ops if beer was available, a night away from their wives; in ordinary times they would have been home, perhaps the nine o'clock news and then to bed. Many times the old Pig and Whistle at Quenington opposite Godwin's Works had the sign closed on the window but regulars were quietly drinking inside.

Outside the Pig and Whistle c.1935. From left: Tom Woodman, Mr Townsend, Ray Cox, Tom Lemon, George Harris, Mr Tarrant, unknown, Bert Edwards, Bert Vincent, Dan Barrett.

Saturday 18th December 1982 – My friends at work took me in a van on Wednesday 15th December to the Foss Dog Hotel on the Cirencester/Swindon road where I found a 12 month old Labrador bitch. Trixie Sims – she has brought life and friendship to me. She is fast, playful and very pretty.

Christmas Eve 24th Dec 1982 – Have a phone call from Mrs Moore of Sturminster Newton to say my Uncle Bob was unwell. He went to the Swan for a brandy, was took with a stroke and is in a hospital somewhere. Have phoned Roy Scammel who was going to have my Uncle Bob for dinner and tea on Christmas Day. I'm sad – my Uncle looked after his mother and also his sister Lou. They have all been very independent people. I am of the same stock. We lose out on the welfare state by it though. But we are all of a different generation. I am glad I went with Mr Hunt and his son of Quenington to see my Uncle in October and found him well. Walk to the church, call on the way for Jennie, but she had gone on and when I got to the church the lights were on and she was lighting the candles we had fixed earlier in the evening. The candles were the gift of Lady Howard of Dean Farm. No ringers. The church was full of people from the five parishes.

Sunday 26th December 1982 – Walk to church for 8am Communion. The Rev Cowmeadow had lights on also the lights on the Christmas Tree. R Sims tolled the Sanctus Bell. No one came. We carried on with the service. My people slept on. The words "Sleep on now and take your rest" apply to my parishioners today.

Wednesday 29th December 1982 – Have a visit from Mr John Winfield of Coln St Aldwyns – a good man, a parish counsellor for Coln and a Buffalo. He wanted to see my new dog Trixie and had some fun and games with her. We talked of how times have changed in these small parishes of ours. Lots done for the old aged pensioners and how there is scrounging and some wish two Christmas parcels from the Hatherop Castle Schoolgirls' Chrismas Gift Fund. All the material comforts of modern society but people have not found contentment, perhaps we never will. It is very quiet here and I spend a lot of time alone but a lot better now I have my labrador bitch Trixie.

Jan 2nd 1983 – The Fairford Bed Race is on – the beds with a competitor on were pushed past this Lodge. From Fairford they will go round the three villages and back to Fairford – all sorts of beds on wheels. The Lions van came up at the rear to pick up those who fell out of the race.

Jan 13th 1983 – Have purchased the June Lewis book – Farmors, Fairford and Primary Schools – price £2. I loaned Miss Lewis two old photos; one of school children late 19th Century and one 1902. The three girls

Villagers welcoming Mr Gardner Bazley home after his wedding in 1903. The 3 girls in the road are Alice Griffin, Mamie Moulden and Beatrice Sims (Reuben's Aunt Beatie). Right hand side against the railings – Mr Moulden (Head Gardener at Hatherop Castle) and beside him, Charlie Barnett. Centre in the road is Wilfred Barnett (later Butler at Hatherop Castle).

standing in the middle by the archway are left to right: Alice Griffin, Mamie Moulden and my aunt Beatrice Sims. By the railing far right is Mr Moulden, the head gardener. Miss Sims, [*not Beatrice mentioned above*] mistress at Coln School, may have been someone to do with Charles Sims, my grandfather's brother who was carpenter on the Coln Estate. They have come out well in the book. Rang Miss Lewis and thanked her for her work on her book.

Saturday 22nd Jan 1983 – John Winfield rung me up on the phone. He is cutting up a large wood bay window which has been taken out of the Bennett's house, opposite his lodge. The window was on the east side where an extension is being built. The timbers are pine, lovely pieces of wood about 7" x 3". I drove to Mr Winfield's house and found him, his wife and Mr Smith of Fairford cutting and splitting the wood for the fire. He gave me two pieces of wood on which were written Charles Sims 1890 and Boswell Sims 1890. Charles Sims was my grandfather's brother – carpenter for the Williamstrip Estate and buried in Coln churchyard. According to the late Mr Percy Mustow who ran the mill opposite, Boswell Sims married into the Mustow Family. Mrs Winfield said "They were not afraid to put their names on their work". How true, my people were craftsmen not jack-of-all-trades-master-of-none. I have brought the two pieces of wood home to keep.

Jan 29th 1983 – Trixie is like a tornado. Rushing down the path from the duck's house she slashed her face near her left eye. I rush her to Baxter at Lechlade who operated on her. I fetched her at 5 o'clock, cost of operation £17.25p. She is now quiet in my kitchen. The vet said how boisterous she is. I have to be much firmer with her. That is difficult. She wears me out with her pace, hope she will slow down in time. The shooting has now finished thank the Good Lord. A man with a shot-gun or a chain saw will make this country a desolate place, void of trees or wild life. He puts nothing back into the countryside.

Feb 2nd 1983 – Harry Day of Dean Farm died at Fairford Hospital around 7am – he was eighty years old. Harry was a real Cotswold countryman, spoke the Cotswold dialect like we all can should we desire to do so. He was a wonderful Home Guard – many times I have been out with him on night schemes at the Moors and at Barrow Elm at 4 o'clock in the morning. He could catch a fish with a looped wire on a pole, shoot a rabbit – he was a wonderful shot – and knew all about nature and farming. Liked a drink and smoked strong tobacco: Black Beauty. He is the last of the Day family at Dean Farm. At the Dean the people look after themselves like a community on its own. In the Hatherop Church Records now deposited at Gloucester it states John Mills of Dean Farm was Church Warden of Hatherop Church in 1746. He placed his X at the end of the vestry minutes. Harry is to be buried in his brother's grave at the west end of Hatherop Church.

Tuesday 8th Feb 1983 – Burial Service for Harry Day at 2pm. Walked to the church the night before and switched oil fire boiler on at 8 o'clock. Church nice and warm, it needs 12 hours to get any heat in building. A good congregation for Harry. Lord and Lady Howard and Mrs Susan Vicary were there with Charles Pollard and his family, Charlie Day and his wife. We sung two hymns, Jesus Lover of my Soul, O God our Help and Crimond.

February 13th 1983 – Ice melts on my duck pond about 12 o'clock and freezes again at night. My shirts and pants freeze on the line in the garden. Such is the life of a bachelor. Just creep out, well wrapped up, a good gin inside me and shut up ducks and hens, let Trixie run out in the Park and come back inside.

Mon 14th Feb 1983 – Have a heavy cold. I drive to Fairford at 8.30am to the doctor's surgery at Coronation Street. Saw a receptionist who said as I had no appointment I would have to wait till the end of outpatients. But Dr Henderson, she later informed me, would see me before he started his regular appointments. Dr Henderson is a fine young man with glasses. I shall never forget how, dressed in a red cassock, he played at the schoolmaster Mr Hedge's funeral and then revived a man who collapsed in the church. Then went back to the organ and played again for the service. Dr Henderson gave me tablets and a liquid to take this week. I think of 1942 when my dad died in February. How my Uncle Jim Sims who is buried in Poulton churchyard came over in a car with one gallon of petrol he scrounged off someone – there was no petrol to drive about with then. How my Dad greeted Jim. He said "Good Boy Jim, Good Boy". My father was at peace after seeing Jim, his brother, and how Uncle Jim stopped in the doorway of this Lodge front room and looked at my Dad laying in the bed across the room by the main road window. His wife told me later when he came home he said "Our Bill will not be alive in the morning". How true he was. My Dad died in my mother's arms around 7am after she told Mrs Barnett to call me. I rushed down the stairs. My Dad had raised his hands to heaven and the Good Lord received him. It will be the happiest day of my life when the trumpets sound for me on the other side and in the presence of the Almighty, my Dad, my hard working mother, and my young sister will be there to greet me and what a reunion it will be.

Tues 15th February 1983 – I am feeling better. My friend Eddie Hunt calls to see me in the evening, we have a drop of gin together – his wife Winnie has sent me up a big cake. We chat about work and also about the new way of having up to five days sick and signing your own sick leave paper. I have never heard of such goings on. Noticed when I drove back from Fairford on Monday to get my groceries that the large beech tree, which stood in Coln School playground by the hedge going up the church path, has been sawn down. It was about 2'6" in diameter. I think it a great pity. It takes one hundred years to grow a fine tree

Saturday 19th February 1983 – I heard the news that George Day of Meysey Hampton had died. He was working for our firm the DOE before he retired about three years ago. George was about the last who helped Baldwin the builder move the Fairford church stained glass windows at the beginning of the Second World War to the cellars of Fairford Park House. He was also at the trials of the SS concentration camp leaders while in the air force in Germany. One was the Beast of Belsen, Kramer. George was a short stocky man, a good gardener and won many show prizes at local flower shows. A bachelor like myself, he must have spent a lot of time alone but was always busy with his garden. God Bless Him.

March 24th 1983 – Have an oak frame made by my father William Sims to fit a painting done by the Rev Sackville Bourke before Hatherop Church was enlarged by Baron de Mauley in 1854. A very interesting picture given by Mr Tony Cotterill of Down Ampney.

Wednesday 27th April 1983 – At 7.30am. Called at Jennie Voaden's house. We had arranged to go to the church and screw on the water colour painting of Hatherop Church. Mr David Mordant of Fairford has fitted it on a maroon background in the frame I have altered which was made by my father. I screwed it on the choir vestry wall. I am sad we have no ringers to ring the bells.

Saturday 28th May 1983 – Mr Hart called at around 10am. I was having my breakfast, arose late. He said there was about £25 per week from our Church Insurance for Mr Cyril Rixon who cut his foot with the church mower. We talked about the bird dawn chorus. I said it was nothing so strong as years ago when the trees were around, of course the 1963 winter killed off so many birds. Parson Lowe then said it would take twenty years to get the bird life back but modern sprays and the elm disease have stopped a lot of that.

Frazer "Farmer" Hart.

Sunday 5th June 1983 – On Saturday bought six hens from battery cages and have put them in my run – they will have a new and wonderful time here. Factory Farming should be banned.

Sunday 12th June 1983 – Cecil Voaden rung me up this morning about 9.30am and told me the sad news that our bell captain George Mustow had passed over at 4.30am in Fairford Hospital. We have lost a good churchman, chorister for 76 years in Hatherop Choir and also bell ringer for many years more than my life time and I am sixty years old.

Thursday 16th June 1983 – Have the day off and go to George's cremation service at 3pm – a lot of people there.

June 24th 1983 – Called at Jennie's house in the evening, she told me Mrs Mustow feels the departure of George greatly and has gone back to bed. Mrs Barbara Holden has written to me to say the ringers of the Gloucester Association stood in silence at the Chedworth ringing meeting the same night we rung muffled at Hatherop in tribute to George Mustow. She also asked me to find someone to take on the job. Jennie does not want it so I shall take the job on, this means opening and closing the tower, after the teams of ringers have rung there on various days or tours. In passing George was always proud of the bell muffs which were made by his father, a cobbler. The muffs are kept in the old church vestry chest in the clock room. I have now to write a piece in the Parish News about George Mustow.

Saturday 2nd July 1983 – Have a visit from one of Dolly Simpson's family from Australia, who are looking up the family relatives. I told them about Jane Simpson who is buried in Hatherop churchyard with the hymn verse on the stone. He told me that the little stone of a Simpson child on the south side by the Mustow graves was a Simpson child who fell out of a window at the old game-keeper's cottage in the wood at Dean Farm. The Simpson family still keep it clean. The gentleman from Australia was amazed at it being preserved so long.

Wednesday 6th July 1983 – Saw Mrs Kathleen Nash at the letter box by East End house in Fairford on my way to work. I asked Kath how Tony Barnes her brother was as he is ill and in Stratton St Margaret Hospital. She said he was very ill and could not be operated on. I am sorry he is now ill at 57 years. Mrs Joan Browning is ill and in bed. I took her a pot begonia last Friday – her eyes are very bad. Mrs Margaret Tarrant is ill and is slightly better and being pushed around by her husband Norman. May the Good Lord look down on all these friends of mine and give them all his peace.

Saturday 16th July 1983 – Took Tom Lemon to a service in Bouthrop Church, Eastleach at 3 o'clock. Keble preached his first sermon there in 1875. Met Mr Ronald Newport there, he is a member of a very old Eastleach family. Dr Henderson's choir led the singing of three Keble hymns. Keble's picture was placed by the pulpit on the chancel arch ledge. The Bishop of Gloucester preached about John Keble and the Oxford Movement. I'm not too thrilled with the Bishop's addresses. I nearly went off to sleep. Bouthrop Church has been repaired and cleaned now it is under the care of the Redundant Churches Commission. It still has those lovely hanging lamps as of old when our forefathers prayed there. Eastleach school was quietly sold for about £16,000 – a giveaway price – school, schoolhouse, garden and playground. Southrop had a poor school but were united to fight closure of their school so they won the day but had to have extra classrooms built on. The closure of these little village schools and the disposal of their contents has been a clandestine operation through and through. Tom Lemon and me went to Mr Newport's house across the clapper bridge from the church and had a nice glass of beer and then drove home around 6 o'clock. Trixie my dog chased the Castle donkeys, naughty girl.

Saturday 16th July 1983 – Dear Joan Browning has passed to the other side. At 2pm the service was held for Joan. The church was full of people including the police sergeant of Fairford in uniform. There were a lot of lovely flowers. Her husband Donald wrote on his wreath card "We are but flowers passing through till we meet again" Donald xxx. Harry Maunders, her brother in law, was very upset. One is so helpless.

Aug 14th 1983 – My great friend and workmate at Briggs, Tony Barnes, who was striker for Fred Parsons the smith and also farrier, is very ill in Princess Margaret Hospital. To be with Tony as we knew him, life was gay and full of fun. I can see him now in the middle war years shoeing Gantlett's and Park Farm cart horses then riding them back to their stables bare-backed and laughing about it – his thick black hair blowing in the wind. Tony could shoe a horse as good as anyone.

Aug 22nd 1983 – A phone call from Mrs Dorothy Barnes to say Tony her husband had passed over at Princess Margaret Hospital. Some of my happiest days were working with Tony. Hard sweating work at the anvil but happiness all around. I am very sad today but Tony has been in hospital for two months and did not improve. What a sportsman he was, footballer, cricketer, dart player, bird fancier, joint secretary of the local Sports Club. He led a full life, always happy and in the centre of things, spreading his happiness to us all.

Wednesday 24th August 1983 – A heavy day. Journey to Kingsdown Crematorium at 9.30am with the Rev Cowmeadow, who told me his daughter had given birth to a son and he was now a grandfather. We hold a small service for Tony's cremation, drive away and come back to Hatherop Church and hold a memorial service there at 11.30am. A tape recorder was switched on by his son Tony, which had the song "One Day at a Time Sweet Jesus" which Tony requested in the hospital many times while he was there.

Thoughts on my friend Tony Barnes: When I was 21 years old on the 11th Jan 1944, I played football with Tony against the RAF on Hook's Landing Field opposite Homeleaze. We had to push a plane off the pitch before we could start the match. The whole team pushed the plane but could not move it very well. One of the players looked back and saw Tony on the tail-end pushing the other way – typical of my friend Tony Barnes. And what a game we played – we lost 4–2 but had a wonderful match.

At 1.30pm I went to Kingsdown with the Barnfield family for a service of cremation for Jack Barnfield aged 79 years – my friend and neighbour. He was the last of Mr Briggs's traction engine drivers with the threshing tack.

Monday 29th Aug 1983 – A good church fete at Quenington House which is now owned by new people after the death of Mrs McFarland. She was nearly 100 years old. Lots of repair work has been done, the fete is held where the old flower shows were held years back. Lots of new people, so much new building and changing hands of property has been done at Quenington over the last fifteen years.

Sunday 4th Sept 1983 – I am thinking about a piece to write in the Parish News on my friend Tony Barnes. His mate, Fred Parsons, was a master farrier in the first war and taught Tony how to shoe the horses. Fred's stock phrases were: "The days are not long enough for what we have to do" and "There is flesh and blood there, we are not driving nails into a piece of board". Fred had shod the cab horses in London before the 1914 war when the pot boy brought the beer round in watering cans. Tony with his black curly hair used the sledge and pounded the white hot metal on the anvil, the forge roaring, Fred and Tony sweating and the anvil ringing all day long. On frosty mornings the pony that pulled Mr Raven's bread van and Mr Ryman's milk float pony would be waiting to be shod with frost nails – this went on every day while the frosts lasted so that milk and bread could be delivered round Fairford. They were happy, hard working days. I stood with Tony in Mr Briggs office when he sold the firm to Mr and Mrs J Arnold and he gave us all a pound for each year of our service. I had £16, Tony I believe, had £13. In his address Mr Briggs said "we were more like a happy family than a firm". A lot of the humour and the nature of Tony Barnes made it so.

Monday 26th Sept 1983 – Jennie told me Charlie Taylor the organist at Southrop was found dead in bed. The Harvest Festival at Eastleach was sung without the organ.

Friday 30th Sept 1983 – Heard that Mr Cyril Sly of Northleach the Undertaker has died after an operation in Cheltenham Hospital. Cyril was a fine business man and also gentle and polite. A fine gentleman. I think of the times I met him at the lychgate of Hatherop church at night with his brother Lou and wheeled our departed up the path and into Hatherop Church the night before a burial and how well everything was carried out with reverence and dignity. God Bless him always.

Saturday 1st Oct 1983 – Ring Mrs E Hill of Courtbrook, Fairford (Joyce Alder) to tell her I am bringing the Parish News with a write-up about her brother Tony. Joyce is still the same girl as we all used to dance in those wonderful times in Coln Village Hall. The youth of today do not know of the times we had dancing. No bars with drink, just cups of tea and some sandwiches. She said she was 61 years on Sept 29th – just a little older than me. How easy it is to talk to people on the phone today.

Sunday 2nd Oct 1983 – I think of times in the war years when, with my friend Tony and Charlie Pollard, we went to Eastleach village hall on our push bikes, danced there all night, bought some cakes which were home-made for about 1 shilling. The dance was 1 shilling also. Fine times – do not get times like it now. The drive-ins for cars, people have more money, go to the supermarkets in Cirencester and buy all their needs. Gardens put down to grass, very few plant allotments. Plenty buy from the green-grocers at the Spar in Fairford Market Place and the old greengrocer Smith over the bridge in Milton Street. The young do not congregate at the Pump House in Hatherop village as they did when I was a young man. Discos and drink, clubs etc. Yes, a new society has emerged. But the work of the Lord goes on.

October 29th 1983 – Have had a letter from a Mr Michael Sims of Billingshurst, West Sussex. He is tracing the Sims family tree. On a recent visit to Arlington Mill, he saw the book of John Sims 1818 which I had placed there and wondered if I were the same family. I have written back to him. Neither I, nor my people, knew that Robert Sims, a brother of my grandfather, had moved to Dorking in the last century, this Michael Sims has three sons around eleven years of age.

Saturday 5th Nov 1983 – I went to Coln and practised in the afternoon on that lovely Coln Church organ. Before doing so I walked down to the lower grave yard by the Village Hall. I looked at the old Hall which gave so much pleasure to our parents and my generation and I felt very, very sad. Some of the window panes are broken. Ivy is growing up the back wall and clogging the gutters. Parts of the roof crest are broken. The old Hall is slowly decaying through lack of maintenance. Oh, the glorious nights we had there. In the War years, when no one could travel far, black outs and cycles, Mrs Gaiger's band on the trestled stage at the church end. Who cared, we danced all night. Yes, my heart aches to see the old hall neglected and sold. So much public money was put into the modernisation which did no good. The nights we had there in the physical training team with Sgt Major Austin and Sgt Finnison of the Hatherop Castle SAS in the last war. All lined up in the centre of the hall, then touch four walls

Amateur Dramatics in Coln Village Hall. Front from left: Gilbert Burge, Eric Cole, John 'Pat' Patheyjohns. Back: Delma Burge, Harold Burge, two unknowns, Jean Bullimore, unknown, Margaret Loving.

and back again, great stuff. The fancy dress dances, the whilst drives, the Co-op meetings, the Church Mission displays, the Sports Club Dinners. The amateur dramatics on the stage all gone but lovely memories. That was village life which is no more.

Sunday 6th Nov 1983 – Play three hymns on that sweet little organ in Coln Church for Holy Communion at 9.30am – about twenty people I would say at a guess. The Rev Peter Murray read the lessons from his wheelchair as he has a job to walk now. What a fine cheerful man he is.

Wednesday 9th Nov 1983 – Catch Marchant's bus at 1 o'clock and go to Cirencester Hospital for a check up. Sit with Mrs Rose Bailey and we chatted about the old times we had dancing in Coln Village Hall. I told her how sad I was at the condition of the hall today. We both agree how much better the hall was before it had the new floor in and how we dressed up at the fancy dress dances together with Gwen and how Mr Rixon dressed up as the little old lady and what fun we had. Rose was a shepherdess, Gwen was a fortune teller, and Mrs Gaiger's band playing. Also Mr Vic Cox with his radiogram playing all the records – tunes like So They Made Him a Major, a Blooming Sergeant Major, His Hat Won't Fit Him Any More; Beloved Be Faithful; I'm Dancing with Tears in My Eyes; Apple Blossom Time; Anniversary Waltz; Who's Taking You Home Tonight; One Day We Cried Together; Three Little Sisters; The Hokey

Kokey; the St Bernard Waltz and Palais Glide; You Are My Sunshine; Moonlight Becomes You; I've Got Spurs That Jingle Jangle Jingle; Yo Ho Ho the Sailor with the Navy Blue Eyes; You Will Never Know How Much I Missed You; I'll be Seeing You in All the Old Familiar Places; I'll Walk Alone; and many more like Silver Wings in the Moonlight and Coming In on a Wing and a Prayer. It is dark now – floor half way up the windows and difficult to heat. A small stove was put in to try and put heat up the stairs but not much good. The catering section, under the Godwin girders, was never finished and never used much. One piano is left on the stage upstairs, one piano in poor condition downstairs. All left there after the Earl St Aldwyn sold the building.

Sunday 13th November 1983 – The Remembrance Service was held at 10.30am in Coln St Aldwyns Church. Mr Henry Bennett played the organ. Jennie Voaden, Tom Lemon, R Sims and ex-serviceman Mr Ernest Tarrant who during the service laid the wreath, given by the Fairford Branch of the Royal British Legion, on a stand in the chancel. After the service, preceded by the Church Wardens and the Rev Cowmeadow, Mr Tarrant took the wreath and laid it on Coln War Memorial. Earl St Aldwyn read the names of the fallen of the three parishes. A good muster of girls from Hatherop Castle School. At 6pm a service was held in Hatherop Church. We all sat in the choir stalls – Lady Howard, Mr and Mrs Wood from Coln, Mrs Cowmeadow, Jennie Voaden, Chris Harrison, Tom Lemon. A very poor congregation for Remembrance Sunday. The old estate workers made so much difference.

Saturday 19th November 1983 – Have had another letter from Mr Michael Sims of 9 Silver Lane, Billinghurst, West Sussex RH14 who is a descendant of Robert Sims, my grandfather's elder brother. One house he called Arlington, after Arlington, Bibury where he was born. This house was sold last year after his Uncle Robert died, having been in the same family for about 110 years. My family never knew where the other brothers and sisters of my grandfather went to, except Aunt Avis who had a house and died in Oxford. Through giving old John Sims woodworker's book to Arlington Mill, I have found out there are plenty of Sims family around in the Sussex area and also Ickenham where Joseph Sims went and was a good carpenter. Also they were true to tradition and good churchmen.

November 23rd 1983 – Shot guns were fired in Mr Lander's fields between 8 o'clock and 9 o'clock, lots of lights from a land rover. The wild life gets little peace here now. Pheasants reared in Stoneyhurst's cover for shooting. Very poor sport, they are so tame and have to be driven so much to make them fly to shoot them down – the sport of the privileged classes.

Monday 5th Dec 1983 – My dog Trixie gets out while I see to my bedroom, goes out to the road and is knocked down by a car. The postman called and told me, I go out, dog lying in the road. The driver of the car very distressed. I thought she was dead but she moved when I touched her so get her in a sack and take her indoors. Ring Mr Baxter of Lechlade who said bring her in. Trixie has a dislocated back leg now fixed in plaster. I fetched her home at 5.30pm – she is very quiet and stiff. Glad she is no worse.

Sunday 18th Dec 1983 – I have had a heavy cold for a week now. Did not wake up to go to my Hatherop Church for 8am service. A day at home by the Rayburn Stove. Mr Hunt my great friend from Quenington came yesterday and brought me a bottle of cheap Co-op whiskey. We sampled some of it and I have drunk a great deal today to get rid of this cold. I have failed the good Lord today. I have not been to the Church of God to repent my sins. Mr Philip Bullimore came this evening and we talked about Coln Village Hall and all the good times we had there, how television and cars had changed our lives, how we are all struggling to maintain our so called standard of living.

Mr Phillips and Mr Hart have had their weekend shoots of killing the wild life. £7 a day is paid to the beaters who drive up the pheasants to be shot down by the privileged classes. A so called sport which delights these over-subsidised farmers who do not grow swedes, mangles or kale.

Sunday 25th December 1983 – Walk to church at 7.45am. See the lights come on in church east window. The Rev Cowmeadow had arrived. I switch on the main church lights and also the Christmas Tree. We choose two hymns: "Oh Little Town of Bethlehem" and "O Come All ye Faithful". About a dozen people arrive and we start the service. I played "Hark the Herald Angels Sing" to finish the service and we all came away. With a Christmas card and a bottle of sherry for Mr Bayliss and Mr Cyril Rixon who do so much for our church with clock-winding and keeping the churchyard cut then spent the rest of the Christmas Day with my friend, Mr John Iles of Lechlade.

Jan 11th 1984 – Reuben Sims's birthday. I am 61 years old. Have some nice cards – one from my cousin Rose Wallbridge of Chandler's Ford, Hants. Mr Norman Tarrant came along in the evening and brought me a packet of cigars from his wife and himself. I gave him a tot of whisky. Norman's wife has been poorly for some time.

Feb. 6th 1984 – Fairford Silver Band meeting tonight at 8 o'clock to see if the band can continue as the players are young and few. I have played with them since 1947. I am still a member although no longer play. Am trying a baritone – the instrument I started with. A great gale is blowing tonight. This wild gale blew down a lot of trees and branches. A large cedar by the side of the Williamstrip Lodge, on the right hand side going from Hatherop to Coln and by the drive which goes across the road down through the meadow, blew down in the night and across the road. Mrs Victor Cox, an elderly widow on her own, lives there. I am told she got up in the night because of the storm. It must have been a frightening experience for her – it is good the tree did not go down on her house.

Tuesday 14th Feb 1984 – Went to the Coln Lodge Buffalo Dinner at the New Inn, Lechlade – a very good meal enjoyed by eleven of us, wives and all. Very frosty and a thick fog for the drive home at 11 o'clock. Several young ladies about eighteen to twenty in the New Inn drinking or having a meal with their boyfriends. How different when I was that age – a good night digging on the allotment in the summer and at home or night school at Fairford in the winter. When the war was on the girls had no lovely clothes like they have today and only older, married ladies went to the local pubs like the New Inn at Coln.

Friday 24th Feb 1984 – Go to church for funeral service of Mrs Joynes aged 85 years. Mrs Joynes was the wife of Mr Joynes who is buried by our old churchman Jim Shepherd. Mr Joynes worked as gardener for Col Gibbs for many years and then moved to South Farm and worked for Mrs Townsend. She and her daughter were at the funeral. From Hatherop there was Mrs Maunder, Mrs Cyril Rixon and R Sims.

March 11th 1984 – Service at Hatherop Church at 11am. Ringers from Harrow on the Hill rung from 10.15 to 11 am – the first time I have heard a ring of changes in Hatherop Tower since the Second World War. Before the war there was always a band of estate ringers at Morning Service but since the War, Mr Jim Shepherd and also George Mustow used to chime three bells. Bob Hutchings and me joined just after the war and learnt to chime in the morning and we used to have a side for Evensong. Lots of people liked the bells ringing today. The 18th century coffin stool has been stolen from Coln Church. The other one was taken some years back. People in cars are very mobile today and it is so easy to pillage these little country churches.

March 19th 1984 – Went to Fairford Band practise in the chapel schoolroom in Milton Street – the first time for five years since I finished cornet playing when my teeth were finished. I played a baritone instrument and quite enjoyed it.

April 25th 1984 – Mr Dennis Bartlett in the last fortnight is turning the blacksmith's shop at Coln into a bungalow. A lot of work involved.

May 6th 1984 – I have read the two books by Kitty Hart who was at Auschwitz Camp. All people should read these books on the evils of man.

May 13th 1984 – Had a look at the graves at the back of the old village hall at Coln. People there like Mr George Kiddle who had a waxed moustache, his son Fred who ran the bus called the Mascot into Cirencester, also his wife Maud who outlived him and was interested in church and local affairs. Fred Kiddle was wicket-keeper in Williamstrip 2nd XII before the war when I started cricket.

Willliamstrip Cricket Club 1931 Back row from left: 1st George Mustow, 3rd Albert Bayliss, 4th Sandy Moaby, 5th Charlie Winstone, 10th Edwin Griffin. Middle row from left: 6th Fred Kiddle, 8th Charlie Mills, 9th Ernie Tarrant. Front row from left: 2nd Charlie Burge, 5th Jesse Blackwell, 7th Harry Rogers.

Six houses up for sale at Hatherop. The Lodge at the bottom of the hill by the iron bridge where Mr Messenger lived who was the chauffeur for Hatherop Castle; The old Reading Room, now a bungalow; Mr Mowat's house by the church lychgate where George Wheeler lived when I was a boy. He used to work for the Rev Davis at Church Mead. He was an old man when we were at school, in the playground we held out our hands and he used to give us a good whack with his hand – a good stinger he called it, then he used to laugh; The Gardener's Cottage opposite the school is for sale where George Moulden lived who attended to the greenhouses in the Castle gardens and also stoked the school boiler; also No 41 next to this Lodge where Mr Arthur Iles lived with his family – he was a gardener in the Castle Gardens. His son John who lives at Lechlade has been a good friend to me.

May 14th 1984 – Talk at the Buff Lodge with Bro. Roger King, Bro. John Winfield, Bro. George Jones, Bro. Wilfred Franklin and Bro. Dennis Bartlett about the Coronation Times of Queen Elizabeth II in 1953. At Coln they had a dance in the Cadet Hut in Coln Meadow. John Winfield made up a 9" television set out of two radar sets. He got about 400 yards of cable from the air base to get the electricity to the cricket pitch for the radiogram for the sports held there.

May 25th 1984 – Drove Jennie to the Archdeacon's Visitation at Fairford Church at 6 o'clock. We could not see him until after his address at 7.30pm. He also stated in his address that Mr Verey of Barnsley had died and spoke of the many books he had written on Gloucestershire. Jennie and I went in to the vestry and saw the Archdeacon. Jennie told him how the Vicarage at Coln leaks in the roof like a sieve. He said he would contact the Parsonage Committee right away. R Sims told him there was no letter box on either door at the vicarage and how many more vicarages had no letter boxes. The Archdeacon said he would deal with it. (The Parsonage Committee are a poor lot, no architect, they fiddle and muddle along). Archdeacon Eric Evans is a wonderful man with a wonderful gift of oratory in the pulpit (should be a bishop).

June 16th 1984 – R Sims played the organ at Hatherop for Matins at 11am – what we would do without the girl's school at the Castle I do not know. There is very little support from the new people who have bought the old estate cottages. I'm told the cottage at the bottom of Hatherop Hill, where chauffeur Messenger lived, has been sold for £80,000. The Castle School has sold the old Reading Room. It is said that Mr Mowat's son bought the estate agent's house known as Sharringtons, the house that was built for my grandfather. When he was removed as foreman carpenter by Mr Gardner Bazley, he lived in the School House and died there. My grandfather left Sharringtons in 1910 and died in the School House in 1918.

Sunday 8th July 1984 – HE at Hatherop Church at 8am. Church was decorated with white carnations for a funeral on Monday afternoon of a 12 year old boy knocked down by a lorry in Manchester. He is the son of one of the girl pupils in past years at Hatherop Castle Girl's School who requested her boy to be buried if possible by the de Mauley chapel doorway.

July 19th 1984 – After a long illness of about two years Margaret Tarrant, wife of Norman Tarrant, passed over at 7.30am in Fairford Hospital. She was a Lancashire lass who came down south and married Norman in 1956. A grand, jolly girl who loved life. Norman and his family cared for her most wonderfully.

Wednesday 25th July 1984 – Funeral Service for Margaret at 12 noon. Lots of local people present. Some fine flowers were on the two iron stands by the pulpit and by the parson's pew where the lectern now stands. We carried Margaret shoulder high down the church path to the memorial gate. Laid her in the hearse and drove to Kingsdown Crematorium for a short service with the Rev Cowmeadow. Margaret Tarrant's casket will be buried privately tomorrow.

August 12th 1984 – Tom Lemon took me round the old Manor House at Coln where he does some part time work. The house is well kept up by an architect firm. The old stones in the passage way to the kitchen are well worn with the tramp of many feet with the meals being carried out and the old dresser is still there filled with crockery. An Aga cooker is going in the place of the old range. I thought of the days when my mother worked there for old Lady Lucy, the present Earl's grandmother. A swimming pool is now built in the lawn where, in the war, we performed as a physical training team of the Home Guard under Sergeant Major Austin of Hatherop Castle SAS. The large kitchen garden is still there but it needs six gardeners to keep it going in the old style. The tool house with apple racks and the fire place which kept out the frost is still there. The summer house which used to face the tennis courts is leaning and needs putting upright. This is a fine English Manor House.

Hicks Beach Family 1909. Back: Lady Victoria Hicks Beach, Hon Michael Hugh Hicks Beach, Sir John Keane, Lady Eleanor Keane (nee Hicks Beach) Front: Vicountess St Aldwyn (Lady Lucy, later Countess St Aldwyn) Hon Mrs Michael Hicks Beach (nee Marjorie Brocklehurst), Viscount St Aldwyn (later Earl St Aldwyn).

Thursday 16th August 1984 – John Plaister of Swindon picked me up in his car at 7.45pm. We met Mr Mervyn Bayliss and Jennie Voaden my Co-Warden and went up the tower and decided to have a winding jack for the clock from Gillett and Johnson. John and I went on to Coln Church, met Baden Powell and the Rev Cowmeadow and went up the tower and John Plaister advised them on a winding jack for Coln Church clock 1857. A fine old clock but of course the Hatherop clock is the real thing of beauty. Took John Plaister for supper at this Lodge – he likes my grandfather clock.

Saturday 1st September 1984 – Fairford Band played at a cricket fete at Poulton in the field by the church. Lots of cars and people there, how times have altered. Saw Mrs Bert Ayers who was there with her daughter Janet. She said she knew no-one at the fete, all strangers, that's how the Cotswold villages have all changed since the days when we had bucket lavatories emptied in the garden or wheeled to the allotment with ashes mixed and no baths, only a tin bath and water boiled in a copper, which held nine gallons and was used for wine making as well as washing, boiled up and then rinsed in a cold tub. I get into awful trouble with Fairford Band who in my time had such wonderful players of contest standard – Bert Cuss, solo cornet, who had a lip like a piece of tin; Alf Cook Junior who played euphonium far above the average player and is retired now; also Dick May who played the trombone – he had such a lovely tone, he is now dead. These were the players under Mr Alf Cook Senior who was Bandmaster and a Traction Engine driver for Mr Briggs who were the corner players when Fairford Band won at contests at Reading in the fall, Witney and Oxford in the spring. It was always said the Cooks and the Cusses held Fairford Town Band. I am playing baritone now and find it so different from a cornet but I'm 61 years and I'm still trying. I get out of favour with the band people because I stick to the rules which are on a card from 1947. This is the rules of Fairford Band after the Second War in which they dropped the name of Fairford Silver Prize Band, to Fairford Silver Band. I love Fairford Silver Band, it has given me so much pleasure in my life, playing with such fine players. Bob Hutchings and his wife Pat called this evening from Cheltenham and we talked over old times when his father was keeper at Williamstrip Lodge. Lovely old days of peace and contentment.

Sunday 16th Sept 1984 – Harvest Festival at Coln Church at 11 am. Coln Church very pretty with flowers and colour prints in the Sanctuary from Williamstrip House. The old candle brackets on both sides of the sanctuary have been polished and look lovely with the electric light bulbs, the first time I have seen them polished. I took down a basket of damsons.

Plastic oranges in the porch did not go down very well with some of the congregation. People do not grow the vegetables our fathers did.

Saturday 6th Oct 1984 – Tracey Voaden's wedding – rise up the bells ready for ringing after the wedding. Drive home, wash and change. Drive to Mrs George Mustow at 33 Hatherop and take her to the Castle archway and see her up the steps into the church. The groom and the best man are being photographed outside the church porch. Mrs Morris's choir is in the church. Mr Tim Morris is playing the organ. I light all the candles. The service starts at 1 o'clock. Mr Cecil Voaden walks in with his youngest daughter Tracey on his arm, she looks lovely. I go out after the Blessing and go up the tower to greet Mrs Eileen Godwin, Fred Harding, Chris Harrison, John Reeves and Mike Adams. Mrs Godwin did the calls and we pulled away. After half an hour we stood the bells, toasted the bride and groom with a bottle of wine placed on the ringing table with six glasses the night before by Mrs Jennie Voaden. I drove to Southrop Village Hall for the reception. The rain had kept away – the church was heated and warm – in all a good, pretty wedding. The village hall at Southrop was full of guests. A long table at the stage end had the wedding cake and the bride and bridegroom and the near relations; a long table in the centre was full of food to eat, lots of small tables around the hall full of guests. Telegrams were read by Nigel Voaden, lots of photos taken by Stella Voaden. After a good meal and wine we parted our ways. Jennie Voaden wore a lovely blue hat. After Tracey Voaden's wedding I drove Tom Lemon to Quenington Chapel for the Harvest Supper – we had a good meal for 50p. Rose Bailey, Ellen Townsend, Betty Lawrence, Pam Holland were there, all local ladies of my school days or just after. A film show of Africa followed the meal and we all came away at 9.15pm. Coming up to Hatherop, cars were all lined along the village road from the green to the old rectory. A disco was held at Hatherop Working Men's Club for Tracey Voaden's wedding.

Sunday 14th Oct 1984 – Ernest Tarrant of the Mill Cottage collapsed and died in his garden around 12 noon. A fine built man was Ernest and a nice man to talk to. A great shock to Flo, his wife, Stella, his daughter and Steve, his son.

October 19th 1984 – Go to the funeral of Ernest Tarrant at Coln Church at 1 o'clock. R Sims read the Lesson and gave a short address on Ernie who married Flo the Land Army girl after the Second War and worked around here as groom and gardener. Since 1960 he has worked as water bailiff for Earl St Aldwyn. Ernie was in the Gloucester Hussars during the War and was in Italy in 1944. He laid the Legion wreath in Coln Church

Ernie Tarrant with daughter, Stella and son, Steve.

last Remembrance Day. After the Chapel Supper on the 6th Oct at Quenington Chapel I asked him if he would lay the wreath at Hatherop this year which he readily agreed to do if no one else in the village would do it. But the Lord decreed otherwise.

November 11th 1984 – I go to Fairford for the Armistice Parade. I'm glad we could do it as Fairford Band nearly broke up early in the year. But with a very young band we play in the church and march the Legion men to the Market Place as has been done for many years. A young cornet girl from Lechlade, Miss Falkner, played the Last Post in Church. A good effort for a girl of seventeen.

Saturday 24th Nov 1984 – We seem to all have phones now. This idea with us ordinary folk seemed to catch on in the late seventies – our parents would never dream of such a thing. When I was a boy the only phone you could use was at the village Post Office No 33 which is now Mrs George Mustow's kitchen. It stood on a shelf to the right of the doorway leading into the living room. You held the ear piece up to your ear but people seldom used it, only Miss Enie Smith who kept the shop with her aged mother. The half penny box with sherbet and liquorice and a few small sweets. The big iron scales which she carefully weighed out on. The Woodbine cigarettes at 2 pennies for five cigarettes in a paper packet. Players cigarettes 11½ pennies for twenty but men like my father never bought them – always rolled their own with shag tobacco at 8 pennies per ounce. Oh, but what happy times with local people all together, not striving to go better, there was no money to do that.

In the evening Bill Brindle of Fairford picked me up in his car and we went to Arlington public house, the Catherine Wheel, and played skittles with the DOE Rissington and Fairford. Rissington won. Saw Mrs Twining, nee Gwen Bailey, and her husband there. I had not seen Gwen for years – we did so much dancing together in Coln Village Hall in the War years and after. Gwen like me is getting older now. She said "We can't be beautiful always". But she still has those lovely twinkling eyes under large black eyebrows. A beautiful girl.

Sunday 9th December 1984 – Canon Creswell took the service. The Castle School girls were in attendance. R Sims played the organ. Very poor singing – hard work playing for that service. How pleased we all are when the school has gone on holiday and the church is left as a house of prayer. The oak strip for the book rest in the choir stalls has been knocked off. Saw Mr Mervyn Bayliss after the service – he will glue it back on again. Mr Mervyn Bayliss and his son Mr Lee Bayliss are not pleased with the way the furniture of our church is knocked about. In the old days when I was a boy Mrs Cadogan would not have had it on any account.

Christmas Day 1984 – Walk to Hatherop Church at 10.10am. Jennie Voaden caught me up at the kissing gate along the church path and we walked to the church. We both commented that there may be about 12 people present but that you can never tell in these days of mobile people. Jennie went to Midnight Mass at Quenington, she said it was full. We put the lights on, I switch on the Christmas Tree lights and also the spotlight on the crib scene by the War Memorial which has been laid on a table by Hatherop School children. Mr John Chudleigh and his wife Marion were there, Marion sang in the choir. John took the service of matins. Jennie issued out the carol sheets from the Bible Land Society – she had to get the other fifty sheets from last year, so many people arrived. When Jennie came into the choir stalls to sing at the start of the service she said "Where have they all come from?" (Only the Good Lord knows). How inspiring and also for me how concerning with so many present. But the carols went off well. Lesson for all church workers: You never can tell how many will turn up.

Boxing Day 1984 – I had a lovely dinner with Mr Norman Tarrant, his son Carlton and his daughter Ruth. Also there was Mr William Smith of Quenington. A good day.

December 31st 1984 – I spend a quiet New Year's Eve at this Lodge. I thought about Keeper Hutchings who I rang up the night before and is retired at West Wallow, Hants. I was brought up with his son, Robert Hutchings, who is married and lives at the Park, Cheltenham. It was lovely to hear the old keeper's voice on the phone – he said he was ninety-two years old and still upright. How I remember the old army stories him and my old Dad talked about in the little front room over a jug of homemade wine when I was a boy. I also had a chat with Robert on the phone. He said when Earl St Aldwyn got married about £200 was raised to redecorate Coln Church for the wedding. My days of youth with the Hutchings family at the Williamstrip keeper's lodge were very happy days indeed.

New Years Day 1985 – The Fairford Bed Race is on this morning and lots of young lads and girls have gone by pushing beds, complete with whistles, streamers and balloons.

Monday 21st Jan 1985 – Have phone call from Mr Roy Scammell of Shillingstone at 10.45pm to say my Uncle Robert Upshall, my mother's brother, had collapsed and died at No 1 Council House, Broad Oak, Sturminster Newton. The police had to break into his house as he would let no-one have a key. He was 84 years. God Bless Him evermore, he was so good to his widowed mother and sister Louise. He is the last of my mother's family. Now they are all united at last.

Bob Upshall (second from left) working for Dorset County Council in the 1930s.

British Legion Darts team 1939 – Back row from left: Wilf Robbins, Mr Lovings, Charlie Alder. Front row: Charlie Mills, George Winfield, Jesse Blackwell, Jack Winfield, Herbie Card.

In the Home Guard he was a Sergeant and used to instruct on the Lewis Gun which was the weapon he was familiar with in the First War. He was the chairman of the local British Legion of Coln, Hatherop and Quenington. The coffin was draped with the Union Jack and we carried Charlie shoulder high to his grave by the west window. Mrs Mills did not attend the service but the right hand aisle was full of members of the family. Molly Mills (Wheeler), who I went to school with, is in America – she has a son ill in New York so could not attend.

Wednesday 8th May 1985 – Forty years have now passed since VE Day 1945. On that morning, a fine warm day it turned out to be. Bob Hutchings cycled down from Williamstrip and together with Stan Clack, who lodged with us, we drank some damson wine by the back door. Bob Hutchings said "We have all been spared the horrors of war" – how true. We put some posts up in the garden round the curved wall and hung up some crepe paper chains left over from the King's Coronation and also a lot of flags. The hunt came through and the huntsman shouted to my Mother "We have got it right this time". The troops in the park put their roller racks for moving panniers at the disposal of children to slide down in the afternoon and in the evening. In the large blister hanger in the park opposite the old people's bungalows, concrete slabs were laid down and tarpaulins were laid on top. A large radiogram was brought in and we danced the evening away till it was dark. The school master, Mr Garner, came and watched. I shall never forget the smile and the look on his face as he saw all us people dancing; of course when we went to school we had no dancing lessons but picked up the steps in Coln Village Hall through the war years. Mr Charles Barnett dancing with Nurse Wearing; Mrs Gladys Wheeler and her husband Harold, lots from Coln and Quenington. Miss Joan Moulden, now Mrs Sid Radway and others. A grand night. The war was over, thank God

June 2nd 1985 – In the Parish News for this month, it writes of the death of Mrs Frances Hughes, second daugher of Sir Thomas Bazley's father Gardner Bazley known to my Mum and Dad as Miss Frances; she was our Cub Mistress when I was a boy and we had wonderful times running the grounds of Hatherop Castle and in the top rooms over the garages. I have the photo of Mr and Mrs Hughes after their wedding taken outside the Lodge at Hatherop Castle. She was very much like her mother Mrs Cadogan.

Saturday 22nd June 1985 – Perhaps it is worth recording that a lot of farms round here have the stables turned into houses. Manor Farm at Eastleach the stables were turned into houses and sold for around £80,000. Park Farm at Fairford and the Fairford Estate yard buildings have been converted the same. At the present time Gauntlett's Yard at Fairford, named now Keble Close, has been cleared and levelled, the old barn has been stripped of tiles. The roof trusses are still there and I believe going to be made into a house. A big dig of Saxon remains is going on at the present time in a field at Lechlade by the new council houses. Lots of Saxon remains have been uncovered and will be placed in Cirencester Museum. The local council wants to get on and build more houses but Lechlade is plenty big enough as it is. The three houses built in Williamstrip Gardens are nearing completion with ½ acre to each house. The roof repairs to the Old Vicarage, known when I was a boy as Church Mead (now Severalls) is well on its way.

July 25th 1985 – No-one at Hatherop has held any event to raise money for Hatherop Church. So Jennie Voaden held a coffee evening on her cottage lawn at 6.45pm which was well attended by the villagers. A draw was held for bottles of wine and a draw for a lovely cake. The evening was fine and warm, the Almighty smiled on us. Cecil Voaden got together a collection of brass band players from Blockley and Fairford and we played for about an hour and half. The music was heard at Coln and Quenington. Mr Baden Powell took charge of the cake draw. The cake was won by Mrs Summerton. Mrs Bartlett the late blacksmith's wife from Dean Row won a pot of honey I bought from Coln Stores. £206 was the total raised for Hatherop Church and we were all pleased. Mrs Florrie Legg, Mrs Jean Maunders, Mrs Mona Rixon and many more helped with the evening and Mr Norman Tarrant parked the cars.

Thursday 30th July 1985 – A great tragedy – Bob Soule of Southrop hanged himself in his barn, he was found by his wife I am told. Bob was a wonderful man, very strong and powerful, a man who worked at tree felling, hay baling and any other haulage or agricultural work. He was a good collector of old machines and tools, and had several open days at his home at Southrop. It is so sad his life ended in this way. In his youth he was a member of Swindon Wheelers – he cut the ash planks for me with his circular saw from timber he had for Hatherop Church belfry steps. I fitted them some years back. It cost the church nothing, it was Bob Soule's gift. Bob was such a fine man but ill health was more than he could bear. His funeral service is on Wednesday 7th August at Southrop at 2pm.

Friday Aug 2nd 1985 – Charlie Alder of Faulkner's Close Fairford passed over this morning, I am informed over the phone by his daughter Joyce. He sponsored me for the Buffalo Order in 1947. During the war years we had some wonderful dancing nights at Charlie's home in Quenington when everyone was young and single and times were grim but comradeship abounded. Charlie was 86 years old. I rang Charlie Pollard of Dean Farm who is home with broken legs after a car accident and told him the news. At his funeral on 8th August the Buffs and the British Legion members lined the path from the church door after the burial service and we dropped ivy leaves over Charlie.

Saturday 7th Sept 1985 – Farmer Hart came up the Eastleach Road with his land rover at 9pm. He stopped and said he was going to boycott the Quenington Harvest Festival tomorrow because the harvest is not in. I told him I will not boycott the house of the Lord. He drove away smiling to himself.

Sept 8th 1985 – Journey to Quenington Church at 6pm for Harvest Festival Evensong. A small bunch of corn at the main north door. Flowers in jars in the windows, a cooked loaf on the altar in the shape of a sheaf of corn. No vegetables or fruit. R Sims took a large marrow and placed it in the north side window in the choir stalls then sat with Mr Tom Lemon and sung the harvest hymns. The young choir we were promised was not there. The poorest Harvest Festival I have ever known – no farmers there, all out in the fields with their combines gathering the corn in the evening sun. And the Good Lord looks on. It does not seem the one Harvest Festival for the three parishes works out very well. Our people still like the service in their own church and will give produce and flowers then.

Sunday 15th Sept 1985 – I am writing a report on the Home Guard for Mr Grace, school-master of Ashton Keynes, Cirencester. He cannot find any records of what went on in the forties and of course a lot of the old Colonels who were of the 1914 War have passed over. It seems what records there were at Cheltenham have gone. I told him I have still my father's LDV card, also I have Home Guard lapel badges and two labels of the evacuees who came down from London. I am told by one evacuee it was three days before war broke out on Sept 3rd 1939.

Sunday 6th Oct 1985 – Mr Peter Grace has replied to my letter on the Home Guard – he would like more information on Hatherop Castle SOE if I can find it. But it was so different in the War Years. "Walls have Ears" was the slogan.

Saturday 19th Oct 1985 – Eighteen years ago today, my Mum passed over, God Bless her for evermore. Life has not been the same for Reuben Sims since she fell asleep.

Sunday 20th Oct 1985 – A fine autumn morning – arrive at Hatherop Church for the 11am service. Mr Edward Bennett from Coln, Miss Rachael's son, playing the organ – he plays well. "He Who Would Valiant Be" is one of the hymns and we sing with great gusto. Mr Bennett pulls out all the stops, a good service.

Talking to Mrs Bartlett, wife of the late Coln blacksmith Charles Bartlett, she told me she used to work in the Vicarage at Southrop when she was a young girl in the time of Martin Squire's grandfather who was Vicar there. He was a small man with a beard – he suffered a lot with lumbago but would always attend the service and used to preach from a bath chair. He was also very good to his parishioners although the living was only £100 a year.

Nov 9th 1985 – The farmer's wagon with straw bale seats for the beaters is parked here in the driveway. The farmers are driving around in their land rovers – guns are being fired at the pheasants who have been walking around here so nice this summer. The farmers wipe everything out, rabbits and hares but they are more choosy with their pheasants which they rear and bring up on subsidised corn. Lots of farm workers and boys around. No old coats with binder string round the waist today. Good green Wellington boots and good green anorak clothes. £7 for beaters. Judas Escariot money. Iva Pelly passed away today – she was one of the old aristocracy who saw the change through the welfare state. The following Obituary was written by a Quenington villager: "With Iva's death on November 9th a well-known figure has passed from the Quenington scene. She came to live at the Court shortly after the war with her mother and sisters before going to live at the Little House. She was a good knowledgeable gardener, a keen follower of sport and took part in all the village activities. For some years she was a member of the Parish Council and was intensely patriotic. But what she will be remembered for is her great love of people. Never happier than when she was entertaining at home, she was equally content to have a long talk with someone met casually in the street. She was a very kind and caring person, helping wherever help was needed."

Sunday 17th November 1985 – I do not go to the house of the Lord today – want to get rid of this cold. Eric Hobbs, Eric Tilling of Quenington before he was married, called to see me. He has been visiting his aunt, Mrs Mills, today – the wife of Charles Mills in the bungalows. We talked of old times, when we were at school with Mr Percy Garner, how Miss Arnold cycled up the Park from Quenington each day. Miss Moot in the other class, in the long room and how people have it so good in these welfare state days. I gave him a photo of Hatherop School 1931 which is the same as the one in the belfry of the church – he was very pleased.

<u>**Hatherop C of E School 1931**</u>

(Back Row) Aubrey Puffitt, Cyril Moaby, Eric Moulden, George Winney, William Dixon, Charlie Day, Basil Avery, Bert Puffitt, Jim Shepherd, Dennis Crew, Roy Russell
(5th Row) Miss Joy Arnold (Teacher), Kathleen Smith, Betty Minchin, Joan Dyke, Eileen Cole, Peggy Moaby, Irene May, Violet Mills, May Ash, Margery Sharps, Kitty Harpe, Dolly Herbert, Eileen Dyke, Audrey Hayward, Miss Moot (Teacher)
(4th Row) Lucy Bartlett, Hilda Ash, Beryl Roberts, Flora Smith, Norman Westall, Jessie Mustow, Reuben Sims, John Garner, Charlie May, Eric Tilling, Fred Cole, Elsie Puffitt, Lily Shepherd
(3rd Row) Betty Tye, Margery Bartlett, May Dixon, Betty Coatges, Percy Garner (centre - Head Master), Molly Wheeler (Mills), Sybil Mirichin, Joan Moulden, Helen Day, Evelyn Avery, Megan Ferriman
(2nd Row - Kneeling) Bernard Iles, Lambert Smith, Fred Herbert, Stanley Bailey, Charlie Rose
(Front Row - Seated) Robert East, John Iles, Joe Binks, Frank Avery, George East, Harry East

Sunday 24th Nov 1985 – I still have this cold, I'm weary with it and ache all over at times. I'm at work but want to do little when I return. I did not go to Holy Eucharist in the House of the Lord today at 11am. It is also the first night known when the Church of England members "Protestants" visit the Quenington Chapel for public prayer. A very good thing. I am sorry I do not feel well enough to go but hope to go to the carols at Advent on Saturday 30th November. Building at the chauffeur's house at the bottom of Hatherop Hill continues. No Cotswold villager will ever be able to afford to live there now.

The house by the Park Gate where, when I was a boy, Dapper Higgins lived with his son Ben Higgins and Beatrice who looked after them (and where for a good number of years Mr Donald Browning lived with his wife) is now up for sale. Mr Browning has gone to live in an apartment at the Folly home of Sir Thomas Bazley, his house has been cleared out, the pigeons and wild life of which he took great interest in have gone. £90,000 is asked for the property. Ben Higgins used to walk to Williamstrip Farm to work night and morning. In the Home Guard he always made Bob Hutchings and yours truly keep the rifle by the bunk beds when we were on patrol at the Reading Room.

Saturday 7th Dec 1985 – Have received a Christmas card from Mrs Helene McCann-Clemens of Defiance, Ohio USA who wrote me about Georgia Ward-Jumper. They were both nurses in the USA forces during the last war and helped my mother get my sister on the train at Fairford to go to Oxford Hospital. They came out to see us while at Fairford Park Hospital in 1944. I have kept in touch ever since. Have also a ring from Mr Lou Sly to say Mrs Shepherd has passed over. She was about ninety years old. One of the last of our old inhabitants and a Wheeler who grew up in this Lodge. The Wheelers were the first inhabitants and kept the gate open for the carriages in the back drive years ago.

December 10th 1985 – I go to Hatherop Church at 11am. Mrs Effie Shepherd is being buried at 12 noon. She is the last I know of the old estate wives who looked after their husbands and family on the estate and helped at the local rummage sale and the treats for the children. Mrs Shepherd was well respected in the village, a lady of quiet nature and attended church at Hatherop with her husband at Evensong. Jim stoked the old boiler, cut the churchyard, rung the bells and sung every Sunday in the choir and was also with us boys on our choir outings to Bristol Zoo and Weston-super-Mare. Mrs King came in who was a neighbour of Mrs Shepherd when she lived in the old people's bungalows, also Mrs Harry Maunders. One other elderly man I did not know. On the right hand side the pews were full of Mrs Shepherd family, Jim the son, a fine man and his wife Lucy. Mrs Dorothy Barnes and her elder sister Lily, who had her mother so long to stay with her, and also her children and grand children. We sung two hymns: "Jesu Lover of My Soul" and "The Day thou Gavest". Mrs Shepherd was then carried shoulder high from the Chancel, down the church and buried in her husband's grave at the west end of the church.

Saturday 14th December 1985 – Journey to Coln St Aldwyns in my three wheel van in the morning. Coming back from the post office I stopped by the bottom Lodge where Mrs Victor Cox lives and I looked at the opening up of the covert showing the Castle and the vast amount of trees that have been sawn down. Planning permission has been given but in these times when timber is so scarce and conservation of wild life is threatened it seems such a shame to me, a Cotswold man living here all my life, to see so much of our local countryside cut down to suit those who will live in the bottom Lodge where Mr Messenger, the Castle chauffeur, lived.

Chauffer Messenger with the Sunbeam 1932.

Although controls are put on things, the power of money always finds a way round. In ten to twenty years time Hatherop will be haven for the middle class of society in cottages which were rented out to estate workers at 2/– per week, their wage being 11/6d per week, and very few

Cotswold people will be left. Also I have found out from Mr Mervyn Bayliss that the old pump house which supplied the water to the estate has been sold to those who have bought the Lodge.

Monday 16th December 1985 – R Sims played the piano for carols with the Brownie pack at their party at Hatherop School to which the elder ladies belonging to the Quenington Wednesday Club were guests at tea. R Sims sat down with them for a good tea. Tables down the centre of the large school room, candles in candle-sticks, lots of sandwiches and cakes, one glass of sherry, lots of tea. Badges were presented to the Brownies by their leader, Mrs Gee. Present as leaders were Mrs Sue Mckenzie and Mrs Richard Lander. The late Mr Ewart Lander's wife was also there, known as Grannie Lander – well in her nineties. The Brownies sang the carols well and a good time was had by all. R Sims sat with Mrs Freda Blackwell – nee Cole, and Mrs Lucy Thomas – nee Bartlett, who he went to school with 50 years ago in the time of Mr Percy Garner who used the cane God Bless Him. Also there were Miss Moot who married a deaf and dumb man and Miss Ivy Arnold, whose brother I worked for at the East Glos Engineering Works. Also present was Mrs Beatie Day – nee Smith, who was at the school when I was a small boy before it was changed to Hatherop being senior school for the over seven year olds.

Sunday 22nd December 1985 – Today a Hatherop Christmas supper at Hatherop School, laid on by Mrs Frazer Hart, is to be held at 7pm. I wrote to Mrs Hart and stated I would be there after the Carol Service at 6pm at Hatherop Church. After the Carol Service we all walked along to the Village School which was ablaze with electric light. A supper had been prepared, cooked on the kitchen extension unit. Hot mashed potatoes, green peas and cooked turkey – very good, plenty of food. Mrs Susan Vicary was giving out sticky labels which were stuck on our clothes to say how long we had been in the village. Lady Howard's was 1934, mine was 1937!! Met very nice new people who have bought the Nurse's Cottage and also a nice gentleman who has bought one of the £80,000 houses built in the Earl St Aldwyn's Estate gardens. The other two have yet to be sold. About 100 people were present. Mrs Summerton and a good singing friend played songs on guitars. Mrs Hart played the piano "And a Partridge in a Pear Tree". Mr Gee from Dean Farm, a pig man there, came in as Santa Claus and gave the children presents from a sack much to their delight. R Sims gave a vote of thanks to Mr and Mrs Hart for the supper and all concerned.

Christmas Morning 1985 – Hatherop Cathedral looked fine, candles lit, red carnations put in by Jennie Voaden in the choir stalls, beautiful, good singing. Jennie Voaden sang well, she has a wonderful voice. Her husband and her unmarried daughter were in the congregation. Church three quarters full of people. I drove to Lechlade, had a drink with my friends Stan Bray and his wife, had a good dinner with John Iles and his wife, came home to Trixie about 9.30pm. Walked down Eastleach Road, all quiet, so to bed.

Monday 30th December 1985 – At 2.30pm we hold a service in Hatherop Church for Tom Ambidge aged 78 years. Tom worked at Rissington Air Base for some years and also for Leonard Jones, Jeweller of Cirenester in latter years. A bachelor, whose mother used to go to Quenington Chapel years ago, Tom was like his father, a man small in stature, loved a good talk, went to Coln shop for his shopping and lived in Golden Row. His father was for many years a gardener in Hatherop Castle gardens in the time of my grandfather. Tom Ambidge had no relatives but the funeral was well conducted by Norman, Trotman and Hughes who have taken over from Mr Sly of Northleach. Jennie Voaden was there, Mrs King, Mrs Maunders, Reuben Sims, one other lady not known and Mr and Mrs Brooks, neighbours of Tom who had seen to all the affairs. They put a lovely wreath on his coffin. Sir Thomas Bazley the Estate owner came and sat in the Bazley pew. Tom Ambidge left his estate to Fairford Hospital League of Friends – £4,000 odd.

Wednesday 1st January 1986 – A very hard frost this morning. The Fairford Bed Race around Coln, Hatherop and Quenington finishing in Fairford Market Place started this morning at 11am. The first bed team went by this Lodge at 11.25am at a very fast pace. The others came along at intervals of 5 mins or so. With horns blowing the American Fire Section went by – a great morning.

Jan 10th 1986 – The first ever meeting of Church Wardens of the five parishes which make up CHEQS was held at The Vicarage, Coln St Aldwyns at 6.30pm. Earl St Aldwyn, warden at Coln was not present. At the long table Rev Cowmeadow poured out sherry and a toast was drunk to Reuben Sims birthday the following day. After about two hours the services for the year for the five parishes were decided. Southrop and Eastleach were satisfied as they had been seeking to use clergy of their own choice. This had been refused by the Bishop of Gloucester, John Yates. All in all a good meeting.

Jan 11th 1986 – Jennie Voaden brought Reuben Sims a birthday cake. I'm 63 years old today.

Thursday 16th January 1986 – I am told by Mrs Eddie Hunt of Quenington that the little water-wheel which drove a Thomas Pump, and provided water for Leafield Farm and Far Hill Farm, has been cut up and the parts are outside the little wheel house by the Cascades. The Thomas Pump single barrel was put in about 1938 to replace two old pumps. Mr Briggs of Fairford had the work and a small Petter Engine was fixed there while the new pump and repairs to the water wheel were done. We used to ride up the Park Drive on our bikes and go down the Pleasure Grounds and across the Park to the Wheel House. Bert Agers and Ray Cuss Jr used to catch some trout there. The little wheel was about 5' in height and about 3' wide with sheet metal vanes bolted each side to the wheel rim. A lovely sight running, when the little hatch was raised. I'm sad it's gone.

Saturday 18th January 1986 – Mr Hart and Mr Richard Hinton and their gang of beaters are out killing the wildlife again. Three times they have shot in the Long Cover here. Complete with tractor and covered wagon with straw bales in for seats for the beaters. Expense does not matter to satisfy their lust for killing the wild-life.

25th January 1986 – An article in the Standard on Charlie 'Bubbles' Rixon aged 90yrs. "Long Life Recipe: tea bags and cider." My mother used to fix him up with an old lady's Sunday dress and we used to go to Fancy Dress Dances at Coln St Aldwyns and Fairford. His late daughter Barbara's 21st party dance at Coln Village Hall was a wonderful time. Band on the stage, lots of merry making and dancing until 12 midnight. Charlie went to the New Inn and invited all the people there. A wonderful night. He still rides his cycle around Hatherop today.

Rixon family outside the Post Office, Hatherop 1946. From Left: Nora Rixon (nee Tombs), Cyril Rixon (sitting) with Dinah the dog, Barbara Rixon (later Patheyjohns) with Bobby the cat, and Charlie Rixon.

Long life recipe: tea bags and cider

THE RECIPE for old age, according to Hatherop's oldest inhabitant, Mr. Charles Rixon, is tea-bags for the eyes each morning, a raw onion each day, warmed cider on a winter's evening — and, above all, an ability to enjoy life.

And in his case the recipe certainly seems to have worked — because at the ripe old age of 90, fit and active with a resplendent head of white hair he still rides a bicycle, goes for long walks in the afternoon, and does the occasional spot of gardening for friends in Coln and Hatherop.

Casting his mind back over the years, he has many a tale to tell. Like the time he took a football team from Hatherop to Southrop in the village milk float. "After the match we got drinking, having a good time and watching the old men sitting with their clay pipes," he reminisced.

"I used to sing a bit in those days, and so the lads stood me on the kitchen table and got me singing 'I'm forever blowing bubbles' — I've been called 'Bubbles' ever since.

"But then when we all got up in the milk float to come back home again, some of us a bit thick in the head, the pony got nervous and reared up and tipped us all out into the street. The talk of the town, it was, in Southrop for many a Saturday night!"

He never knew his father, who was head gamekeeper on a large estate in Berkshire, and who was shot one night by poachers before the turn of the century.

But one early memory he does recall from the time before he moved to the Cotswolds is of being the first boy in his village to own a bicycle.

"I used to get up early in the morning to pump water for a farmer, and then walk one-and-a-half miles to school," he explained.

"But I was saving up the pennies that I earned for an old Cushing bike that was up for sale. The bike cost 15 shillings — and one day, when I'd saved 5d the farmer called me in and said he'd put up the rest.

"So there I was, the only one in the village to have a bike — and I've been riding one every since."

He first moved to the area more than 60 years ago, when he took lodgings at Netherton before moving to Eysey near Cricklade to work on Stanley Barton's farm, where he was for more than 30 years.

He also worked in Evans' butchers shop in Faringdon before moving to Hatherop to run the village shop and post office.

He recalls Christmas Eve drinking sessions in the Earl Grey in Quenington when the "lads" would finish at 2 a.m. out on the street singing and women would call down from the windows of houses, "Why don't you lot get yourselves off home!"

"Jimmy Strange, the landlord, he was a real character, and a good pal of mine. He would start the singing, and then when we had all got going he would bring out the brown bread and Gorgonzola, and we'd have a fine old do."

But the memories are not all good ones. There was the time when he caught anthrax from ointment he used to rub down a horse. "I was monstrous bad. And I think I would shoot myself before I went through that again.

"They called the specialist doctors in, and I pulled through — but I was so weak for a long time that I couldn't stand up. I just had to sit for hours watching the people to by."

And there was the time when his wife Nora died, after he had nursed her through a long illness,

But despite the hard times, he insists that his life has been "wonderful". He said: "It's how you make life that counts. People these days, they go around with faces that long — as long as a fiddle.

"But I've never hurt anybody — and no matter where I went I was always welcome."

All his old friends are gone now. But his son Cyril lives with his wife next door, and he still goes to the social club in Hatherop for a drink, and rides his bicycle — and three times a week visits Florry Card in Coln for dinner and to do her gardening.

"It's been a good life," he said. "Sometimes I think I've been lucky to get through it all — but I did, and here I am alive and still kicking."

MR. CHARLES RIXON.

Sunday 23rd February 1986 – Feed the birds, have one woodpecker, how nice to see such a fine bird. Yesterday the guns were all firing over the Williamstrip House area. I expect it was a duck shoot. How the wild life is killed off in the cold weather. But there is a better attitude among the younger generation – they buy nuts in the greengrocers to feed the birds – something unknown in my parent's time.

Monday 24th February 1986 – Listen and see economists and politicians talking about the cost of welfare state and how it is favouring the middle class and also how a lot of people prefer benefit to jobs. How after 40 years it needs overhauling but where and how to start is a great problem. So much is said today about the poor but when I grew up before the welfare state we accepted the life we had. My parents never thought about strikes, knew nothing about politics and were very proud of our country and heritage. We worked to better ourselves if we could and also would sing, whistle and laugh. You get very little of that today. Everyone seems to want to demand more like Oliver Twist. It has just been announced that pensions are going up a little. Family Allowance from £7 per week to £7.10p. I'm afraid my parents never thought or expected any money to bring up my sister or me. We had a happy childhood, I think of it often. My sister Edith, who was not strong, had a cooked meal every day when she went to Coln School. My mother paid Mrs Avery who lived in the second cottage on the left from the school – do not know how much – it could have been nine pence a day.

Friday 28th February 1986 – Forecaster on television says the second coldest time of the century. 1947 being a lot colder, I know about that one, very hard frost, snow out of fields into the roads, walked and carried cycle up and down Fairford Road to Mr Briggs Engineering Works. Lots of our folk know nothing of those cold rides, they live in central heated houses and come out and get in a good car with a heater, then creep out again into a hot office, especially in government departments. This present generation do not work like our parents did. In spite of high unemployment people are well dressed, live well with plenty of money for dining out and drink. Our parents were content with homemade wine.

Saturday 8th March 1986 – Another frosty morning but a bright day. I do nothing all day but look after myself. Feel the cold this year more than I ever have before. Three old people died because of the cold weather but there is a lot more care of the aged today than there was years ago. Met Charlie Pollard of Dean Farm at Coln shop yesterday evening – he is getting better after his accident with two broken legs. He now drives a car with an automatic clutch.

Charlie Pollard's wedding to Joyce Bishop. From left: Mr Pollard senior, Granny Pollard, Charles Pollard, Dan Collett (behind), Joyce Bishop, Dorothy Pollard, tall bridesmaid – Pauline Coates, Mr and Mrs Bishop.

The Wilts & Glos Standard paper this week says about the closing of village schools of less than 50 pupils. Coates school is on the cards. Hatherop School, which has had so much money spent on it, is also threatened. Some time ago I asked the late headmaster Mr Erving if I could have one of the old black board easels for Hatherop Church – there were three in Hatherop School made of pine wood. He told me they had been scrapped. The spears and battle axes etc that I gave to Hatherop School belonging to William Smith of Hatherop who was in the South African Police have also gone out of the school. Moral – never give to County Schools.

Thursday 13th March 1986 – Clean up six of my old pictures of Hatherop to place on show in a collection of pictures in the Quenington Institute when it is reopened after modernisation this coming Saturday.

Saturday 15th March 1986 – Drove my three wheel van to Quenington to Carey Cottage – home of Mr Eddie Hunt. With his wife we go to the old Institute building which has been modernised and a new kitchen and toilets added. A lot of new Quenington people there – lots of pictures on display. The Hundred Club is still going – we pay 50p per month for a draw prize. The hall is very warm and cosy, quite big enough to cater for the village needs. The late Alexander Abel Smith's son spoke. Mr Polityer, who gave about £10,000 to the restoration, was given a piece of framed embroidering. We all clapped him and sung "for he's a jolly good fellow". Mrs Lucy Thomas was there, Mr and Mrs Gordon Timms, who used to keep the Earl Grey Public House, Mr and Mrs Hunt, Mr John Moaby, who is in business as an electrician, Reuben Sims and lots of new people to the area. Also Mr and Mrs Wilfred Smith, his wife was Rene King, daughter of Bert King of Hatherop who led the cows in to be milked when I was a boy from Green Islands to the Glebe Farm at Hatherop at 5.30am. Hot coffee and tea was served and also sweet meats etc. Mrs Don Collett was in the kitchen doing a lot of washing up. Her husband Donald is a great country man. I knew his blacksmith father and his mother.

March 21st 1986 – Drive to Coln and get my shopping from the stores, meet Mr Tom Lemon and we look at the new entrance being made today into the old Manor Gardens in the Manor Drive. A new house is going to be built in the garden. The old tennis pavillion is to be pulled down. It is sad to see the old gardens with little box hedges and the old apple trees cut down but such is the time in these modern days when the cost of gardeners at £100 per week would not be profitable. Six men used to work in those gardens years ago at about 15/– per week. We looked at the old stables which had been converted for habitation. Jim Hunt's old carpenter's bench was in one part of the stalls – I expect my dad's coffin like many others was made on it. The old joiner's shop has been made into a house, such are the changes. We both looked at the cemetery, no stone to Mrs Atkinson who kept Coln Post Office and who played the organ in Coln church when I was a boy. She was a school teacher and was the daughter of Leonard Miles who worked as a carpenter on Hatherop Estate with my father.

Thursday 27th March 1986 – Drive in the hearse with Mr Lou Sly and take Miss Lucy Barnfield who passed over in the cold weather. She was the sister of Jack Barnfield who did a lot of corn threshing and seed hulling for Briggs & Richards threshing contractors. She had a crippled leg all her life with polio and worked for some time at Mrs Gaiger's shop – next house above the Earl Grey at Quenington.

April 10th 1986 – My friend Robert Hutchings (Bob) rung me from Cheltenham tonight to say his father Hughie Hutchings, who was keeper on the Williamstrip Estate till 1951, had passed over in his sleep this morning. Hughie Hutchings was a fine upright man, a good keeper, and a good Standard Bearer for the British Legion, carried the Standard for many years at the Armistice Parades in these three villages, wearing the white gauntlet gloves and the Standard belt. He was 93 years. I had some wonderful days with the Hutchings family in my youth when they lived in the keeper's lodge at Williamstrip.

The Bristish Legion marching in Quenington with Ernie Tarrant bearing the Standard c. 1950.

April 15th 1986 – The news tonight is full of the American air strike at Libya from where so much life has been lost through terrorists. France and Spain denied air space over their countries – the French have always let us down. They took the pump handles off the water pumps in their villages in my father's time when the troops marched through although, as my father said, they were fighting for the French. My father suffered all his life through trench warfare – as he used to say "I was there". He worked with his left leg black and leaking ulcers. His stomach and right arm full of shrapnel – it was never taken out. There was no welfare state then – only Dr Blocksom, my mother and me ever knew of his suffering.

May 25th 1986 – Have listened to parts of the serial on the Life of Edward VIII and Wallace Simpson. I remember the time well when I was a boy and my mother and father talking about it. Mrs Simpson died a month or so ago at a great age and has been buried at Frogmore with her husband Edward VIII. Not a lot of pomp and show – of course many of her time have passed over.

May 30th 1986 – Jennie Voaden my Co-Warden rang me up this evening to say she is living apart from her husband and has found a job as a warden for old people in Cirencester. With her husband Cecil and her family they have been wonderful people in the Parish. I'm very sad.

Jennie Voaden at the Victorian Fair 1979. From right: Ivy Smith, Jennie Voaden, Mary Brazier, Mrs Cowmeadow.

June 7th 1986 – Farmer Hart called to say there will be a meeting to find a deputy church warden in place of Jennie Voaden. He would like to find out who I would like. I told him I would like a lady to do the work. Jennie Voaden was wonderful at the job. We will have a job to find another lady so good and so loyal at this kind of work. God Bless her always.

June 25th 1986 – Church Meeting at Hatherop School at 7pm. Lady Worsley is elected deputy Church Warden till Easter. Reuben Sims the only Cotswold man there.

Sunday 29th June 1986 – After the service R Sims met Lady Abel Smith who looked at her family graves. She said she could see the new gateway made in Church Meade boundary wall and the 1760 ironwork gate had been moved there from the Castle kitchen garden which the new owners [*Sir Winfried and Lady Bischoff*] of Church Meade [*the Severalls*] have bought. Very good, I'm pleased at that news.

Saturday 12th July 1986 – A fete for the Youth Club and Girl Guides was held at the Old Rectory Quenington at 2pm. The rain, which had been falling, held off after Mrs Curteis [*the authoress Joanna Trollope*] of Mill House, Coln St Aldwyns opened the fete. A large crowd of people bought cakes, plants etc off the stalls. The Fairford Band played through the afternoon – R Sims played the Eb Bass. The American Airbase tug of war team won the event. They pulled against the Keeper's Arms team from across the river which resulted in the Keeper's team getting pulled in.

Sunday 13th July 1986 – 6 o'clock evening prayer at Coln St Aldwyns. The Bishop of Gloucester, John Yates, was greeted at the main door by Earl St Aldwyn and Mr Baden Powell, Church Wardens, followed by the newly formed, robed young people's choir from Quenington. During the service the bishop swore in Rev Michael Austin as unpaid curate to the Rev Derek Cowmeadow.

July 23rd 1986 – The day of the Royal Wedding between His Royal Highness, Prince Andrew and Miss Sarah Ferguson. I rise early and put up my flags and a large picture of the couple on the east wall of this Lodge. Mr Lee Bayliss went by to work and gave me a toot on his car horn. Flags and poster 3' x 2' look well, I'm pleased. It is not a public holiday but I have two days holiday from work and watch the whole ceremony on my TV. Drink a lot of whisky. Lots of people stop their cars and take snap shots. People do not put up the flags as they used too. When I went to school we all saluted the Union Jack and sung "Flag of Britain Proudly Waving Over Many a Distant Sea, We Salute Thee and We Pray, Bless Oh God our Land

Today". Mr. Smith told me, only my flags and one small flag on Bibury Football hut were to be seen around here. Nothing in Fairford either. The whole ceremony from start to finish was marvellous – no nation in the world can do it like the British. A fine day, God Bless them all and no bombs or blow ups.

July 27th 1986 – Had a phone call from the Rev Cowmeadow. He liked my flags flying for the Royal Wedding. He said he put the flag up on Coln Church Flag Pole. I'm pleased as I was very disappointed at the lack of flag flying by our people – they seem to have lost the pride that our people had with our National Flag. Money, not God or Nation today. Lady Worsley came and took a snapshot of my flags.

Saturday 30th August 1986 – Heard from Mr Dennis Bartlett at the Buff Lodge on Wednesday 27th that Mr Reggie Dingle of Quenington died on Tuesday 26th August. He was 91 years I believe. For years when I was a boy, through the Second World War and after, he ran the bus to Cirencester about three times a week, and did all the shopping for people on the route. Of course they had no cars like today and Cirencester Market Place was always full of the local village coaches: Little of Poulton, Norton of Lechlade, Harvey of Chedworth, Kiddle of Coln St Aldwyns. My mother told me Mr Kiddle charged 2s 6d to go to Cirencester return. When Mr Dingle started he reduced the fare to 1s 6d. Mr Dingle always said he was the last to go to bed at night after the picture bus came home. Also after the last war, when petrol was more available, he took tours to Weston and Weymouth. The war was on for six years so it was quite a treat. I believe his Bedford bus is still in his garage at Quenington. He drove a large brown diesel bus after that. When I was a boy in the thirties he drove home from Cirencester with a bus full of people – it was a fourteen seater and my father William Sims and Mr Fred Ford came home on top of the bus on the luggage rack. There was a ladder at the rear of the bus to climb up. Mrs Dingle took the fares on the bus and on the last bus out of Cirencester, with people standing all down the aisle on the thirty two seater, she would still get to the back of the bus for the money.

August Bank Holiday 1986 – Extensive alterations are being made to Coln Manor to make it into flats. What my mother would say I do not know. An extension is being built to the bottom lodge at Netherton by the river. A fine arched doorway seems to be created, lots of stone used.

Sunday 7th Sept 1986 – Trustee Savings Bank shares are coming up for buying, also Gas shares. If Labour get back in power they will renationalise the Telecom and Gas. I hope they do not get in, they waste so much money. One million council houses have now been sold to home owners.

Hatherop Street is full of cars at weekends. About fifteen cars line the street when the footballers play in the Park. Gone are the group of young men on cycles standing by the pump house by the green of a Sunday, waiting for the Wall's Ice Cream man and his ice creams in a large box on a three wheel trike. 2 pence for a wrapped vanilla ice cream, 1 penny for a snowfruit in a cardboard holder. More money about today in spite of large scale unemployment in our industries, plenty of cars, lots of young ladies driving, plenty of them wear jeans and a blouse worn like our old shirts on a man but hang outside the jeans. When I was a young man this would have been called outrageous.

Times Remembered: The old Reading Room now turned into a bungalow was closed during the summer months. Mr Oliver Puffitt, now 70 years, told me a steward was in attendance every night, darts, cards and dominoes were played, the small billiard table was used, a small charge of 2 pence per game. They were never short of money and sometimes a visiting Reading Room team would come and play billiards – the home team usually won because of being used to the small table. The Hatherop Reading room never opened again after the War started in 1939 – the Home Guards had it for headquarters all through the War. After the War the Estate used it as an office.

The week of the 14th Sept 1986 – Three oak trees, about three feet in diameter, have been pulled down in Green Islands by heavy tractor diggers. I suspect they were in the way of Mr Hart's combines so were rooted up. A very sad thing. Green Islands has been burnt of straw in various strips. Also beech and chestnut trees, about two feet in diameter, have been felled in the spinney at Barrow Elm and also in the small coppice across the road from this lodge at the right hand turn going down the Eastleach Road. Never in my time has any trees been cut down here. The corn carting on tractors and trailers continue till 9pm with lights on. Glad when the noise is over, when man and wildlife can get some peace. Glebe Farm is getting like an American ranch with its felled trees.

Saturday 27th Sept 1986 – A birthday party in the Barn at Glebe Farm, the barn has been whitewashed out. White canopies at both doorways have doors in them.

Monday 6th October 1986 – Go to the funeral service of Mrs Kathleen Coates of Coln St. Aldwyns. A full church of mourners – Cotswold people. It is sad to see my people in distress. Kath was 64 years old. I played a lot of cricket in Williamstrip Park with her husband, Douglas Coates, and also football in Hatherop Park with Charlie Pollard, Kathleen's brother.

Molly Mill's daughter, adopted to Mr and Mrs Charlie Mills of Williamstrip Farm, has gone back home to Atlanta, USA. She came over to see Mrs Mills, now a widow living in the Piece bungalows. I went to school with Molly and also in 1937 rode to Fairford night school at old Farmor's School with her and Norman Westall – subjects arithmetic and book-keeping. She cycled from Williamstrip those winter nights from October till Easter. One would not do that today with these violent things happening to girls. She sent £65 to Fairford Hospital when Mr Charles Mills (Windy Night) died. Molly has made it very well – she and her husband run a carpet business in Atlanta. They stayed at the New Inn at Coln St Aldwyns but moved to the Bull at Fairford where it was more comfortable.

Armistice Sunday 9th November 1986 – A sad Evening Prayer in Hatherop Church at 6pm. R Sims forgot his glasses so no organ.

Sunday 16th November 1986 – We have had a spate of cot deaths all buried opposite the de Mauley door. Two Hatherop Castle School Girls have been expelled for stealing goods from Tesco in Swindon. A great pity, two fine girls, there is so much temptation to young people today. But justice must be done and standards must prevail.

Saturday 22nd November 1986 – Bert Harding of Quenington has been buried. A First War man and Sergeant in the Local Home Guard in the Second War – a fine upstanding man. Worked for many years on Godwin's outside gang.

December 8th 1986 – Very wet for some days now, heard that Jim Brindle, "Dickie", Kathleen Brindle's brother had died. Jim Brindle was quite a boy for the ladies. When I was a boy in the thirties he was our idol on the Hatherop football pitch. He rode a racing bike to Godwin's Works where he was a turner. When I played cricket for Williamstrip before the war I played some games with him. He was a good bowler and used to like a good average. Mr Mervyn Bayliss remembers when Jim went to Ford's of Dagenham for a job and picked up Mr Wilfred Barnett, the Castle butler, who went with him for the day out on Jim's motorbike. Wilfred got up late and was buttoning his coat up as he got on the motorcycle. Jim roared away down the Castle drive. A few days later Mervyn saw Jim and said "You were cutting it fine the other morning – Wilfred was buttoning up his coat as you drove off". "Yes" said Jim "and he was still buttoning up when we got to Wantage". Jim had a job at Ford's and received £4 per week. My mother and father could hardly believe it. The average wage then was around £2 per week. Jim was 77 years old and his wife had died about three years ago.

Christmas Eve 1986 – Reuben Sims played the organ in Coln Church for a children's service organised by Mrs Mandy Weston and Mr and Mrs Curteis. The church was full of parents and young children. A nativity was held in the chancel – a horse came in with a child on its back. A little live lamb was there. Lots of little girls and boys were dressed up as sheep. I was busy playing "Once in Royal David's City" and "Away in a Manger" – everyone sung well. Coln Church is good for musical sound. Earl and Lady St Aldwyn were in their family pew. The Earl has just survived a car accident coming back from London.

Sunday 28th December 1986 – Forgot to say that on Christmas Eve Mrs Hart brought about fifteen young people round by my back door and they sang carols – no money required – just to bring the spirit of Christmas. How lovely it was to hear the young folks sing. This has not been done for many a year.

Saturday 10th January 1987 – One of our parishioners, Mrs King who lived in the old people's bungalows, was buried on Thursday 8th Jan. The funeral service was at Hatherop Church. We shall miss Mrs King at our 8am communion services – she was a regular attendee and did much for the older members in the old people's bungalows, may the Good Lord bless her family.

Sunday 11th January 1987 – My birthday – I am sixty-four years old. Walk to the Parish Church at 7.30am and meet the Rev Cowmeadow wearing his black cossack hat. My Brother of the Buffalo Order, Mr Roger King, looks very sad – how helpless we are at the time of bereavement.

Thursday 15th January 1987 – The Hatherop/Fairford Road blocked with snow – straw bales put across the road outside. I feed my hens, keep indoors. Have a visit from Mrs Gordon Legg and her young son to see if I am all right. I say I am, told her I'm walking to Coln to pick up my shopping. She wanted me to have her son go with me, I declined – she said I was too independent. I like it that way. She is a wonderful woman and will reach heaven with all her good works. Go to Coln with two haversacks, Coln Hill has been cleared.

Friday 23rd Jan 1987 – Snow banks still line the sides of the Hatherop/Fairford Road. BT engineers go on strike on Monday – a great pity – lots of old people today have a phone. It was unheard of 20 years ago. People would have thought then that you were well off or snobbish. There is not the village community spirit today as there was when I was a boy and all our people worked on the Hatherop Estate. Three parts of the cottages are sold and properties here fetch around £50,000 and there are people who will pay this kind of money. I remember when I was a boy, about 10 years old – that would be 1933, a lodger my Mum put up who was working at Hatherop Castle wanted to get in touch with his firm so my mother told him there was a phone in our local post office and shop run by Miss Enie Smith. I went along with the lodger to the shop which was No 33 Hatherop. We went into the shop and the lodger told Miss Smith what he wanted to say and she let him use the phone which stood on a shelf in a corner of the shop. The phone was the old upright model with the ear piece on a cord which clipped to the side of the phone. He phoned his firm and did the business he wanted. Miss Emie Smith never left the counter in the shop. This was long before any phone box in the village. How different today when all the young are used to answering the phone. So much has been done to make life easier for us all. But people are not as happy and content as they were in the old days with so little. Moral what you have never had, you never miss.

Thursday 5th February 1987 – When I look back over 1986 I remember Swindon Railway Works closing down. Am told the hooter was turned on and hooted till it would hoot no more. A lot of the railway work is going north. The GWR which I used to travel on with my parents and my young sister when I was a boy, going down to Sturminster Newton in Dorset, were days I shall never forget on those great steam trains and their glorious whistles. The smartness of the station staff, the cleanliness of the station and the rush of the porters to get the tips for moving luggage is all gone with the motorcar owned by the general public and the big lorries taking goods straight to their destination. The government buying out the old railway companies promoted the finish of those great days. The scrap dealers have made a fortune.

Saturday 7th February 1987 – Mrs Fanny Mustow, the late George Mustow's wife aged 83 years, walked along to this lodge this afternoon and asked me if I would sweep her bungalow chimney so that the Southern Electricity Board could seal off her fireplace and finish fixing her central heating electric radiators. The Electricity Board have been fixing these radiators in all six of the Piece old people's bungalows for about a fortnight. They are working overtime this afternoon in the next bungalow which was occupied by the late Mrs Edith King so that a new occupant can move in on Monday. The chimney sweep from Northleach will not come for one chimney. I collected my rods and brush and swept the chimney. Mrs Watts, 80yrs old in the nearest bungalow, was there to sweep up. Mrs Mustow gave me a lovely cake to come away with, she is a marvellous cook. All's well that ends well.

Friday 13th Feb 1987 – We live in a society which has a terrible disease called AIDS, also lots of child abuse and children sexually assaulted. One judge has jailed two youths for raping and assaulting people. The public did not agree with his light sentence of three years. Tonight on the television, a female judge has sentenced another man for rape to sixteen years in prison. He was a man who claimed to belong to a religious order. The death penalty and birching should never have been abolished.

Feb 19th 1987 – We have had two deaths this week: Mr William Sharps of Coln St Aldwyns known as "Buster". A great country man, his father and mother lived at Hatherop for many years in one of the houses in the centre of the village. His father used to play a mallodion outside the house in the summer when I was a boy. He played football for CHQ and was a forestry worker and general farm hand on Coln Estate previously working on Hatherop Estate. He had been retired some years. Mr Frank Vincent of Quenington who lived at Fowler's Hill died in Fairford Hospital. A tall, fine man, also a farm worker, retired some years now, he was a great gardener and also a regular attendee with his wife at Quenington Chapel. I loved to talk to Frank.

Buster Sharps.

Saturday 21st Feb1987 – John Iles of Lechlade rode over on his motor cycle to see me this morning. We looked round the garden and talked about 17 Hatherop, a house in Golden Row, which I have been offered. I approached the Estate Agents, Smith Woolley Woodstock, some while back about a smaller house then later changed my mind. I have lived here sixty years. Wonderful years with my family, always Sunday meals in the front room. John Iles, my lifelong friend, thinks it would be a good thing to move out now into a smaller place with not so much garden. We have always kept poultry here to help keep it tidy. I am considering it.

Saturday 7th March 1987 – Snowing all day, about 2 inches of snow in the night. Last night, heard of the tragedy of the Thoresdon Ferry capsized coming away from Belgium – about 300 people trapped in her. This morning the television is full of the tragedy. I see no one, have a good hot drink and go to bed.

Friday 13th March 1987 – Times remembered: 1942 Bill Allan in the allotments one evening, said he was not going dancing with his wife again in Coln Village Hall in civvy clothes as the last dance he went to he was the only man in a lounge suit – all the others were in uniform.

My mother put up two lodgers from the Forest of Dean, woodcutters, one a man in his late fifties, one a young man, his son around nineteen years old. They cut down some large elm trees at the side of the Eastleach road opposite the long covert. The elder man said his son cried when he saw the size of the trees, nearly 6 ft in diameter. Three men also lodged here from the Post Office and did work on the telephone line. The foreman, Mr Twogood and one called Harry, walked to the Pig and Whistle every night for a drink. Albert the older man stayed with us and helped Mum and me pick the damsons. Harry had his call up papers come. Later he dropped in for breakfast when the Arnham practice drop was held one spring morning in 1944. Another man stayed some days when a corn dryer was fixed in 1944 at Mr Stanley Barton's Farm at Williamstrip. The airbourne drop was held at that time. Carter Card at Glebe Farm said he stopped his horses at plough and the men dropped down all around him. Stanley Clack tool grinder of Godwin's came and lodged with us in 1943. He was a jolly lad, and cheered my sister no end. His money of 15s per week helped us a lot. Before that a man used to stay about 3 days cleaning the chandeliers in Hatherop Castle. Hill Upton's electricians, Mr Chaundry and Ted Butler, came many times to see to the 100v electric plant at Hatherop Castle driven by the turbine in the wheel house by the bridge. All these people helped us live in the thirties. Jim Dix, groom for Mr Horniman, lodged with us when Mr Horniman stayed at Glebe Farm with Mr Arley Barton. Jim had been in the Lancers abroad and had an Arab's headdress sent from home for a fancy dress dance at Coln Hall. Mother washed it to get the blood stains out. He was not too pleased about that. He also had two daggers with it. How my dear Mother worked for us all and kept my invalid sister clean and bright long before this welfare state era.

April 2nd 1987 – Just after 5pm talking to Mr Norman Tarrant by the Lodge kitchen window, about the fallen Scotch fir tree Reuben Sims passed out. [*He had a heart attack*] When he awoke he was in a bed at the Cirencester Memorial Ward Medical Side. An awful lot of trouble for Mr Tarrant who got an ambulance to take me to the hospital. A lot of friends visited me in hospital, including Mr and Mrs Mervyn Bayliss, Mrs Bill Godwin, Mary Vigor and the finest support of all from Coln St Aldwyns Buffalo Lodge: Brother Winfield and his wife, Norman Tarrant who fed my chickens for 11 days and also walked and fed my dog Trixie. Dennis Bartlett who brought me home with his taxi and also brought me 5cwt of coal. George Jones who visited me in hospital and Brother Wilfred Franklin. The whole Lodge was very good to me. Brother Alf Kent visited me from the PGL. How fine the Order is when you are down as I was then. I had a visit from my friend John Iles who came into the hospital to have a thumb dressed which he had cut a week or so previous with a power saw. Mr Eddie Hunt visited me many times, what a good man he is and I had two visits from the Rev Cowmeadow and a visit from Lady Worsley our new church warden, very nice.

April 13th 1987 – Mr Dennis Bartlett brought me home to a nice clean and warm house, washing all done by Mrs Winfield. It's good to be home, in Cirencester Hospital I was given every attention, they were wonderful.

Easter Sunday 19th April 1987 – The first Easter Sunday I have not been to a service in Hatherop Church. I am told the church was beautifully decorated. I walk slowly now, but getting stronger.

Tuesday 5th May 1987 – Meet Mr Leigh Pemberton of Smith-Woolley for Hatherop Estate to see how I was in health and how I felt about the move to Golden Row No 17. I told him I felt a lot better and to continue with the move. Mr Hart had called the previous evening to say the lady who was occupying No 17 could now get a property in Fairford belonging to Mr Sid Bayliss in about five weeks time

May 7th 1987 – I have lived here sixty years today. It is a lovely sunny morning as I write this, apple blossom coming out, hens feeding in the large run in the top half of the garden, Trixie my dog asleep in the back doorway. All is peaceful. I am slowly getting ready to move into the village. Tears roll down my cheeks as I write this. Mr Lander's cattle are grazing in the park – a lovely sight. God's World.

At 2pm Mr Solomon and Mr Smith of the DOE, Fairford come to the Lodge and present me with a pewter tankard, a large card signed by all the staff and a barometer on my retirement aged 64. Mr Eddie Hunt came as well. Mr Solomon could not understand the round pillars at the cross roads – he thought he was on private property not a public road. He had never seen such lovely country.

Reuben with his retirement presents in the garden of the Lodge.

Wednesday 27th May 1987 – Funeral at Hatherop Church at 2pm for Donald Browning aged 60 years. John Parry brought the British Legion wreath – Donald was in the local Home Guard then went into the Coldstream Guards in the last war. He was very knowledgeable with nature. Sir Thomas Bazley and Lady Abel Smith were present. He was buried with his wife. For some while now he lived at the Folly, his cottage by the Park gate, now sold, has a notice saying planning permission is sought to extend the house and build a double garage. So many of the old Hatherop Estate tenants are going.

Friday 29th May 1987 – Hatherop Downs buildings for sale. In 1900 when my father was fifteen, he carried water to fill a trough from which the 10 horse-power portable steam engine took in water while driving the large circular saw, cutting wood for the estate. While sawing one day a lady looked in and saw the engine and said "Oh I see, a new engine". Joe Thorn the engine driver with an iron crook on one hand said "Yes madam, twenty years ago". I guess the elm for St Andrew's Eastleach Church roof was cut here.

June 5th 1987 – The battle for power in government goes on apace. Labour want to scrap nuclear arms, Conservative want to keep them. Alliance in the middle with David Steele and Dr Owen. I watch a lot of it on the TV. Mrs Gordon Legge called yesterday afternoon. She told me her house is a listed building. This is the two cottages on the left of the farm drive way at Glebe Farm. She said Charlie Barnett told her that at one time it was a bake house with two baking ovens and part was a shed for the horse and trap. The oven places were discovered about twenty years ago when the house was modernised. In my time Dobin Russell, the carter who never saw the sea, lived in the first one by the road, and where Mrs Legg lives was Mrs Hemmings a great pianist, and her son Marine George Hemmings.

Thursday 11th June 1987 – Polling day: I go to the polling station at 4pm which is held in the new school building erected behind Hatherop C of E School. Mrs Hart is inside, also Mr Robinson the retired school teacher from Barn Ground Cottage, a returning officer and a lady police officer. Stay up late looking at the television about the election. Go to bed around twelve o'clock. Wake up at 3am, come down and switch the TV on again – find that the Conservatives have won a good majority. I'm pleased, Maggie is pushing the country along, there is more respect for Britain abroad and more money in the country. I remember the words of the late chorister George Mustow who said "There are no poor today Rube". How true in spite of three million unemployed.

Friday 26th June 1987 – Church Council Meeting at Glebe Farm 7.30pm. Mr Hart told me when I arrived, he had bought 45 The Lodge. Have a good meeting round a lovely long oak table. Have a good argument with the Rev Cowmeadow over the Castle School unscrewing all the brass candle tops on the candlesticks in the choir stalls for their choral singing (why we have to have this church bashing I do not know). Mr Hart has a new puppy called Ebony. The curate forgot to attend the meeting. The Rev Cowmeadow said "Although he drinks a great deal he can speak seven languages". He deserves a better job than here.

Wednesday 1st July 1987 – Mr Lander is making hay in the fields near the Park, it does not take long these days. No long nights of cocking up the hay and loading the elevator to make a rick. Hay is baled in large rolls. Too much food stored in refrigeration in Common Market, intensive farming has produced too much food and milk but people starving in the world. Lots of land will have to go back to natural farming and tree plantations. The subsidy given to farmers has made them well off.

Talking to my friends at the Buffs, heard that Mr Morris, who is now retired into a house by the Coln river at lower Quenington, pulled down three Cotswold stone barns including Shagbarrow Barn and sold the stone. One barn, according to Mr Richard Cole who used to farm Coneygar's, had some stones of Roman origin in it. Earl St Aldwyns some while back pulled down a lovely large Cotswold Barn on the left hand side going to Aldsworth called Knoll Barn. We used to meet there in the early mornings and before sundown in 1940 in the LDV sections to look out for German invaders.

Mr Bennett at the bottom of Coln has walled across the waterway for cattle to the river and planted a rose garden there. (But it is still a waterway.) Keble Barn belonging to Earl St Aldwyn is coming under discussion to be made into a house as is being done on lots of farms. Such are the changes, not all for the good. Also found out that the Hatherop Castle private swimming pool, where the water fetes were held when I was a boy, was ruined when the Hatherop Castle maintenance men drained it when the water table was well up and the weight of water pushed up the bottom – how crazy can one be. I believe a new heated pool is there somewhere which must be better for the school pupils.

Saturday 4th July 1987 – At 9am a large red car drew up outside this Lodge and a stocky lady who was travelling in the car got out and greeted me by the gate. She said she had heard that I knew her mother Mabel Ponting known as Queenie. I said "Yes I did". Joe Ponting and his wife [*Queenie's father and mother*] came to live at Barn Ground Cottage down the Eastleach Road before the last war and Joe Ponting was a milker for Mr Arley Barton at Glebe Farm. Mabel Ponting worked for the Miss Kebles, at Keble House, Fairford and used to cycle there from the Barn Ground cottages which then were two cottages. The first one Joe and his wife lived in; the far one, Shepherd Hawkins and his wife lived in. Shepherd Hawkins and his wife used to walk to Quenington for the harvest festival at the chapel at the top of the little hill going down to Quenington Church opposite the bottom farm buildings. The chapel is now a private house as also are the farm buildings opposite. The lady I was talking to was the eldest daughter of Queenie. She was born in 1937. Queenie Ponting had two children, the war was on and she went away with a soldier called Travers. The lady said she had four children of her own. She lived Marlborough way and her husband worked for a farmer who had a daughter boarding at Hatherop Castle School. It was through the girl at school that Queenie Ponting's daughter had found out about her Mum who is buried in Hatherop churchyard, no stone, grave lost like so many, levelled down as the years go by. Told the lady where her mother lived at Barn Ground Cottage and the car drove away to see it.

Sunday 5th July 1987 – I look in Register of Deaths book in vestry. Found the entry of Mabel [*Queenie*] Ponting's death entered under the name of Mabel Travers. May 21st 1944 – died at Evacuee Hospital Cirencester – buried by the curate Edward Green during the war years. Mabel was 22 years old. A quiet, soft spoken girl. Of course to have children out of wedlock in those days simply was not done, or if it was, the poor girl was not approved of. Today they are known as one parent families and have the social services behind them – there is no stigma any more. Queenie's daughter told me that Joe Ponting and his wife are buried in one of the villages near Marlborough in Wiltshire.

July 11th 1987 – Cyril Rixon, our churchyard worker, has fallen off a load of hay bales and is seriously ill in the Radcliffe Infirmary. A good man for Hatherop Church, looks after the churchyard well.

Sunday 12th July 1987 – A lovely warm morning. HE at Hatherop Church at 8am. Two new people there who have bought Mr Harold Godwin's house [*Mr and Mrs Mick Barham*]. The Rev Cowmeadow was pleased, he said "They are church people". Lady Worsley came on her cycle – she parks it by the church porch. We pray for Mr Cyril Rixon who is very ill in the Radcliffe Hospital. Take some eggs for Mrs Mona Rixon and a bottle of wine for Cyril's father who is in Cirencester Memorial Hospital.

Tuesday 21st July 1987 – The young man who lives at 41 Hatherop has come tonight with the paper "What's On" and asked me about the records of Hatherop. He is on the Parish Council and says that my grandfather Reuben Sims has his name in one of the books. He has had a letter from a Mr Silk. All I could say was that I heard my people say that Ann Silk was housekeeper at Hatherop Castle, also Caroline Silk, who according to her tomb stone by the church path was housekeeper at the Castle for forty years. Ordinary people years ago had little say in the running of the parish. My Aunt Beatie Humphries told me that when she was a girl a lady used to come down from Golden Row with a shawl covering her face. I believe this must be Caroline Silk. In the church burial book it states she was at Gloucester Asylum. All the new people here want to know about the past in the village. There are only about 14 properties left unsold. I am still waiting to hear about this Lodge, I have let the garden go wild but still keep the hens. The letter offering the house at Golden Row was in February this year. Of course I had a sickness spell in Cirencester Hospital for ten days in April which delayed matters. Had a visit from Lady Abel Smith to see how I was getting on and we had a good talk on the old days at the Castle and how her father, Commander Cadogan, read the Lesson to the Legion Men in Hatherop Church on Armistice Day and how her people used to call my mother Saucy Kate.

Brigadier Sir Alexander and Lady (Henriette) Abel Smith.

Wednesday 22nd July 1987 – Up till this year I always planted the garden since 1942 when my father died and Mr Fred Ford came to this lodge and said he would see I planted onions and potatoes correctly in the Hatherop Allotments. Mr Fred Ford and my father William Sims were great shots in the Coln Malt House range before the 1914 war. Saw Mr Weston who now owns the Malt House and told him of the shooting range in the Malt House before the 1914 war and how I have a cup and medals won by my father there. He was very interested. Also saw Mrs Lucy Thomas of Quenington, we talked about the canvas swimming pool fed from the river in the meadow at the back of the cottage by Clifford's Mill, placed there by the Bazley Family. I write these notes, as things come into my head. I remember Mr Fred Moaby, who was a fast bowler for Williamstrip Cricket Club in my father's time, standing in this Lodge's front room and saying a toast as he drunk some homemade wine: "When wars are on and danger nigh, God and soldier is the cry. But when wars are over and peace reunited, God's forgotten, soldier slighted."

Sunday 2nd August 1987 – Earl St Aldwyn I believe is in London for an operation. Lady St Aldwyn has crashed a car.

Friday 7th August 1987 – Warm days now, corn fit to combine late though. Smoke from the straw burning Coln St Aldwyns way. I am told there are only five men working on the Earl's Farm such is the use of tractors and machines today.

August 9th 1987 – Reuben Sims oversleeps, does not go to Hatherop Church for Communion with his Lord.

See the Rev Michael Austin and his wife in Coln Stores when I drive down to get my paper, the Sunday Telegraph, once the paper of the rich and famous but now read by ordinary folk who buy some shares. Unheard of in my father's time. Apologised to Rev Austin who told me Farmer Hart pulled the bell, Lady Sally Worsley was home so she saw to the people coming in.

Monday 10th August 1987 – Post a Standard paper to the Williams family in the Oregon USA including a paper written by Mr Ian Curteis on the roof repair at Coln St Aldwyns Church – £21,000 needed. Also a paper to my school friend Mollie Wheeler in Atlanta USA, she will be interested in the price of property here. When we went to school a house would fetch about £60 if you could buy one. There were none for sale on these estates. Mr Fred Harding of Quenington told me he went to The Court at Bibury where his brother Bert's house was auctioned. It made £68,000. Fred said his brother bought it from the Church Commissioners for £400. In Canon Lowe's time an old lady lived there when I was a boy and the windows were painted black. I did not like going by there.

Wednesday 12th August 1987 – A good Lodge meeting of the St Aldwyns Buffaloes in Mr Dennis Bartlett's caravan at the blacksmith's shop Coln St Aldwyns. Landlords in public houses charge too much rent today for a weekly meeting and want pool tables and gaming machines on their property.

Thursday 13th August 1987 – Have a good old dust up with Mr Hart on the phone about cutting Hatherop churchyard now Mr Cyril Rixon is ill. Mr Tim Mowat and Mr Hart, with Lady Worsley's approval, have decided that contract mowing of the church yard at £16 a cut is the way to do it. I do not agree. I think someone from the parish should do it if they wish the Lord's building to be kept open. But I expect the contract work will go ahead. Two men from the Manpower Services Commission came to see what they had to do to cut the churchyard on the appeal of Mr Tim Mowat. I told them the hedges wanted cutting but they did not know whether they could cut the hedges, just general clearing and grass cutting. They could not walk the long church paths as they had a van and power tools. Ten people would come. Such are the times in which I live.

Thursday 20th August 1987 – Phone call from Reverend Cowmeadow to say William Parker had died from a heart attack in Fairford Hospital. Bill and his wife and family lived in Golden Row before the Second World War. He had an injured leg and for many years rode a bicycle with a loose pedal crank and a fixed wheel drive. Later on after the war he drove a motor-bike and sidecar. A nice quiet man was Bill.

Tuesday 25th August 1987 – Walk to Hatherop Church with Trixie and see "Garden Maintenance" Herby Harris and his son cutting the churchyard with a garden tractor mower and other portable mowers. Mr Cyril Rixon our churchyard worker has been unconscious for six weeks in hospital. Twenty years ago, our people would have wanted the work for the money but no-one wants the work today. The funeral service for our old parishioner William Parker took place today at Hatherop Church at 2.30pm. The local villagers came: Mrs Jean Maunder, Mrs G Legg, Mr Gerald Hartshorn and Mrs Mervyn Bayliss.

Monday 7th Sept 1987 – A fine warm day. Stand in the road-way with Mrs Richard Lander while Mr John Lander and his son Richard bring the cows up the Eastleach Road and across the road into the Park. Mr Richard Lander commented on the Common Market rules of less milk production. Some of his fine cattle have to go. How strange while there is so much poverty in the world. Farmer Hart's tractors are working the land after the harvest of the corn crop. Mrs Richard Lander said they have done contract baling with the new machine which puts bales in large rolls lifted by fork lift on the tractors. How times have changed on the farm. No more bumpy rides for farm workers on a sledge towed behind the baler, knocking back a bolt, and letting four bales go off at once, or the short tine bale forks where two men lifted the bales on to the trailers. All the work is now done from the tractor seat.

A large pile of Cotswold tiles are in the garden of the house by the park gate where Mr Donald Browning lived. Before him was Mr Dapper Higgins with a large beard and his son Ben. They were looked after by Miss Beatrice Higgins who came here from service to look after them after Mr Dapper Higgins wife died on the condition there was no wine making. They had a barrel of beer instead.

Saturday 12th Sept 1987 – A wonderful Children's Fete and Flower Show was held in the Manor Farm Barn. Mr and Mrs Weston of the Malt House Coln St Aldwyns and many of the new people who have come to live in Coln St Aldwyns worked hard for the show. Also they all work very hard for the Coln Parish Church roof repair fund. If the Coln nave roof of the church repair was left to the ordinary Cotswold people I doubt if it would ever be done. The new people bring in their talents of drive and business ability, also ideas for raising money and carry it through. We Cotswold people have good intentions but come from non-industrial, low paid estate and farming backgrounds and have not the money or the business drive.

Sunday 13th Sept 1987 – Farmer Hart's tractors are working on the Lord's Day.

Saturday 19th Sept 1987 – Went to the Harvest Supper in the large barn at Manor Farm, Coln St Aldwyns in the evening at 7.30pm. I am 64 years old and this is my second visit to this fantastic barn – its length makes the mind boggle. Earl St Aldwyn has the lambs reared there. The new people of Coln worked awful hard and put on a good supper and entertainment. The barn was decorated with ivy and electric light bulbs of various colours hung on the walls. A stage was erected from which the announcements were made. The barn is nine bays according to the roof trusses. Lady St Aldwyn sat with us all, also Earl St Aldwyn. How nice the Class War is over. Peter Hicks Beach was there also. I did not feel too well so I left quietly after the dinner. Nothing like this in aid of Coln Church has ever been done before, a wonderful evening. Came home, sat in my chair quietly in kitchen at this Lodge and saw the last part of the film "A Bridge Too Far". Took me back to those old days of 1944 when the airborne troops dropped in one morning in the spring time all over these fields with their scooters and folding cycles etc. One was standing

Tom Lemon (right) with Ricky Lait at the Harvest Supper 1987.

by the stone pillar across the road from this Lodge kitchen window and as I ran round the house to see what was going on he said "Did I wake you up this morning?" They were fine men – the Flower of our Youth. At that time my mother took in a lodger who put in the dryer apparatus for the combine at Stanley Barton's barn at Williamstrip Farm. He saw a lot of men jump from the Dakota airplanes – one man's chute failed to open.

Coln Village Hall, now called Vicarage Cottage Barn, is a memorial to the young airborne troops who danced the hours away till midnight in this hall before the Arnham drop. They were wonderful dancing nights before the great slaughter of our men. Gwen Bailey and Rosie Day both made dresses out of the parachute silk and they looked wonderful.

Sunday 4th October 1987 – 8am Holy Communion. R Sims overslept and arrived at 8.10am in time to take the collection. 8 communicants including Mrs Bartlett who he had seen at supper the previous evening. She said "I won't take you to supper again Reuben, you are late!"

Thursday 8th October 1987 – Go to the Hatherop Working Men's Club and pay my last six months rent to Smith-Woolley & Co. Have the key for No 17 Golden Row. Am now making plans for moving before the cold weather.

Friday 9th October 1987 – A dry day, go with my friend John Iles of Lechlade to look over No 17 with its carpeted floors and stairs. We clear out some of the rubbish in the hovels outside for coal and a washing machine place. Look at Park Ray stove and heating radiators.

Saturday 10th October 1987 – Ring John and decide we will visit No 17 again on Monday. Today Mr and Mrs Donald Collett and his son come to The Lodge with a pick-up truck and take 13 hens, one hen house, 5 bantams and the house and run, also take my Norfolk greenhouse attached to Lodge tool house wall. I miss the hens very much, a lot of life gone from the Lodge.

Monday 12th October 1987 – Drive to Lechlade – pick up my friend John Iles who came back with me and we made three trips to Golden Row with my garden tools and tool boxes. Also he had made up some coat hangers on a board to fit in the small hall. Mr Harry Maunders came and took down the chicken run and posts. Play Eb Bass for Fairford Silver Band in the Chapel School Room at the Congregational Chapel in Milton Street. Our buxom young lady conductor from Gloucester put us through our paces with the piece The Snowman. I played wrong in a place or two and had good reprimands. I enjoy playing with the band. When I joined in 1947 I could not blow a note then but have had some wonderful times through the years. Have a glass of beer with Frank Law of Highworth in the Bull afterwards, Frank plays baritone and loves it.

Tuesday 13th Oct 1987 – We take more tools etc. from the Lodge to Golden Row where I am to be moved on Wednesday 21st Oct. I came to this Lodge on the horse and cart May 7th 1927 from Netherton so it is quite a wrench leaving here. Go back to Lechlade with John and have dinner with him and his wife. Come home and rest. I am not so strong as I used to be before I had the heart attack.

Wednesday 14th Oct 1987 – Have a ring from Mr Silk of Shrivenham who talked about his ancestors at Hatherop. Ann Silk, he said, was married to James Silk born 1800. He took part in the 1830 agricultural riots at Quenington, smashing a threshing machine and was sentenced to deportation to Australia but did not go. He was six years on a prison hulk at Portsmouth, then released. Came back to Hatherop, fell off a ladder on to a pitch-fork, died after 30 odd hours and is buried in Hatherop churchyard (no stone). His daughter Caroline has a stone by Ann Silk. She was forty years at Hatherop Castle it says that on the stone. James Silk died 23rd October 1845.

Friday 16th October 1987 – Drive to Lechlade, pick up John Iles and drive back to the Lodge. Make three journeys to Golden Row with china and home-made wine. We have moved a lot of small things. Do not stay to lunch with John and Rachel but come back with a good lunch of lamb and a good sweet on plates covered with tin foil. Van front wheel breaks down at South Farm, two woodmen help me push it on the grass verge. Ring up Hammonds repair shop in Cirencester. Pete the mechanic came out with a van and towed my van back to Cirencester, repaired broken frame and brought van back at 6pm. I'm very pleased, I can continue now on Monday, taking more stuff to No 17.

Wednesday 21st October 1987 – I rise at 6.30am. Let Trixie out round the Lodge grounds for the last time. My friend John Iles comes and at 8am Barnes removal van draws up, a large van, three men, including Mr Barnes, load my furniture and clothes etc on to the van. They like my grandfather clock and my commode which look like pieces of furniture which are both worth a lot of money. The commode my mother had from Barrow Elm house for a few shillings and we used it a lot in the front room at the Lodge with my father ill in bed there. I rang my friend Eddie Hunt on the night before the move to say good night from the Lodge for the last time. He told me he had heard from Fiji a few days ago and that his son there had been in an accident and lost an arm. He was in hospital recovering, a great worry for Eddie and his wife.

My friend John Iles, a very handy chap, took the door off in the archway of No 17 Golden Row and the removal men unloaded all my furniture and household effects. My father's carpenter's tools were put in the garage I have with the house. This little cottage is packed full of furniture now, I shall have to get rid of quite a few things. Go to Lechlade for lunch with John and his wife, how wonderful they have both been to me. In the afternoon we bring away a lot of small things from the Lodge and light the Park-ray fire. There are three radiators upstairs. John rides his motorcycle home. The Rev Michael Austin came in and we had a glass of whisky together. I retire early to bed in the bedroom over the archway. I'm very tired.

Sunday 25th Oct 1987 – Mrs Fanny Mustow, wife of the late George Mustow, passed over sometime on Saturday evening and the police had to break in on Sunday morning. Another of our faithful church worshipers has gone. She missed her late husband George very much, she was a wonderful woman.

October 30th 1987 – Cremation service for Mrs Fanny Mustow in Hatherop Church at 2.30pm. A lot of people present as she was well liked. Mrs Sue Sly carried out the arrangements. Tom Lemon and Reuben Sims in the choir. Some Hatherop Castle School girls brought some flowers.

George and Fanny Mustow.

October 31st 1987 – Sir Thomas Bazley's 80th birthday party at Hatherop Castle from 6pm to 7.30pm. R Sims helped pour the wine. Plenty of bottles of white and red wine. Lots of tenants from Eastleach and Hatherop present, also lots of the new property owners. A happy party.

Sunday 8th November 1987 – Fairford Silver Band played for the Armistice Service in Quenington Church at 11am. A good place for a band in the chancel of Quenington Church. The band was conducted by Helga Perry, our lady conductor from Gloucester, in a red uniform.

Sunday 13th December 1987 – Am getting used to living in Golden Row, quite peaceful here and as I am getting older now it is nice to be near neighbours.

Thursday 24th December 1987 – At 5.30pm have a visit from Lady Sally Worsley who gave me a lovely white flowering plant and a card. Her daughter and son would help with the collection and light the candles at 11pm. Hatherop Church is noted for its evening candlelight services. Walk to church at 10.30pm. Lady Sally Worsley came in with her daughter and son, a collecting bag each. The ladies had decorated the church well. We lit all the candles, the organist from Quenington, Colin Walters, played the organ. R Sims pulled the Sanctus Bell, the congregation came streaming in, lots of young people. The ladies had the lights off except the far light opposite the main doorway and the candles did the rest. Only the main altar and choir stall lights were left on. I thought it was a pity really with carols to sing and the church packed to the doors with people but variety is the spice of life they say. Our top people were there – Lady Abel Smith, Lady Howard, Lady Worsley, Lady St Aldwyn and her son Peter. The Rev Derek Cowmeadow and his curate the Rev Michael Austin officiated.

Christmas Day 1987 – Drove to Lechlade to my friends John and Rachel Iles. Had a good Christmas Dinner and listened to the Queen's Speech on the Television. She looked her age this year.

January 3rd 1988 – Look at the extra ground the Hatherop School Governors have given the school. It has been taken off the garden of the school house so when the occupant comes out of the house he is confronted with a children's area. When my grandmother lived in that school house my father used to plant potatoes there. Today the young do not want to do gardening. They would rather drive around in their cars. In a report in the Church magazine, the first ever, it says the teaching staff has been increased from three full-time teachers to three full-time and one part-time. Sixty-four children in my day, enough play area, three teachers full-time and out to work at fourteen years. I don't know why everything has to be done in an expensive way today.

January 6th 1988 – Meet Mrs Farmer Hart at the Church at 2pm and greet a surveyor for the employment schemes for work for unemployed about white-washing the church interior. It was last done by Mr Clem Peyman of Fairford in 1951. The trouble is the height of the nave. Farmer Hart has some drain rods and we put them up the nave wall. It is somewhat around thirty feet. De Mauley put the roof up five ft – I presume to get his Victorian windows in. The surveyor said it was the height which would stop his men doing the wash as fifteen feet were their limit. Mr Peyman did it off a ladder in 1951.

Walked back home along the church path, had a phone call from John Plaister of Swindon about the winding of Hatherop Church clock. He said he now had a winding jack. But I told him, with the money left to Hatherop Church by Mrs George Mustow, we thought it would be a better memorial to both her and her husband George that we had the clock automatically wound. When Mr Mervyn Bayliss gives up the winding three times a week, the clock will stop.

January 8th 1988 – Walk Trixie down the Park in the morning and back past Home Farm to Barrow Elm. Saw Mr John Lander by his new milk parlour. He said he has had to give up the Barrow Elm Downs land as there is development there. Also the Barrow Elm Farm buildings are to be developed. The changes we see today, our fathers would never have dreamed of all the people with wealth who are coming into this area. Twenty years ago there were bucket privies here in this Golden Row. No baths, ordinary fireplaces and paraffin stoves provided extra heat. The village baths, two in number at the back of the Reading Room, were looked after by Mr Jim Shepherd, the bell-ringer and chorister. He cleaned the baths, took the money. The fee was four pence when they started but later rose to one shilling. How Jim carried on if you used too much hot water or overstayed your time of half an hour in the bathroom. The baths were put in when I was walking to Coln School so they were in operation all through the 30s. If you did not go to the baths you bathed in a bowl or had a long tin bath with hot water from the copper. We did this quite often at the Lodge. Of course there was no electric light at the Lodge. It was too costly to put the power on. This was done when the old people's bungalows were built in 1967. I shall always be grateful to the late Mr Percy Mustow when I went down to Coln Mill Cottage and asked him if I could rent the cottage while the Lodge was modernised and he immediately said 'Yes, would you like the key to have a look round?' A wonderful man.

John Lander

January 11th 1988 – Reuben Sim's Birthday – He is sixty-five years old and feels it sometimes. Walk to Coln Post Office with Trixie and get my first week's pension.

January 12th 1988 – Meet the architect Mr Barry Lloyd together with another gentleman, Lady Worsley and Mr Hart to discuss re white-washing the church last done off a ladder. This time, staging has to be erected. This is the Rev Cowmeadow's idea but he would like the walls back to their original stone. The architects are doubtful this can be done once limed.

Tuesday 26th January 1988 – I am writing about a chat I had while in Fairford car park about a fortnight ago with Mr Tom Woodman. He told me he bathed Mr Herbert Stephens, the farmer at Manor Farm, Coln St Aldwyns for two years every night before he departed this life. He also said Mr Stephens walked from Wantage to Manor Farm, Coln St Aldwyns with a threshing machine and three horses with £90 in his pocket. When he died he left £70,000. He always went around on horseback at hunting weekends and also went to Coln Church in the forward right hand pew in Coln Church. He was a teetotaller. I remember how Tom Woodman said that he went to Hatherop School before my day. His Dad was gardener for Colonel Conley who lived in Church Mead. The Colonel used to walk along the church path when we were boys going to the church services and used to wave his thumb stick and always said to us young folks who walked in front "Get out of my way boy, get out of my way!" Tom said they lived in No 9 which was the gardener's cottage for Church Mead. His father disagreed with old Colonel Conley and knocked him down so he said they were moved out the same day. Such was the thing in those days.

Sunday, 31st January 1988 – Have a visit this afternoon from Bob and Mrs Hutchings of Cheltenham in their Fiat Sports car. We had a lovely chat of old times. How nice to talk to an old Cotswold villager. I really enjoyed it. 1928 was the year Bob Hutching's brother Jim was born and also when a great gale blew down the avenue of elm trees lining the front drive to Hatherop Castle. I remember the traction engine pulling the tree trunks when I walked to Coln St Aldwyns School.

Wednesday 3rd February 1988 – Visit Mr Charles Rixon at his son's home No 8 in the afternoon. His daughter-in-law Mona had gone to Swindon to see her husband Cyril who is still unconscious there.

Sunday 14th February 1988 – The roof is being repaired on the Hatherop Downs Barn, believed sold for £250,000. The house by the Park Gate of Hatherop Park is being rebuilt quickly by Mr Lipscombe's firm, Bibury. To think his father and mother came down to Quenington in the last war from London and lived in old carpenter Leonard Miles's house in the Conegar Road.

Tuesday 23rd February 1988 – Escort two clock repairer men up the Hatherop Tower to price putting automatic winding gear on the church clock. One man was from Smiths of Derby, the other from Public Clocks of London. We want to put automatic winding in without interfering with the glass case which protects the clock so much.

Thursday 10th March 1988 – Mrs Cyril Rixon is clearing out Mr Charles Rixon's home at No 10 Hatherop where Mr and Mrs Chater lived when I was a boy. I visit Mr Charles Rixon who now lives with Mrs Cyril Rixon which is a very good thing now Charles has grown old and we have a good chat about the old days when Mr Watley was the shoe mender and had the wood shed in front of No 40 and about Bert Wheeler who lived with his brother at Homeleaze. Charlie said how he whistled and we remembered how he rode to Hatherop every night to see Enie Smith who lived with her mother and kept the bread shop at No 33 before George Mustow lived there and how Enie came down to the gate to see him off back home to Homeleaze. Poor Bert Wheeler died – Enie most upset – so courting over, the Smiths left Hatherop for the east coast in 1937. When old Mrs Smith died, Alfred Hope, Enie Smith and Beatrice Sims played hymn tunes on violins under the trees at the shop – 33 Hatherop. I am writing this at 6am. I got up and made a cup of tea at 5am.

March 13th 1988 – Mothering Sunday – Good service in Hatherop Church at 11am. The Rev Michael Austin took the service. Mr Morris played the organ. The Castle girls, Tom Lemon and R Sims in the choir. Posies made up and given to all the children from the altar rails, brought up by Sue Mackenzie and another young lady. Posies and flower arrangements by Mandy Weston. Two ladies played guitars and children sang at the chancel steps. The Rev Michael Austin forgot to read the bans for the second time of Charlie Pollard's daughter so he read them from the Chancel steps in the presence of Reuben Sims, Mr Tim Mowat – synod representative and some others who had not gone after the service.

Tuesday 29th March 1988 – Had a visit from my old friend from Kidderminster, Stanley Black and his wife Beryl. We went to Eastleach, saw the daffodils and had a ploughman's lunch in the Victoria Public House, very nice. I gave Stan a martingale (horse brasses) which I bought off his uncle Sid Black when he worked at Maccaroni Downs Farm. He told me he had it made at Burford.

Thursday 31st March 1988 – Mr Charles Pollard of Dean Farm gave me £18 to pay the six ringers for his daughter's wedding at Hatherop Church on Saturday 2nd April. Charlie said at one time they were all related in the Dean Farm Cottages and all worked there. Now only one person works on the farm and all the rest of the cottages are let and no one does a garden where they all used to do their gardens and his father always planted potatoes whenever Easter Monday occurred. They were always self-supporting at the Dean. It will be good to have a wedding at Hatherop Church.

Saturday 2nd April 1988 – 2.30pm ringers from Fairford arrive and ring the bells [*for the Pollard wedding*]. Rev Cowmeadow and Rev Richard Austin officiated. The church was full of people. Mrs Hart and Lady Sally Worsley had decorated the church and candlesticks. The bride came in late all in white. The yellow Rolls lost its way and could not find Dean Farm, home of the bride. The bridegroom was in a grey suit, also the Best Man. Charlie, in a smart black suit led his daughter in. The cameraman was there, plenty of cameras clicking. Lord and Lady Howard and family in the Bazley pews. Three small bridesmaids in red dresses and an older girl dressed the same all with white shoes – a fine show.

Easter Sunday 3rd April 1988 – Drove to Coln church for 11am service of sung Holy Communion. Church as always well decorated. A bank of purple and red flowers stood each side of the altar supplied by Williamstrip Estate. The Hayward boys who live in the old Wilkins almshouse are wonderful gardeners. The organ was beautifully played by Mr Morris. The church was full of people. The service was taken by the Rev Michael Austin, a tall, well built man with black hair and a rounding face, in his white Communion robe. We all came away and I forgot to get my paper from Coln Stores so went without. TV broke down so went without. Went to Hatherop Church at 6pm. No bells. Church beautiful with the flowers of yesterday's wedding. The Rev Derek Cowmeadow played the organ. He plays very well. Tom Lemon and Reuben Sims in blue cassocks and white surplices walked up the aisle with the Rev Michael Austin like we did years ago and we all sang the hymns, Psalm 150, the Magnificat and Nunc Demitis. Lady Sally Worsley told the Rev Michael Austin he was not wearing his cape correctly and he should be tidier. In all a good Easter Day. Saw Mrs Legg in the street a few days later and she was not pleased that Lady Worsley had shown her husband to the south side pews and she had to sit in the choir stalls [*at the Pollard wedding*]. One does get these little kick-ups from time to time. Mrs Hart and Lady Worsley stayed in the choir vestry during the service. No confetti was thrown in the churchyard much to my disappointment.

Monday 4th April 1988 – The new homes being built in the fields by Lovers Walk, Quenington Road, were offered for sale. People queued to buy them. Some were priced at £120,000, but still sold. To get £1,000 for a second-hand house in Fairford after the last war was wonderful. Mr Briggs bought Southcott, a fine house opposite the Hyperion Hotel (previously Fairford Vicarage) for £2,000 from Mr Crook the local tanner – considered a good buy.

Monday 18th April 1988 – Forgot to say that I went to the Memorial Service at Hatherop Church for Miss Pieper, a school teacher at Hatherop Castle School. Dr Moorhead gave the address. Mr Barraclough read the lesson. Dr Moorhead said we should not be sorry for Miss Pieper as she had suffered so much with cancer. She had had a very hard life, lived in East Prussia, was branded by the Nazis because she and her family would not join the Party. She served in labour camps when the Russians overrun Germany, got out of Berlin at the third attempt and made her way to England. Told by her doctor how long she had to live, she said "I want to live long enough to see my girls though their exams". A very courageous and marvellous lady. Miss Ingelore Pieper was 61 years.

May 1st 1988 – The Gloucester Cathedral Choir and Organist led the Thanksgiving Service at Coln St Aldwyns Church for the redecoration of Coln Church. Mr and Mrs Curteis had the Cathedral Choir to tea. The choir boys eating nearly cleared them out of food. Fine singing by the Cathedral Choir.

May 21st 1988 – Mr and Mrs Farmer Hart held a soup lunch at Glebe Farm at 12.30pm for Christian Aid. Lots of new people there. A fine lawn at Glebe Farm. This is where the old kitchen garden used to be. A confirmation service at Hatherop Church at 3.00pm. Mrs Susan Vicary stood in as Warden as Lady Worsley was away. The Bishop John Yates was 15 minutes late as he was held up in traffic jams coming out of Gloucester. We all had tea in the Castle library where the section has been built across. A Bed and Breakfast sign has been put up on the large tree by Mr Mowat's house. This is the house which was built for my grandfather when he came to Hatherop in 1888. This Bed and Breakfast sign is the first in Hatherop.

Sunday 22nd May 1988 – Mr Dennis Bartlett took his wife, his mother and me to the Corinium Court Hotel in Cirencester for a Buffalo Dinner at 1pm. It was nice with the St Aldwyns Lodge No 6723 and their wives. This hotel is in the area where Aubrey Rees Agricultural Engineers were. When I started work for Mr Briggs at Fairford, Aubrey Rees was a great competitor in the field of agricultural repairs and agent for International 10/20 tractors – a very good tractor. Mr Briggs was agent for Standard Ford & Sons. They were not as strong as the International and the Land Army Girls in the Second War sometimes had a job to start them with the handle.

June 5th 1988 – Have a petition notice put in my letterbox from a developer who wants to buy the New Inn at Coln St Aldwyns and turn it into three dwelling houses. The new residents of Coln who have bought the old Coln Estate houses are up in arms and are forming a Coln St Aldwyns Society. How times have changed. It is only the last two elections that people have put up party candidate posters in their window. I have written to the Council opposing the plan.

The Coln St Aldwyns Society: Don Courtney – Secretary, David Trudgill – Treasurer, Edward Weston – Chairman.

June 10th 1988 – The petition against the development of the New Inn being turned into dwelling houses and the coach house into flats heats up. Large notice and petition board outside Mr and Mrs Mandy Weston's house [*the Malt House, Coln*].

Mrs Ewart Lander, mother of John Lander, has died at 99 years.

Sunday 12th June 1988 – I played the organ in Coln Church at 6pm for evening prayer. Saw Mr Carter after the service and he wants Tom Lemon and me to meet Central Television at 10am tomorrow to state our views about the closing of the Coln public house and so it goes on.

Monday 13th June 1988 – Meet Douglas Coates and Tom Lemon at the New Inn. The television crew arrive. Also Mr Carter from the Mill House. The crew get filming. Mr Carter tells how the developers want to close the Inn down and make it into houses and also build more houses out of the Coach House and garden at the rear. We go into the Inn – only the front door used now – the side saloon bar is closed. The landlord poses and calls time for the cameras. Earl St Aldwyn talked about the Inn and said it would be a great shame if it closed or words to that effect. The interviewer said 'Didn't he regret selling it?' but the Earl said 'One could not do that but we must do what we can to keep it open'. Tom Lemon spoke and said he agreed with Earl St Aldwyn and it would be a shame if the Inn was closed.

One of the Central Television crew was a Midlander from Tom Lemon's own county and called for a pint for Tom, Doug and Reuben and went off without paying. We paid up. Tom said 'Wait till we see him again!'

Funeral of Mrs Ewart Lander. A large congregation. Mr John Lander and his family, also many older people because of the age of Mrs Lander. Ninety-nine years – she died on her birthday.

Charlie Rixon's house is for sale now he has moved in with his daughter-in-law at No 8. This is the house where Mr and Mrs Chater lived and who lodged the school teachers Miss Evans and Miss Moot (she had her wedding reception there and all the choir boys went).

Sunday 26th June 1988 – Mrs Bartlett, the blacksmith's wife is not well. Cyril Rixon, our churchyard worker, is still unconscious in Swindon Hospital. His father has come home after a fortnight in Fairford Hospital to give Mrs Cyril Rixon a rest.

Wednesday 6th July 1988 – Meet Mr M Bayliss, Farmer Hart, John Plaister of Swindon, Lady Sally Worsley, Sir George White – Diocesan clock adviser and Mr Meecham and his partner who have a clock winding unit which John Plaister of Swindon does not approve of because of the method of driving the clock. Lots of clock engineering talk going on between Mr Meecham, his partner and John Plaister. We listen. This job had nearly been given to Mr Meecham and his partner by Mr Hart before we had the advice of John Plaister of Swindon. We could not get John Plaister on the phone as he was out doing clocks. Mr Ted Pearce of Lechlade found him for me at a funeral of one of the Traction Engine Rally members. After the discussion for about an hour and a half and after looking at the unit in the back of the car and a discussion between ourselves and Sir George White, we decided the equipment was not good enough and Public Clocks should be consulted again. Mr Meecham said in the tower that winding should be fitted and a teenager could be trusted to wind it twice a week if paid well. I told him in modern society with the money they have, cars, televisions, a cold frosty time in the winter, who would do it twice a week? He disagreed with me but the fact remains I can get no young men to mow the churchyard now. No bell ringers, no choir nor young people at church at all to my regret. If the Hatherop Castle School was not there the church would close.

Friday 8th July 1988 – Go to the funeral service of Mrs Cynthia Burge at Quenington Church – one of the last of the laundry maids at Hatherop Castle. My mother was a great friend of Ethel Burge when they were at Hatherop Castle in their single days. Mrs Cynthia Burge was a great dancer and held classes for a great many years.

Tuesday 12th July 1988 – Drive to Eastleach to see Mr Ron Newport. I park by Causey Barn and collapse. Taken by ambulance to Cirencester Hospital.

Tuesday 19th July 1988 – Rev Cowmeadow brings me back from hospital. The Buffs looked after my dog and my house while I was away.

Thursday 21st July 1988 – Cyril Rixon was buried in Hatherop churchyard after a cremation after a year and a week in a coma in Princess Margaret's Hospital, Swindon. His wife Mona drove to see him nearly every day. He was a good working man and worked hard in Hatherop churchyard.

Saturday13th August 1988 – Watch the German film 'Heimat' at night – about the war years in Germany. The German people suffered a lot in the war, like every other country.

Sunday 14th August 1988 – Holy Eucharist at 8am. Gillian Akers and her boyfriend came in, also Mrs Townsend and her daughter Mrs Backhouse. Mrs Mona Rixon, Miss Hobbs and one more lady from Coln. The Rev Michael Austin officiated and read the marriage banns of Gillian Akers and also Miss Colby of the Hornbeams.

Wednesday 17th August 1988 – Douglas Barnes came and tuned my piano and I'm very pleased with it. Now I can pass the hours away here amusing myself. My fingers are not as nimble as they used to be but I get a lot of satisfaction in music. I am always grateful to my Dad and Mum for paying half a crown tuition with Mrs Hedges, the Fairford school master's daughter. Walked to Coln, as the New Inn is still under threat of closure, for a radio interview outside the New Inn with John Winfield and Douglas Coates. It will be broadcast Saturday morning. By the time I walked back to the Coln Buffalo Lodge at the Blacksmith's yard I had had enough to drink. If this situation has arisen twenty five years ago the deal would have gone ahead without question by the Cotswold working class but today there are a lot of writers and intellectual people who have bought estate houses in Coln and they are fighting this closure.

Friday 19th August 1988 – The front page of the Standard local paper says the local villagers have put in their own proposals for the New Inn and have also offered Mr Clarke the developer ½ million pounds for the New Inn.

Saturday 20th August 1988 – Overslept this morning so do not know if the broadcast on Coln Public House took place. See no one to talk about it. Did not go to Coln Flower Show at the Malt House. The doctors will not let me drive my little three wheel van so did not go to Steam Engine Rally at Fairford.

Wednesday 24th August 1988 – Have small freezer delivered from Gardiner's of Cirencester so that I can keep my bread better. Go to Buffalo Meeting in the evening. Mr John Winfield said the copper pans and brasses in the New Inn were being taken away yesterday. The fight still goes on by the Coln St Aldwyns Society to save the New Inn.

Saturday 27th August 1988 – Wedding at 12 o'clock of Mr and Mrs Colby's daughter from the Hornbeams. Flowers were placed in the church yesterday and posies with ribbons hung on the centre aisle pews. The flower stands are used, one in the sanctuary, one in the far arch from main door. The candles were lit by Lady Sally Worsley. She had no main lights on (strange), a good organist and choir of the St Oswald singers. Mr Terry Keen brought six ringers and they rung the bells before and after the wedding. I was so pleased we could do this as it is not easy today with no ringers in the Parish. The times I have seen in my church life. I pay the ringers £18 and another church day over. I was told that the broadcast of our interview at Coln New Inn was broadcast this morning at 8 o'clock and I did not hear it.

Tuesday 30th August 1988 – A fine morning. Have been writing since 5.30am. Came here October 19th 1987 and I am just getting used to retirement. Living on my own so long, work was my companion, seeing the men at work, a chat and a good laugh at dinner time. Once retired, all that finished. A new style of living emerged. Friends at work at Fairford Air base seen every day gone – only walks with the dog. No family to come and see me – only clearing out a lot of my mother's things. She saved everything: 'We might want it' was her stock phrase and so it was before the Welfare State days. All my boyhood friends married with their families. As I grow older, my older village friends of boyhood days passed on – only Bob and Jim Hutchings and Desmond Westall on the Hatherop Section Home Guard picture still alive. Of course we were all local in those days. I also remember Mr Gaiger from Quenington talking to my father on the same seat about the bombs that dropped behind the Williamstrip Estate Park wall opposite the lodge by the iron bridge and all across the park east of the cricket pitch. Mr Gaiger said he had seen shell holes in France in the 1914 war a lot bigger. My Dad agreed with him of course. Those were early days – the old LDF [*Local Defence Force*] days of arm bands and shot guns. Sid Hearne, butler to Lady Margaret Watney [*at Williamstrip House which she rented 1935–1946*], rode as messenger on an auto-bike – the first little motor bike we had seen – to Fairford Croft chapel headquarters on the schemes we had. Our headquarters then were at the Hatherop School and Sid on one of these schemes said 'I have gone all the way to Fairford and back and now they are not ready' and how the Colonel used to say 'We will go forth to battle and Hearne will go forth on his scooter'. At some of the target practices across the river at the bottom of the Coln, the Schoolmaster of Hatherop said 'If there is any more bad language, I shall not come again'. Gas masks in cardboard boxes tied on the cycle carriers to work.

Wednesday 31st August 1988 – John Winfield said that on August Bank Holiday Monday the New Inn closed down. The battle royal goes on. Sally Beauman and Joanna Trollope, writers who both live in Coln, have written an article in the Daily Mail about the developers and how they can wreck village life.

Sunday 4th September 1988 – Go to Church at 2.40pm. Light candles on altar and put out cards for the christening of Hannah Johnson. The parson arrives from Minster Lovell or that area. The ladies and gentlemen arrive, the christening takes place. R Sims played the organ and we all sang Crimmond at the end of the service. We all go to Mr and Mrs Johnson's house for a strawberry tea in the walled garden of their home – the old head gardener's house opposite the village school. A very happy time.

Wednesday 7th September 1988 – Go to Buffs in the evening and hear that the application by Old Minster Securities to alter the New Inn into small houses for the jet set has been turned down at the Council Meeting. The Coln St Aldwyns Society has offered to buy the New Inn for £500,000.

The Coln St Aldwyns Society meeting to save the New Inn
held under the horse chestnut tree at Coln.

John Winfield and Douglas Coates were well under the weather after a meeting and party at the Malt House at Coln.

Thursday 8th September 1988 – Ambulance called and picked me up to go to the New Hospital at Cirencester for results of my scan at Swindon hospital about 2 months ago. The doctor told me my head was alright but I must give up driving my little van. I can ride a horse or a cycle so I must get my bicycle out again. With no shops or post office here now you are cut off without some transport. The bus service comes through at various times for Cirencester.

Wednesday 14th September 1988 – Went to Cirencester on the service bus. Fare £1.15. Have my old age pension tokens 20p each. Bought some meat at Jessie Smith's, had cup of tea at Ann's Pantry, lost bus back but brought home by Mr Keith Harris, an ex DOE worker. My luck was in.

Thursday 15th September 1988 – Walk to Church at 1.30pm for the marriage of Gillian Akers. Ben Smith said hello. He was getting his wife out of a car parked near the Memorial Arch. Marjorie has both her legs off from sugar diabetes but is still a very jolly girl. Sue Sly from Northleach turns up and Muriel Percy brought the other four ladies so we had a good team of ringers. I light the candles, switch the lights on, plug in for the organ and the organist started to play. Ben Smith wheeled his wife Marjorie in and she had a good view by the font. The ringers rang the bells up, the Rev Cowmeadow in his coloured habit started the ceremony. The cameraman arrived. After the service I call up the tower stairs and the bells rang out. Photos were taken by the west window and lots of confetti. How lovely. I do like to see confetti mark a joyful occasion. A lovely Cotswold wedding. John Akers, Gillian's father, gave £10 for the plate.

Saturday 17th September 1988 – Have heard that Desmond Westhall has died. He is on 'The Stand Down of Col Gibbs Home Guard picture 1941. It now leaves Bob Hutchings, Cadet Jim Hutchings and Reuben Sims. Desmond had sugar diabetes, was blind and had one leg off, so not much in life. May the Good Lord give him Eternal Peace.

Fairford Market Place c. 1920.

Thursday 20th October 1988 – Ronald Newport

of Eastleach called and took me to Fairford for shopping. Go to Betteridge the butcher in London Road. He took over Perry as butcher. Lots of apples, carrots, all sorts of green stuff etc as well as meat. A lot of shops do this kind of thing today. 98 pence for a dozen free range eggs. When at the Lodge I used to put four in Trixie's bowl!!

Tuesday 25th October 1988 – See Mrs Mona Rixon in Hatherop who said Charlie would be going into Fairford Hospital for a fortnight. It will give her a rest. Meet Mrs Ellen Townsend and Mrs Rose Bailey at No 17 at 2pm and we go to Hatherop Tower and I show them the photographs and the clock and bells. Ellen could see her father and her husband on the 1941 Home Guard stand down picture of Col. Gibbs and Rose her father and brother-in-law.

Monday 31st October 1988 – Pack up some things belonging to my mother and carry them to Coln St Aldwyns Post Office to go to my cousin, Mrs Gladys Yarrow of 3 Richmond Road, Parkstone, Dorset. She is my mother's brother Jack's daughter. Draw my pension at the Coln Post Office. Walk to Coln Church and have a look around the building. At our last Parish Council Meeting at Hatherop the Rev Cowmeadow said they have been ordered that the Coln Church take down the plastic guttering. I must admit it does not look good on such a fine building. What the architect was thinking about I do not know

Saturday 5th November 1988 – Go to Hatherop Castle Gardens and buy a good cabbage for 75p. Talked to the gardener there about the old days when the gardens were dug with a fork and little box hedges surrounded the dug plots. About four men used to do this work then go to the Hatherop allotments and dig their own plot in the evening. Those were the days when men earned around £2.50 a week. As the gardener said 'You could not afford it today at £100 per week per man'. In the evening, lots of fireworks going off. Trixie barks. She does not like the bangs. Fireworks should be £10 each.

Wednesday 9th November 1988 – Catch bus to Fairford at 9.20am. Bus shelter full of camera gear and two men. The high steel wire fence has been taken down by the school arch. Lots of laurel bushes in pots placed each side of Memorial Arch to School entrance. The street full of parked cars. Yesterday I am told it was the same. Some filming job.

Friday 11th November 1988 – Talked to Mrs Owen who lives in the old nurse's cottage and has it on the market for £120,000. She said the film company chose Hatherop School out of 300 schools because it has not been altered and gave the school £500 for the permission to do their filming. We live in a strange society where money is flung around like water.

Sunday 13th November 1988 – Get ready for the service with black bow tie and blue cardigan. The dress today. Nobody seems to want the old military style uniforms. Go to church at 9.45am. Mr Voaden comes in, also Mrs Susan Vicary and her son who put the books ready for the congregation. The congregation came in – among them Dame Lady Abel Smith, Lady Howard, Countess St Aldwyn and her son the Viscount who read the names of the fallen and laid the poppy wreath during the service. Col Malet read the lesson (very well). The pupils of Hatherop Castle School filled the choir stalls and the side aisle with the band in front. Very few Second World War men. Time goes by.

Monday 21st November 1988 – Walk to Coln Post Office to get my pension and pay my bill at Coln Stores. Came home to stoke up fire and think of the many frosty mornings through the years I cycled to Fairford to work when I was young, scarf over cap on head, sandwiches in tin and bottle of tea put behind stove in the main shop with cork loosed for lunch break and dinner time. Bert Ayres of Poulton used to put some onions in front of the stove to cook for dinner time and we sat round the stove on trestles or oil drums with a sack on when it was nice weather. We closed the main doors, had a cut out bat and a tennis ball and played cricket. Bert Ayres was a good footballer and cricketer. Jeff Hatton used to join in if he came back early from dinner. Jeff had a three wheel car with a V Twin engine in the front. You had to shout at one another when you were going along. We used to go to Coln Stores butcher's shop at Bibury in it to decoke the diesel engine in the time of Mr Stan Lewson, manager, whose name is on Bibury's War Memorial now. Go to Band practice in the evening with Mr Cecil Voaden and come home with Mr Frank Law who is still feeling the loss of his wife. We had two pints of beer in the Bull Hotel.

Wednesday 23rd November 1988 – Go to Buffs at night and have a good chat with my fellow Buff Brother, John Winfield, who said Sally Beauman, the author who lives in the first Cotswold house on the right going into Coln from Hatherop, has had a visit from burglars who took antiques worth £400,000. The burglers had beer there during their visit in the day while she was away. Also he said he had, after a great deal of effort, found the first Parish Council Minute book and in it Mr Fred Kiddle complained about the railings in the centre of the village round the chestnut tree in Coln, the old parish pump area, as there might be an accident there with all the fast moving traffic. This was around 1931. Also, it says that years before that, the old Sir Michael Hicks Beach wanted to put a bridge over the river by the sawmill at the bottom of the Stoney path across to the path that leads past Mill House to the main Coln/Quenington road. The Stoney path led round somewhere through the sawmill area. The bridge was built, although the Parish Council refused permission, but no mention in the parish book that permission was refused. Mr Douglas Coates told us that years back in the early fifties, when Mr Jesse Miles died and they cleared the house out in Coln which was up Main Street above the New Inn [*No 8 Casina Cottage*] that all Mr Miles's carpenter tools in a large box were burnt out in the garden. The Miles were carpenters for years and a very clever family. Jesse Miles was foreman on Coln Estate. What a shame, as these kind of tools are now valuable as collector's items.

Tuesday 29th November 1988 – Have visit from Tim Saunders who bought my three wheel van for £1,000. I cannot drive so it is no use keeping a car.

Tuesday 6th December 1988 – Practise carols on piano for Brownie party next Monday. A small bus picked me up at 7.15pm to take me to the New Inn at Lechlade for a dinner with Ted Pearce, Eddie Hunt, Tony Marsh, Stan Dennis, Ron Newport, Harry Gardiner, Airman Ossy of the USA Airforce, Frank Blackwell. Except Ossy, all pensioners. A good meal – turkey. Eddie and me had pheasant, crackers and table wine. The price of the wine is a rip off. But it is only once a year and no washing up!!

Thursday 8th December 1988 – Hear news of big earthquake in Armenia on radio. Go to Fairford with Eddie Hunt at 1.45pm and go to the men's ward. The nurse told me not to stay too long. Charlie [*Rixon*] as always was glad to see me. He had grown so much older and looked his age now. He was propped up in bed and his voice was faint. We talked about old Gunner Wheeler at Quenington and his grey horse and how they used to saw the wood up with a circular saw and about homemade wine. He said you do not know anyone that comes in the Ward these days. Of course that is true. So many new people around here and the hospital caters for a large area. The ward is very nice and warm, well decorated and the nurses look after the patients well.

Saturday10th December 1988 – See Mrs Mona Rixon – said I had seen Charlie but she said he did not know I had been and also he was very weak. I came away and walked with Trixie to Coln. Mrs Cox from the Lodge called me to get her the Star paper which I did and put it on the doorstep when I returned. She said her husband's father and brother built the Lodge. Also the gate pillars nearby that lead into Williamstrip Park. She said her husband's father was turned out of Coln for having something to do with the Liberal Party. Of course, this is long ago. We have some good laughs together about the changes we see today on my walks to Coln Stores. On my way up Hatherop Hill, Mrs Rixon pulls up and said 'Charlie died early this morning'. She would let me know details later. I am very sad – another of our old characters has gone.

Monday 12th December 1988 – Get ready for the Brownie Pensioner's party at Hatherop School at 5pm. Large table of food and sherry to start with. The Brownies waited on us all then we sang carols. R Sims played the piano. He was given a present of pipe tobacco.

Tuesday 13th December 1988 – Walk Trixie through the Grandage and up Snake Drive to the Green at Quenington and down to Godwin's Works. A large building project is going on by a firm called Keene. The old Chapel of the Plymouth Brethren has the slates pulled off the roof. The porch is half gone. Eleven houses are going to be built around here. When I was young several cars used to be parked by the chapel for a service but it has not been used for years now.

Thursday 15th December 1988 – Go to the service and burial of ashes of Mr Charlie 'Bubbles' Rixon in the afternoon. The service was taken by the Rev Cowmeadow and the Rev Michael Austin who gave the address. A lot of people there. Mrs Hart played the organ. Two hymns, 'The King of Love' and 'All Things Bright and Beautiful'. Charlie saw his wife go twelve years ago; ten years ago his daughter; this year his son Cyril. Charlie was a man of great courage, a hardworking countryman who loved the old fancy dress dances we had when we were a rural community and everyone knew everyone else and of course drank the homemade wine. Hatherop churchyard was levelled by him in the late 1960s so that contract mowers can mow it today. He said he rode a penny farthing cycle years ago – the problem was not getting on but getting off the machine. How he loved his horse and trap in years gone by and his cattle. Sir Thomas Bazley came to the service. He usually does to his old tenants. I was very sad. No bell is now tolled at funerals.

Wednesday 21st December 1988 – Mr Cecil Voaden took me to Bouthrop Church now under the care of the Redundant Church Fund. Fairford Band was in the side wing and played for the candlelight service. Mr Hart of Glebe Farm was giving out the lighted candles to all the people who came in. The Church had some of its paraffin lamps going. Holly in the windows. The children sang 'Away in a Manger'. A full church of people afterwards in the large Cotswold Barn. A good glass of wine and platefuls of hot dogs. Mr Arkell is a wonderful man there and Fairford Band played well.

Saturday 24th December 1988 – Mrs Susan Vicary visits me with a lovely iced cake. Mr Mowat picks me up to go to the Crib service at Coln Church at 5pm. The church is full of people and children. We have readings, blessings of the crib and sing carols. Reuben Sims reads the last lesson. Sing well beside Tom Lemon. Only candlelight. Lady St Aldwyn, her son Peter and Lady Howard were there.

Sunday 25th December 1988 – Walk to church at 7.20am. Switch on lights. Light all the candles in the candelabras. Light altar candles. The stands of flowers by the pulpit and rear pillar by the font catch the eye as you walk in. R Sims pulled the Sanctus Bell. Mrs Bartlett came in, Mr and Mrs Colby whose daughter was married earlier in the year. Mrs Wood from Coln was there, Mr Mowat and Mr and Mrs Owen who live in the nurse's cottage with their baby. Fourteen in all were communicants at the Lord's Table. All is quiet in the village although some lights on in some of the houses. Mr Dennis Bartlett from the forge picked me up at 10.30am and took me to my friend John Iles house at Lechlade. I have a good Christmas Dinner. Mr Bartlett picked me up again at 3.20pm after the Queen's Speech and Trixie is at the door to greet me.

Sunday 1st January 1989 – Bob Hutchings came at 11am and drove me to Cheltenham. Had lunch with his wife Pat who is walking on crutches after breaking a leg in a fall off a barge on a canal. We had a haggis and a cream pudding and black coffee. Had a lovely chat about old times and Bob brought me back at 3.30pm. Sold Bob my Sovereign dated 1913 belonging to my grandfather for £50 – the going price.

Wednesday 4th January 1989 – Go to Buffs Meeting at Coln smith's shop in the evening. Brother Wilfred Franklin is in Wroughton Hospital. Brother George Jones is in The Querns, Cirencester. Brother John Winfield has been taking Mrs Franklin to Wroughton to see her husband. Brother Dennis Bartlett is seeing to Brother Jones.

Friday 6th January 1989 – Visit Mr Bill Cuss the wood pattern maker, retired from Goodwin's. He is a very clever craftsman, lives on his own and had the cottage next to him left to him by Mrs Edie Pitt who used to be the postwoman at Quenington for many years. Have a glass of sherry and a good chat with Bill. He said Miss Jackson, who lived in the cottage opposite him, left £180,000 when she died. The cottage is still empty. She was the churchwarden at Quenington for some years. Left Bill and walked up Fowlers Hill and looked in the cemetery. I have not found the grave of Leonard Miles who worked as a carpenter with my father on Hatherop Estate. I rather fancy there was no stone as it was 1941. My Dad and Mum walked to Quenington for the funeral service.

Bill Cuss (left) with Harold Tugwell in the Pattern Shop at Godwin's Pumps.

My Dad had to stop several times on the way because of breathing trouble. I remember how they both used to ride in the trap to Eastleach to work when I was a boy with the old Kitty mare, and then Leonard sat in the cab with Mr Ernest Sharps when they had a lorry which Mr Sharps drove back from Portsmouth. A great thing in those days.

Wednesday 11th January 1989 – My birthday. Have a lot of cards and a phone call from Gladys, my cousin from Parkstone, Dorset. Go to Buffs Lodge in the evening.

Thursday 12th January 1989 – See Mrs Victor Cox at the Lodge. She said Mr Percy Mustow's son Cecil is dead and is going to be buried by the Salvation Army in Coln Cemetery tomorrow. He was a nice quiet man. The Mustow family – very good people. Lovely coloured ducks on the Coln River.

Sunday 22nd January 1989 – Walk to Church at 7.30am. Go up tower. Ring the bell. It rings out clear on this frosty morning. Should have woken those heavy-sleeping girls at the Castle School. The Rev Michael Austin and his wife were all smiles when I came into the church and pulled the Sanctus Bell. Later in the morning around 11am saw Mr John Winfield and Mrs Legge's son by the Workman's Club. It was broken into by thieves last night.

Friday 27th January 1989 – Go to the funeral of Mrs Charlie Mills who died in Paternoster House, Cirencester. Her daughter Mollie came over from Atlanta for the funeral at Hatherop Church at 3.30pm. R Sims spoke a few words about Mrs Mills, then a car drove me to Fairford, Milton Street, where we had some tea and I saw Mrs Mill's sister in her cottage in Waterloo Lane. Came home in the car, Mollie came for the ride.

Wednesday 15th February 1989 – Waited at the church tower for Public Clocks to arrive at 10.30am. They were late 11.15am. I told the man of Public Clocks he was late and also we had paid him £800 prior to the work being started. He was not pleased. But when he came back at 12.30pm he was in a better mood. He said he apologised to Mr Bayliss for being late.

Friday 23th February 1989 – Frank Law, our baritone player, picked me up and took me and his brother who is a retired blacksmith of the Swindon Railway Works, to the Jolly Tar at Hannington for a ploughman's lunch. Frank's brother, Bert, worked all his life in the Railway Works in the old Great Western Railway days before public ownership and said how they worked hard, made everything at the works and had great pride in God's wonderful railway. After nationalisation, more managers and foremen were put in. The mode of transport changed. The large steam engines were stopped being made. The diesel engines were made and engines were made in Germany. The casting shop was the first to close. The large rivets were bought instead of being made. Men were held on when there was no work by left-wing works councils. There was no desire to make profit anymore. The taxpayer paid. The government had to cut its losses and closed it. A very sad end to a fine GWR engineering works. Did well with redundancy payments of £17,000 etc. Another case I can recall was when Mr George Aruthers was estate agent and he told me that, before he came to Hatherop, he did the accounts for a local hospital. They had a reserve fund of about £12,000 when the welfare state was formed. Two officials came to see him and said he was not doing the books right. He said he was doing the work for nothing so told them to take the books. A willing helper lost.

Tuesday 28th February 1989 – Walk to Coln. Buy some fruit for Miss Marjorie Brindle who lives on the Fairford Road end No 39 Hatherop. See Miss Marjorie Brindle and give her the fruit. She was very pleased. She gave me an electric clock that needs a battery. I shall go on the bus to Fairford tomorrow and get the clock fixed up at Barnes electric shop next to Radways Bakery, opposite the church.

Wednesday 1st March 1989 – Catch the service bus to Fairford. Buy two herrings in the market which is held every Wednesday, also a new pair of

Wellington boots in Peyman's shop. Go into Radway's bakery shop and visit Mr William Radway who cannot get around very well and we have a good chat. Get a new battery fixed into Miss Marjorie Brindle's clock, come back on bus at 12.15pm and take clock to Miss Brindle who will be eighty years old in April. She is very pleased with the clock.

Thursday 2nd March 1989 – Keeper Smith's son known as 'Digger' has been buried today at Coln Church. Keeper Smith is the retired keeper on Coln Estate. His son had a blood disease. Lord rest his Soul.

Thursday 9th March 1989 – See Mr Mervyn Bayliss outside the Estate carpenter's shop. We talked about the bothy house where the grooms used to lodge in days gone by. Also the carpenter's shop must have been used. Mr Bayliss took me down to the Estate lorry shed and outside, under some bushes, was the old hydro machine. Two laundry ladies turned the handle, got the drum spinning, then put it into a higher gear and spun the clothes. It is a rare machine and should be preserved. The washing was done in 4 large clay sinks. Two very large coppers boiled the water. The ladies did the stoking. There was also a machine with a lot of rollers over which was a large box full of gravel which pressed out the clothes. In my time Mrs Flo Card, Mrs Cynthia Burge, Mrs Bert Tennerman, Queenie Ackland and Mrs Charlie Barnett, head laundress, worked there. The laundry wash-house was entered by a door at the bottom of the steps under the archway leading to the church. I remember Mrs Barnett saying about a handrail there which she told her girls always to wipe as the housekeeper, Ann Hocking, used to run her hand along to see if there was any dust every time she went into the laundry.

Tuesday 14th March 1989 – The Public Clock men call at 10.15am. I give them the keys to go up the tower to start work on the automatic winding. Run Trixie in the Grandage after hearing Mr Lawson's budget speech. When you are on a pension it does not matter much.

Thursday 16th March 1989 – John Moaby calls at 8.15am and gets me out of bed for the tower key. Public Clocks' two clock fitters are fitting the motors etc. At about 1.30pm the Public Clocks fitter came and gave me his key and said the clock is going. I'm surprised and very pleased. Thank him very much and ring Mr Bayliss to tell him and meet him at 2pm and we watch the weights going up and down as the chimes go off. Such small weights compared with the old ones which are left in the weight box. We are both pleased with the job and hope it will go alright. So March 16th 1989 Hatherop Church clock winding goes automatic. No more going up the tower twice a week in all weathers to wind the clock.

Friday 17th March 1989 – Mr Bayliss tells me the chimes have stopped so I ring Mr John Plaister. He says he will come out tomorrow morning.

Saturday 18th March 1989 – John Plaister came approximately at 11am with Mr M Bayliss and we all went up the tower and Mr John Plaister corrected the faulty chimes. He said it will take a month or two to settle down. Lots of ducks on the River Coln – a lovely sight.

Palm Sunday 19th March 1989 – Go to the church for 11am Holy Eucharist. A costly fancy book has come from the Diocese about the Vicar and other church matters. I fail to see why such things are printed in this day and age with so much poverty and suffering in the world. We have too much printed material in the Church of England. We all come away from the service with our Palm Crosses. I take the Rev Cowmeadow up the tower and show him the new automatic clock winding.

Friday March 31st 1989 – Get up late. Trixie wanted to go out twice during the night so I'm tired. Do not feel well. Lady Sally Worsley rang to see if I was going to Fred Cox – the Southrop church warden's funeral. I said no, not feeling too good. She said look after yourself and would ring the Rev Cowmeadow to get a lift to Southrop Church. Fred died in his church on Good Friday. He was a wonderful warden for Southrop. The Good Lord will receive him. The coalman for Mr Rollins of Lechlade told me there is a funeral service at Eastleach Church tomorrow for the death of Mrs Martin Squires of Macaroni Downs Farm. I am very sorry.

Tuesday 4th April 1989 – Sunday night, the Hatherop Club was broken into for the third time. This time entry was through the roof as Mr John Winfield has had steel plate bolted onto all the doors. The police cars are in the street like yesterday. Go to the Club in the afternoon to pay Smith-Woolley the rent. In the morning, around 10am had a call from Mr Mervyn Bayliss to say the clock man from Public had arrived to look at the clock chimes which do not work. I walked to the church with Trixie after I had had my breakfast of eggs and sausages. John Plaister of Swindon, the clockman Mr Adams and Mr Bayliss were there. Mr Adams put an extra weight on the chimes. Gave him a bottle of my dandelion homemade wine.

Thursday 6th April 1989 – Mr Mervyn Bayliss called and said the clock had stopped. We decided to go up the tower and see if twigs from the jackdaws or anything else had got into the drive or else would have to get John Plaister of Swindon. We both went up the tower but could see nothing which caused the hand drive to jam, so decided to call John Plaister of Swindon.

Saturday 8th April 1989 – John Plaister of Swindon got the clock going again. Something to do with the chime work.

Sunday 9th April 1989 – Mr and Mrs Oliver Puffitt of Meysey Hampton called. Oliver said he was born in this cottage. Afterwards they moved to the house with the village cross, where I always remember them, but I have a picture of Mr Bayliss welcomed home after his marriage and Mr Puffitt is on the pavement by these cottages.

Saturday 15th April 1989 – Ring up Miss June Lewis of Fairford who wants information and photographs if any of the Second War years. I told her I have a good picture she can borrow of the stand-down of Col Gibbs, Commander of the G.H.G Guard in 1941. She said she would like it. I also have a photo of Eastleach playing the RAF of Hooks Landing Ground. I remember playing in that game well.

Wednesday 19th April 1989 – Got a paper for Mrs Victor Cox in the morning from Coln Stores. She told me when she was a girl she remembers the Grandage was mown by men with scythes for hay and they sat down under the Netherton Road wall eating their bread and cheese for dinner. Mrs Bartlett has been taken to hospital.

Thursday 20th April 1989 – Forgot to say, on Wednesday 19th, caught the service bus to Fairford and called at the East Glos Engineers. Had a chat with Mr Vernon Cole about the days of Reuben Briggs. I wish one of the old account books was still around but it appears they are all gone and the old binder and chaff cutter repair parts books. All through the Second War it was a busy firm with fine sets of steam tackle working. Briggs and Richards, Albert Butler and the Fowler engine. Alfred Cook and the Alchin engine, Herbert Marshall and the Marshall DD2007 still around. Ernest Reeves with the single Marshall, Jack Bamfield and the Alchin, and seed huller. Bertie Gold and the Clayton and shuttle engine, the set of tackle that belonged to Arkell of Lechlade. Another Alchin engine went to Barrington Estate on the rack saw-bench. The steam roller was used to roll Rissington Aerodrome when I was a boy of fourteen in 1937. There were also two or three Rushton straw balers that had self feeds fitted on them and were fixed at the rear of the threshing machines. I ramble on but I walked up what is known as the little alley and saw the old Church of England school with its windows all boarded up and the gate locked. Also the opposite side where the school buildings were built in the orchard and allotments, the gate was locked. What is going to happen to these buildings, now all the schools are in Fairford Park on the Rag Hill road, I do not know.

Sunday 30th April 1989 – Mr Oliver Puffitt came to see me in the afternoon. We played football together against the army and airforce teams in the last war in Hatherop Park. His wife had baked a cake for me which he brought with him. Oliver has diabetes and has had to go on a strict diet. We talked of old times on Hatherop Estate and how all our people worked on the Estates. His father was stone mason for many years. Maurice Dennis and his wife Lucy, Cecil, Dorothy, Gladys and Elsie are dead. Stanley who was groom and car driver at the Castle, Aubrey, Bert and Oliver are still alive. He said at one time three laundry girls lived in No 8. That was before Jim Shepherd lived there and where Dennis met Lucy.

Tuesday 2nd May 1989 – Meet the Smith-Woolley rent man, about a 20% increase in rent.

Sunday 7th May 1989 – Go to RSPCA animal service in Hatherop Church at 4pm. Mr Tim Morris played the organ. Alsatians, whippets and spaniel dogs there. Not a large congregation but we all sung well. A collecting box was in the porch. Did not take Trixie. She fights her own kind. Pity.

Saturday 13th May 1989 – A young couple from New Zealand staying at Mr Mowat's across the street from me wanted to know about George Wheeler as they were descended from a brother who went abroad in the last century. Showed them the records in Hatherop Church. They also went to Highworth to see the Silk family because they are related. They also were interested in the late George Mustow who was a nephew of George Wheeler who was the gardener and coachman for the Rev David at Church Mead, the old rectory. I told them how George Mustow was a great chorister and bell ringer at Hatherop all his life. And how George Wheeler as an old man used to give us a good stinger as he called it when as school children we lined the playground wall, we held our hands out and he gave us a good smack.

Thursday 25th May 1989 – Mr Bayliss called to say the church clock had stopped again. This is three times since it stopped with a power cut during thunderstorms.

Saturday 27th May 1989 – Mr Mervyn Bayliss arrived, then Mr John Plaister of Swindon who started the clock again and went up in the belfry and oiled the chime shafts.

Monday 29th May 1989 – At 1pm Mr Cecil Voaden took me and Mr Frank Law, a baritone player who came from Swindon, to Cheltenham to a fair where Fairford Band played during the afternoon. It was a lovely warm day. Mr Cecil Voaden drove back from Cheltenham, down the Coln Valley, Chedworth, Coln Rogers and Coln St Dennis, Ablington, Bibury then home – a lovely drive in the Cotswolds. Our people pay hundreds of pounds today for a holiday abroad and long airport waits. But all the beauty is here in the Cotswolds.

Wednesday 31st May 1989 – Walk to Buffs in the evening. Mr Douglas Coates came after being in Cirencester Hospital, brought by his daughter in her car. How times change. I remember when the petrol rationing came in early in the Second War when my mother went to Cirencester on the Dingles bus which ran every afternoon. When mother came home she said 'Mr Cadogan was on the bus'. Unheard of in ordinary times. Another item Mr Mervyn Bayliss told me – when the old Reading Room was going before the War, Ben Ash playing billiards on the quarter size table struck a ball which went through the glass widow and landed in the road outside. Quite a stroke!

Thursday 8th June 1989 – Taken by Mr Hart to Dean Farm to Mrs Susan Vicary's house. There a party was being held for the ladies and discussions on making fifty kneelers for Hatherop Church. One kneeler made by Mrs Ruth Mowat was on display. Drinks, sausage rolls and cakes were provided. Mr Hart took me to the large metal barn lower down, where several young men were putting down wood pallets and nailing ply sheets at £8.50p each to make a floor for dancing. The disco band will be in the rear of that. The whole ceiling so to speak of the barn is covered with black polythene sheeting. This drops down like clouds. Dance will go on all night Saturday June 10th. I'll bet there will be some revellry and one heck of a din.

Sunday 11th June 1989 – Walked to Coln Church for Evening Prayer after the Hatherop Castle School girls who visited me in the afternoon said Mr Lemon would like me to sing in the choir. We sang well. A lovely evening. Mr Tom Lemon took me round the manor where a lot of people have flats and nice gardens. Of course, you have to have money to be there.

Thursday 15th June 1989 – Have a visit from Mr Ronald Newport who took me to Fairford Hospital to see Mr John Chesterman of Kempsford who is a patient there. He had a bad leg. A marvellous man who was a prisoner of war under the Japanese. Also saw Mr Morgan, the Fairford School retired woodwork master who is a patient there. Had some wonderful woodwork classes at the old school by the church in the fifties and also at the prefab buildings now locked up by the old infant's school. The Fairford hospital is a fine place now. Go to Hatherop school and vote for members of the Common market. Mr Robinson and the wife of the taxman in number 41 were the stewards. Plenty of money has been spent at Hatherop school. It is a luxury hotel – whether it improves the education of the pupils is arbitrary.

Sunday 18th June 1989 – Trixie laid down in the choir stalls while I practised the hymns for the Holy Eucharist service at eleven o'clock. Mr Robinson of Barn Ground Cottage picked up Tom Lemon and me at 7pm. Drove to Southrop Manor for a farewell drinks on the Manor lawn at Southrop in honour of the Rev Michael Austin and his wife who are leaving for a parish in Sussex and have lived in the cottage next to me here in Golden Row.

Wednesday 28th June 1989 – Talk to Mr Gerald Hartshorn and Mr Norman Tarrant about the number of workers years ago on the farm. How at Williamstrip Farm a large locked box was kept in the kitchen when the command bells were rung. The box was opened for Gold Flake cigarettes for the household.

Thursday 29th June 1989 – Have phone call from my friend John Iles who said the removal people would be coming tomorrow morning to take them to their new house at Wroughton which will be a quarter of an hour's walk from their daughter's house opposite the Iron Horse Public House. I wish him well on their move after thirty-six years at Lechlade.

Saturday 1st July 1989 – Mrs Reginald Dingle died this week aged 89 years. Wife of Mr Reg Dingle who drove his bus around these villages for many years. Edith Dingle was a teacher at Hatherop School.

Saturday 8th July 1989 – Mr Cecil Voaden took me to Quenington Green where the village fete is being held. Fairford Band played under the large Chestnut tree. A good afternoon playing, also a good parade of Swindon majorettes. A traction engine went by sounding the steam whistle. Teas were on sale in a marquee. Lots of side shows including some Amanco oil engines. I had one of those years ago. Gave Mr Charles Richards of Furzey Hill Farm £5 for one and I drove a saw with it.

Friday 14th July 1989 – Moorhen sitting on nests by the railings across the river. Poster on bridge gate saying the Lait family at the Lodge now called Pump House have applied for planning permission to build a house with garage and driveway at the bottom of the hill.

Saturday 22nd July 1989 – The Air Tattoo is held at the Fairford Air Base today and tomorrow. Mr Roger King brought me a Cotswold Life magazine June 1989 with a writing on the three village schools by Miss June Lewis of Fairford. It included the photo I loaned her of Hatherop and its people welcoming home Mr Bazley after his wedding in January 1903.

Hatherop welcomes Mr Gardner Bazley home after his wedding in January 1903. First two boys on left: Charlie Barnett, Wilfred Barnett. Beyond the group of boys: Gran Sims in bonnet and shawl, Mrs Thomas Smith in hat. First man sitting on wall – William Sims, carpenter. Right side: Mrs Thorn, Coachman Messinger and family, Mrs Messinger standing in road. Behind her: Beatrice Sims and Mrs Moulden. Further down, standing near roadway: Mrs William Puffitt.

Wednesday 26th July 1989 – Walk to Buffs in the evening. Took one of the old Buffalo Minute Books and read the passages out of it concerning the Buffs moving to the Keepers Arms, Quenington in 1940 because the troops took over the Lodge room over the stables at Coln New Inn. The Buffs is one of the few organisations still going in the three villages.

Tuesday 1st August 1989 – In the Wilts and Glos Standard, it reports that Dr Moorhead, principal of the Castle School, is retiring. She has been head for some years and is very keen on animal life. Am getting Hatherop ringing chamber in good shape as Mrs Sue McKenzie is bringing five ladies with her on Thursday evening to try out bellringing. Mr L Sly is coming to instruct from Northleach. No men want to ring here.

Thursday 3rd August 1989 – Go to church, unlock the tower and wait for Mrs Sue McKenzie and her band of ladies. They all turn up and Mr Sly showed them how to pull the bells up and down. I showed the ladies the No 3 bell and all the ladies had a go at ringing it. We went on till 9pm. Now we will leave it for two weeks because some are on holiday. It is the first time a local band of ladies have rung in the Hatherop tower.

Friday 11th August 1989 – Had a talk with Mr Bayliss earlier in the week who said Bill Puffitt talked about the three cottages which were made into the Rectory in 1914 when the Rev Cheales came to Hatherop and where my Aunt Beatie used to light the fire for Francis

Smith while he was out tree planting. One cottage was the Reading Room. The Reading Room was built in 1906 out of the quarry stone in Hatherop Park. Bill Puffitt's son Oliver told me sometimes there were a couple of dozen people in the Reading Room. The committee man on for the evening lit the stove and locked up after everyone was out by 9pm. The billiards and darts were one or two pence a game. I have heard that the project in the fifties for the tennis courts and sports grounds in the Grandage fell through when the people of Quenington wanted the project there. Mr Godwin would have helped finance it, had it come about, but instead it all fell through. The Grandage is sold and a large clump of trees have grown up where the tennis court was. Good for wildlife.

Mrs Joyce Bullimore presenting the singles cup to Jim Day c. 1952.

CHQ Tennis Court Committee c. 1952. Back row from left: Vic Cox, Joe Prytherch, Jack Gaiger, Jim Day. Sitting from left: Irene Townsend, Eric Cole, Jean Bullimore, Reg Godwin, Kath Brindle.

Monday 14th August 1989 – Get cycle out. Pump up the tyres and ride to Fairford surgery by the Eight Bells public house and get my tablets. I am very pleased because I have not ridden my cycle for so long and however generous your friends are with their transport it is nice to have transport of your own.

Sunday 20th August 1989 – Get out the bicyle and ride to Coln Church for the 8am Holy Eucharist. About 10 communicants. Rev Cowmeadow and Mr Powell at the main door. Ask them where the annual statement of accounts is for Coln Church as it is not on the notice boards in the porch. They say they were there. The Rev Cowmeadow said they are only there for two weeks. At Hatherop, ours are in the porch for twelve months. No one knows what happened to the £100 the late Mrs Fred Kiddle gave to the Bell Fund which Mr William Godwin started by going round hand bell ringing at Christmas.

Sunday 3rd September 1989 – Spend a quiet day at home. I am tired. Listen to the old war songs on the radio and watch the film 'Bomber Harris'. What a man he was. Bombed everything. All the roads round here to Fairford and Conegar Road were stacked with bombs at the side of the roads. Fifty years ago today.

Sunday 17th September 1989 – Harvest Festival at Hatherop Church at 11am. Colin Walters played the organ. The Castle School girls filled the choir. R Sims pulled the Sanctus Bell. Mrs Susan Vicary acted as warden in place of Lady Sally Worsley who was away. The Castle School girls lit all the candles, the window sills and font were full of flowers and produce. Lovely flowers on the flower stands. The candle sticks in the choir stalls were all decorated. Just like the old days when I was a boy.

Thursday 21st September 1989 – Had a good chat with Mr John Winfield at the Workmen's Club. Mr Winfield has done a great deal in keeping the club running and has put metal on the outside doors because of the break-ins that have been here from time to time. He is a very clever man and always willing to carry out jobs which want doing and does a great deal for the village life at Coln St Aldwyns. Go to the ringing practice at the Church tower at 7.30pm. Mr Sly from Northleach brought three more ringers with him. Mrs Lindsay Sharps, Mrs Ruth Mowat and Mrs Nixon Lee were there and are making good progress with the ringing.

Wednesday 27th September 1989 – Go to Buffs in the evening. Have a visit from the Provincial Grand Lodge, a good night had by all. The Buffs are not so strong now in the affluent society. New people are moving in to Mr Moulden's cottage today.

Saturday 30th September 1989 – Heard that Mr Philip Bullimore of Coln St Aldwyns has passed over. For many years he was head gardener for Earl St Aldwyn. He was a real expert, the flowers he put in Hatherop Castle Hall at the CHG combined church dances were terrific, also at festivals in Coln Church. He and his wife were wonderful dancers at the local dances that used to be held.

Philip Bullimore in front of Williamstrip House.

Tuesday 3rd October 1989 – My friend Frank Law came from Swindon just before 9am and drove me to my cousin's house at Parkstone, Dorset. A fine day and drive down. Lots of motorways and fast cars towards Parkstone but Frank took it all in his stride. Salisbury Cathedral is surrounded by scaffolding. Found my cousin's house at 3, Richmond Road. Showed her my mother's postcard album which was given to her by Emily Ayres in 1913 which has lots of Bournemouth and Sturminster Newton postcards in it. I am giving it to Sturminster Newton museum. See my cousin Gladys Yarrow and her husband. Have a look at the book. Have a good lunch, play Gladys's piano then drive to Sturminster Newton to Mr and Mrs Moore at Butts Pond by the milk factory. They were pleased to see me. Had a good cup of tea and a good look at the album which I left with them to put in the museum. Also my mother's suitcase with KU [*Kate Upshall*] on it which she used to take with her to all the large houses she worked in. Came away with Frank at 7pm and drove up to Westbury,

Devizes and then saw the mass of lights of Swindon. How it has grown these last twenty years. The old railway lines are disused and we have these vast motorways but they have taken up so much countryside and the wildlife has suffered through it.

Wednesday 11th October 1989 – Have a visit from Mr Denny Smith of Quenington who showed me his retirement photographs. Get ready for the funeral of John (Jack) Tovey at 2.30pm. I played a lot of football with Jack in the War Years. We played the Southrop RAF teams and also the SOE troops at Hatherop Castle on the Hatherop football pitch. Also the Poles had a team. Lots of people used to come and watch. Some entertainment in those war years. Mr Mervyn Bayliss, together with his wife, picked me up at 2pm and we drove to Eastleach. The car was parked by the large willow tree by the Eastleach Turville Church and we walked to Bouthrop Church of Eastleach Martin. Jack's son with his mother was there. He is the spitting image of his father. Lots of good, hearty singing. The old harmonium rang out. The Rev Cowmeadow said the prayers and Jack's ashes were buried in the north east corner of the churchyard I am pleased I went to the service for Jack. He was a nice quiet man, lovely to talk to and he was a marvellous footballer (the Stanley Matthews type). God bless Him.

Tuesday 17th October 1989 – Have a visit from Mrs Ruth Mowat who said Mr Sly wanted a box made up for Mrs Sharps who started ringing last week. Made the box this afternoon. Hope I have it the right height for the lady to stand on.

Thursday 19th October 1989 – Go to church bell tower, switch on lights. Mr Lou Sly and Bill and Paul came from Northleach; Mrs Ruth Mowat, Mrs Sue McKenzie, Mrs Lindsay Sharps and Mrs Joan Akers who started last week. We tried the apple box Lew Sly wanted for her to stand on but it was too high. I brought it back home to lower it to nine inches. The ladies are getting on well. Mrs Ruth Mowat brought flasks of coffee and tea and biscuits which we had at nine o'clock when we pulled the bells down.

When I walked to Coln Stores I met Mr Jim Day of Fowlers Hill – he told me 42 houses have been built in Quenington in the last ten years and building still goes on at old Godwin's Works. Some of the new residents who have bought property are very difficult over the fixing of the street lights and also where the money should go from the fete on Quenington Green. Life has changed round here.

Sunday 29th October 1989 – The clock has stopped at ten to two Summer Time which ended last night. Go to Mr and Mrs Bayliss's house – see Mrs Bayliss. She said Mervyn and his son Lee had gone to the tower –

Reuben with his dahlias and Trixie in the garden of the Lodge.

think twig or something has caught in drive cogs. William Brindle of Fairford called with some snaps he took here some weeks back of me and Trixie and my dahlias. We had a good chat about old times and the farming community – what hard work it was for the horses on carts and corn binders in particular. The long hours in the fields in the autumn sunshine, men having their dinner in the fields, paid weekly or fortnightly at the side window of the farmhouse, the shifting day at Michaelmas. How life has changed with the tractor. In the war plenty of Standard Fordsons and Land Army Girls driving them, in the 50s the Ferguson Tractor and hydraulic lifts on the ploughs and harrows etc. Then Fords and all the other tractor companies followed suit, today large tractors with cabs on, drive ploughs or sprayers home to dinner. The stables for the horses turned into houses. The old blacksmith type harrows and ploughs which we used the forge for so much now gone. Three or four men do the arable work on a farm now where it could be a dozen or more.

Monday 6th November 1989 – The geese are on the River Coln. A lovely sight. Saw Mrs Owen in Coln Stores, she and her husband have moved to Cross Cottage, Quenington. The new people in the old nurse's cottage commute to London every day. What a task. After the Second War when Mr Briggs of Fairford took us all by train to the Earls Court Agricultural Show, none of us workmen had ever been to London.

Tuesday 7th November 1989 – Have a ring from Janet Smith of Fairford to say Alf Shakespeare had died at a home in Stroud and would be buried at Fairford on Thursday at 2.30pm. Alf was a bass player for Fairford Silver Band and also secretary for many years. He did a great deal for Fairford Silver Band. He was knocked off his bicycle coming home from work at Yarnold and Gale Millers of Lechlade and had one leg off below the knee but had his car converted and drove some of the younger band girls to engagements for a very long time.

Sunday 12th November 1989 – Mr Voaden picks me up at 10am to drive to Coln St Aldwyns for Armistice Service in Coln Church. Miss Helga Perry our conductress was there with the tenor horn players she picked up at Withington. Frank Law drove from Swindon. Kevin Musty from Swindon way. His father, Derek Musty from Lechlade. Adam Bayliss from Fairford. The church was full of people – the Rev Derek Cowmeadow took the service. Lady St Aldwyn was in the family pew in front by the pulpit. Earl St Aldwyn sat in a wheelchair in front of his family pew. The band was in the chancel. The hymns and National Anthem was sung. The names of the Fallen of the three villages were read out by Viscount Quenington. The new Parson [*Canon Tony Ross OBE*] gave a short address. At the end of the service the Band played the "The Long Day Closes". The people went out and the wreath was hung on the War Memorial. It has not been hung there for some years – it used to be hung by the roll of honour list in the church. Now it is hung in the proper place.

Sunday 19th November 1989 – Forgot to say – went to Edgar (Joe) Murby's funeral at Quenington last week, taken there by Mr Mervyn Bayliss and his wife. Joe was a great farmworker for Mr Tinney at Leafield Farm. He came to Netherton in 1934. I went to school with his daughter Jose and also Mrs Joan Radway, and Ronald (Mrs Joan Radway's brother) who married Jose.

Tuesday 21st November 1989 – See Miss Hobbs who let me look at the bread oven which served what was three cottages below me and are now 14 and 15. It is a wonderful condition. She says it is a great attraction for her friends and visitors. It must be the only one in complete form around here. She said there was a copper at the side but this had gone when she bought the property. When I was a boy there were three cottages. In the one by the road was Mrs Jermans; in the one up, one down was Mr Teddie Barnett who looked after the pump and light plant for the Castle in the Second War; and in the end one was Mr Harry Sharps and his family. The three privies were all under one roof in the building behind the old bakery. That's what made these gardens so productive. Writing about Mr Teddie Barnett and his looking after the pumps reminds me that Mr Bayliss told me that when there were house parties on in Hatherop Castle in the 30s, Mr George Burge who lived in the Grandage Cottages, had to stay at the Pump House all night to keep the turbines running and keep the current in the batteries. It needs a lot of water for electric power. Mr Holton living at the Bibury Mill by Bibury Court could never get enough power for his house until Mr Briggs of Fairford put a turbine in to provide electric power with a generator. We knocked the old waterwheel and millstones out. The axle of the waterwheel was about 12 inches across – we had to drag it out with the tractor. The Mill Stones were pushed out from the second floor – one remained upright and was rolled against the wall opposite and stood upright – this was 1946 just after the war.

Monday 27th November 1989 – Walk to Coln Church and had a look at the gravestone (with a bell cut in same) of a man called Mr Kitchener who was a great bell ringer in the last century – he died in 1911. I heard George Mustow and Jim Shepherd talk about him. He had a wooden leg, and used to stamp it on the belfry floor when they were ringing. How he got up the steep stairs at Coln I do not know.

Monday 4th December 1989 – Have phone call from Bob Hutchings and we talk about old times – when Bill Harding, groom at Williamstrip Farm, said one night in the war years that he must cover up the shining discs of a set of disc harrows because the German bombers could see them. How strange it all seems today.

Thursday 7th December 1989 – Go to church tower in the evening for ringing practice with the ladies. They have got control of the bells now – present were Mrs Joan Akers, Mrs Christine Morley, Mrs Ruth Mowat, Mrs Lindsay Sharps and Mrs Sue Nixon-Lee. We all had coffee and mince pies after the ringing.

Monday 11th December 1989 – Go to Hatherop School at 6 o'clock and have some tea with the Quenington Brownies and Guides then we sang carols with the piano. Kirstie Hartshorn, the girl living next to me at Golden Row, was there in the Brownies. It was arranged by Mrs J Holton of the Saddlestones, Quenington, and we all came away with a present.

Friday 15th December 1989 – Go to the church again at 4.45pm and open up the tower. The ladies come and we rise the bells and ring them round. Mr Nipper Reeves came up the tower and helped. The Rev Cowmeadow came up the tower and rung for a little while but left as he had not had any practice. The bells were left up, I locked the belfry door and we all went into the service of carols and music on recorders by the Hatherop Junior School children. Lots of people in Hatherop Church I had never seen before. After the blessing I unlocked the tower and the ladies lowered the bells. Then they all went into Hatherop School for refreshment. It was the first time Hatherop Bells had been rung for about eight years for a service.

Wednesday 20th December 1989 – Rung up Mr John Winfield of Coln and said I was not going to Buffs, it is a wild rough night. Mr Winfield was on television on Monday at the Coln New Inn when it was announced that the developer's application to turn the pub into flats had been turned down.

Thursday 21st December 1989 – Mrs Susan Vicary of Dean Farm brought me a Christmas Cake. She is a fine lady and helps so much with Hatherop Church. Play carols round the Christmas Tree in the Fairford Market Place in the evening. Have mince pies in the Fairford Chapel room afterwards.

Saturday 23rd December 1989 – Presents from Mrs Mona Rixon and Mrs Mary Vigor of Fairford. Ring Mrs Vigor who said water by the old White Hart had got into the gas main and had stopped the cooking at the Bull Hotel for two days. Went to Glebe Farm in the evening and the youngsters sang carols from the stairs and we had mulled red wine and mince pies. The Christmas Tree outside on the lawn with its white lights looked very nice.

Sunday 24th December 1989 – Take a card to Miss Marjorie Brindle but she was not up. Milk at backdoor. Come home, ring Mr Bayliss about it but he said it was quite all right as she gets up at 2pm. Very sad there is so much trouble in Romania at the present time, hope there will soon be peace. When I walked to Coln St Aldwyns this morning, riders and their horses were by the chestnut tree and they were singing carols.

Monday 25th December 1989 – 10.15am Put on lights, light candles, boiler has packed up. Came home told Rev Cowmeadow on the phone – he said we could do nothing about it. Mr Hart arrives, I tell him about boiler, he adjusts something and boiler started again so it was all right for the service. Mrs Susan Vicary arrived and gave out the hymn and prayer books. Mr Tim Morris came and played the organ. Some good decent singing from Mr Hart's daughters. The Rev Argyle took the Morning Prayer. When I got back to Golden Row, John Iles and his son-in-law Bert Belcher were waiting to take me to Wroughton for Christmas Lunch. Have a good lunch cooked by Wendy, bless her.

Boxing Day 26th December 1989 – All is quiet at Hatherop today. "A Bridge Too Far" on the television – remember those times well when the supply detachment of the Airborne had their tents and cookhouse at the bottom of the old Lodge garden. One of mother's lodgers, Harry who worked on the telephone lines, had his call-up papers come. I reckon this was the summer of 1942. He sold his few possessions at the Pig and Whistle. When the practice drop of airborne paratroops came over Glebe

Farm fields in the spring of 1944, Harry was amongst them. When I cycled home from Mr Briggs Agricultural Engineering works in the evening my Mother said "Who do you think came here this morning?" I said I did not know. She said "Harry called with a mate of his". She asked him how he got there and he said "Just dropped in this morning, Ma". Mother made them a breakfast of boiled eggs and a pot of tea.

Tuesday 2nd January 1990 – Met Mrs C Rixon who said she had heard Mr Ted Twining had died of a heart attack. He worked for the DOE at Kemble. His wife Gwen was with us all in our dancing days at Coln years ago. I'm sad this has happened.

Mr and Mrs Twining making hurdles and feeding cribs.

Thursday 11th January 1990 – Have phone call from Uncle Jack's daughter, Gladys Yarrow of Parkstone Dorset, wishing me a Happy Birthday. I also had a card and a pack of envelopes and writing paper. A card from Mrs Phyllis Ayers and her daughter Mrs Janet Bowler, a card from my cousin Rose Wallbridge of Chandler's Ford, Hants. A card from Katie, a girl from Hatherop Castle School, who came with a teacher. The girls visit me on a Sunday afternoon. My friend Eddie Hunt came from Quenington with a card and I gave him a few Brussel's sprouts I had grown.

Sometime before Christmas Mr Reg Lipscombe died, his family came here from London early in the Second War. He was in the Home Guard physical training team and stood on the tableau we used to make and then all collapse like a pack of cards. We practised this a lot on Coln Vicarage Lawn with Sgt Major Austin and also in Coln Village Hall. I remember the start of all the sessions in the evening was "touch four walls and back". Then over the vaulting horse with the strong Sergeant Major standing at the side helping us over. Displays were put on at the Fete on Coln Manor lawn; the Long House lawn, Quenington and Fairford Park when the Home Guard had a field day there.

Thursday 25th January 1990 – A fierce gale raging. Electricity cut off. Fetch out primus stove, cook breakfast and make tea. Walk to Coln – very strong winds, no lights in shop. Power comes on again around 12 noon. I cook a good dinner, light fire, rest, power goes off again around 5pm. Fetch out my mother's Aladdin lamp – heats this room wonderfully. Make tea with the primus stove. Power came back on at 10pm and Hatherop was soon lit up.

Tuesday 30th January 1990 – Walk Trixie in Grandage. A large beech tree about 2ft 6" in diameter has blown down by the old Artesian spring which used to supply water. The tree has fallen across the river by the wooden bridge which goes to the Pump House. The old cast iron pipes which carried the water to the Pump House are smashed.

Monday 5th February 1990 – Mr Ted Peare of Lechlade called at 11am and took me to Swindon – had a good walk around Regent Street and the Plaza. How different it is today from the times I used to go on the Fairford to Swindon bus on a Sunday with my friend Stanley Black and listened to the Sky Rockets, Jack Jackson and his band and also Billie Tennant. This was at the Savoy Cinema. Spent £20 on three books of wartime music at Duck, Son & Pinker.

Tuesday 13th February 1990 – Walk to post box on the green and see the couple with two children, Mr and Mrs Johnson, are moving out of Moulden House. Loveday's furniture van is there with three men moving out the furniture. I played the organ in the church when one of their daughters was christened. I go and wish them well in their new home in Yorkshire. Mr and Mrs Johnson gave the house the name Moulden – they told me they found the old gardener's gravestone in the churchyard.

Friday 23rd February 1990 – Talk to Mr Lee Bayliss who is doing some woodwork at the houses going into Coln on the right hand side – the Co-op managers used to live in them in years gone by. The butterflies are out – it shows how mild it is. Mr Mervyn Bayliss said that his grandfather had told him there was a brick kiln somewhere around the site of the Glebe Farm orchard.

Saturday 3rd March 1990 – See Mrs Mona Rixon in the street who told me Joyce Alder (her maiden name, she married twice) had died of a heart attack, I remember when we all went to the Coln Infant School together. She was a nice girl – we all enjoyed the dances at Coln Village Hall and at what is known as Cross Cottage, Quenington when her father and mother were there in the war time.

Wednesday 7th March 1990 – Have a letter from Mrs Davina Wynne Jones saying she is selling the Arlington Museum. It is six years since her father, Mr David Verey, died and the mill is a great commitment. She wanted to know if the things I gave to the museum should be returned to me or left to another owner or, if it should be it is not a museum again, should they be given to another museum. I wrote back and saying 'Let them go to another owner or, if not, give them to a local museum – Northleach or Cirencester'. I hope another owner will be at Arlington Museum. Mr Verey made me a Patron of the Mill.

Saturday 10th March 1990 – Mr Frank Blackwell came in the afternoon and we had a good chat and I told about how my mother took my sister on the train to Harley Street to see a specialist and he said that the finest doctors were at the Radcliffe and we could do no more than that. We paid bills for £5 for that visit. How my mother had to hold off people as she got my sister on the utility buses and had to ward off people who wanted to get on the buses at the same time. People have not changed today. This was before my sister had to have a wheelchair. The poor girl knew she was finished when she had to use the chair which we bought ourselves. How different things are today with all the social benefits that are. Yet we were all happy together and Mr Stanley Clack, who lodged with us after my father died in 1942, was a great help to my sister Edith because he was so jolly and full of fun in those war years and when he came home to us late at night my mother was reading the paper and they both had long chats.

Sunday 18th March 1990 – Katie of Hatherop Castle School called and brought me some daffodils – very pretty. Have a good chat with my friend Bob Hutchings of Cheltenham on the phone. Told him Bill Cuss who was the pattern maker at Godwin's had died, also Joyce Hill (nee Alder). Also Mrs Joan Smith of Fairford Road died.

Friday March 23rd 1990 – My friend Eddie Hunt picked me up and took me to Bill Cuss's funeral at Quenington Church at 11am. Bill Cuss was 75 years old and a marvellous pattern maker and woodworker for Godwin's in his time. He was a bachelor and lived in the property of two houses left to him by Miss Edie Pitt who died at Northleach hospital. The house was called "Yew Tree Cottage". I spent many hours there talking to his late father and him. Bill Cuss was laid to rest in Quenington Cemetery. The large mass of flowers are still on the late burial of Joyce Hill. Joyce was the daughter of the late Mr and Mrs Charlie Alder of Fairford – worked at the Macaroni Camp in the last war, married Jack Whittaker, an air force man, in 1945 lived in Yorkshire, buried her husband at Quenington when he died and remarried a Mr Hill and lived at Welford. Her brother Tony Barnes and sister Kathleen, all had many dancing nights at Coln Village Hall in days gone by.

Sunday 1st April 1990 – Walk to church at 7.30am. Mr and Mrs Hart present – we talk about the riot over the poll tax in London's West End yesterday. Lots of police injured. Our young people have had everything provided for them under the Welfare State and this is the result of it all. Lady Worsley will not be present for Easter. She brought me a cake later in the morning. Tonight on the tele it showed a prison riot at Strangeways Jail. Rioting has gone on for ten hours.

Sunday 8th April 1990 – Go to a birthday party at Hatherop School at 12.30 given by Mr Tim Mowat in honour of his wife's 40th birthday. A large white sheet hung in the large front window with "Happy Birthday Ruth" written on it. Lots of white and red wine – also lots of food. The Rev and Mrs Mowat were there – I had not seen them for some years

Tuesday 10th April 1990 – Have visit from my friend Eddie Hunt we have a good chat from the poll tax to the prison riots. Eddie is going to New Zealand to see his son later this summer. It is three years ago today that I retired from work and was in Cirencester Hospital at the time. Retirement is not much for those who live on their own.

Wednesday 11th April 1990 – Go to Buffs in the evening. We talked about who was first in the bungalows at the end of Hatherop next to the field 'The Piece' where Mr Westall and Mr Bert King used to call the cattle in for milking at 5am. They were Mrs Sorrel Taylor, Mr and Mrs Bert King and Mr and Mrs Smith of Golden Row. Their house in Golden Row is now the archway. Mrs Jim Shepherd who lived in number 7 Hatherop, Mrs Westall who lived in the west end cottage of Golden Row and Lucy Bartlett and her brother Jack who lived in number 14 below me. All this occurred when the estate properties were modernised around 1970.

Sunday 15th April 1990 – Easter Sunday morning. The ladies come and pull up the bells. The ladies are ringing well now. They are a very lively bunch. The Rev Derek Cowmeadow came up the tower and wished us all a Happy Easter. More people there than I expected – 38. In the 1950s it would have been 70. Mr Bennett of Coln St Aldwyns, the estate agent for house buyers, came in his wheelchair along the church path which is in poor condition now. My church is a long way for those who come in wheelchairs. Walk to Coln Church for Evensong. Lady St Aldwyn with the Earl pick me up on the way down Hatherop Hill. Mr Edward Bennett played the organ very well. Not very many people there. The lovely brass chandelier needs the late Mr Jessie Blackwell to clean it – it is a beautiful piece of work.

Wednesday 25th April 1990 – Went to a church meeting at the school at 7.30pm. Mr Tim Mowat brought up the question of getting someone to look at the church bells as Mr Lou Sly has told the ladies some repairs need doing to them. Mr Hart wanted to know how much money I had saved in our fund started by the late Mr George Mustow with a £3 donation. I told them I had £90 in the Cheltenham and Gloucester and around £840 in a saving bond. It was agreed at the meeting that Mr Sly should get someone to look at the bells. The Rev Cowmeadow remarked that it may mean thousands of pounds but Mr Tim Mowat said the ladies were prepared to raise the money.

Thursday 26th April 1990 – Worth recording that on a previous talk with Mr Lou Sly of Northleach, he said he had a portable petrol engine which will drive a circular saw which he bought off Mr George Kiddle of Coln St Aldwyns, one-time chauffeur to Lady St Aldwyn. After starting it up he broke his arm. So Mr Sly's father bought it from him in 1919 for £35. This engine will go to Northleach Museum.

Thursday 3rd May 1990 – Go to the tower in the evening – the ladies were ringing with Mr Bill Greenwood of Northleach who was talking at the coffee and biscuits break about how his father made straw bee skips and bound the straw bonds with briers split into long pieces. Then the skips were put on a large flat stone made for the purpose. I have never seen straw bee skips in use.

Friday 4th May 1990 – Mr Ronald Newport of Eastleach came to see me in the afternoon and we talked about everything from the poll tax to the prison riots at Strangeways. How it was left to go on and could have been stopped on the second day but with council elections coming on the government pussy footed around, not to upset the opposition, with the now familiar cry of police brutality etc. The result – a wrecked prison and tremendous cost to the British taxpayer.

Sunday 6th May 1990 – Walk to church at 7.30m. There were nine people present including the hospital anaesthetist who comes to all the 8am services. Also Lady Howard from Dean Farm, Mrs Arkwright, Mr and Mrs Hart. Mr Hart wanted to cut the church lawns this afternoon but I said "Not on a Sunday" so he said he would mow them tomorrow. Prayers were said at the service for Lord and Lady St Aldwyn and their family. Their son Peter died yesterday – he had been ill for some time. He was a tall young man and a very nice gentleman – he was well liked by everyone.

Peter Hugh Hicks Beach.

Friday 11th May 1990 – Walk to Coln church and look at all the bunches of wild flowers on the grave of Peter Hicks Beach. A large vase on the grave full of flowers. Bless Him.

Sunday 20th May 1990 – Met Mr Hart. I told him I wanted a meeting to discuss what we should do with the remains of the oak De Mauley pews which were taken out when we had the dry rot. He said we would not need the meeting as the oak is in a carpenter's shop in the farm back drive. I should like to clear this up, as the pew remains with carving have been there some time now.

Friday 1st June 1990 – Have visit from Mr Anthony Van Oss asking me to make the first draw at the raffle at 9pm at the church fete at Glebe Farm tonight. I have never seen the remains of the old farm barns in Hatherop Park opposite the bungalows in May before – shows how dry it has been. The Fete at Glebe Farm at 6.30pm went off well. They ran out of beer and borrowed a barrel from the club. The barn all lime washed and with the new windows looked marvellous. Lots of stalls there, cake stalls, sandwiches, drinks and bric-a-brac. A three-piece band played at the end of the barn – electric organ and guitars. Skittles, bottle stalls and see the farm pigs for 20p, croquet and other sideshows. I bought a good sponge cake for £1.50p. The bar today is most important, keeps people there. The Glebe Farm house was open to take in children in their sleep attire. A lot of credit for this Fete goes to Mr Anthony Van Oss and Mr James Hart. They worked very hard. I drew a ticket out of the sack at 9pm for Mr Sidney Bayliss – twelve bottles of wine. I came home at 9.45pm – drunk too much red wine.

Friday 8th June 1990 – Meet Mr White of Appleton, Oxon for an estimate on restoring Hatherop Church bells. I unlocked the tower, we all go up and they look at the bells and frame. They say the frame Mr Collett made in 1855 is light and will have to be strengthened. The old bearings will be discarded and the bells would have to go away. The clappers and steeple pins would be looked at, a steel girder put under the frame to stop movement as it now only rests on the stonework. In all a big job. Our ringing ladies said they would raise money. If we have it done there will be a lot to raise.

Sunday 17th June 1990 – It is Mr and Mrs Smith's Golden Wedding. Alfred used to work at Dean Farm for Lord and Lady Howard – he was here when he was a boy and told the Rev Cowmeadow how they went to Sunday School Morning Prayer, both the 3 o'clock service and the 6 o'clock service on Sundays. I remember his brother Bill, now dead, who used to sing the solos in the choir when I was a boy. Alfred Hope used to play the bass, Ernie Smith and my Auntie Beatie the violin and they played the hymns on a Sunday afternoon here. Alfred Smith's son Michael Smith, who worked with me in the blacksmith's shop at the East Glos Engineering Company when he was a boy, is landlord of the Golden Cross in Black Jack Street. Mrs Smith said he is doing very well. Alfred Smith, his wife, daughter and son-in-law have now gone to Dean Farm, invited there this morning by Lady Howard. Go to Hatherop Castle at 4pm for a strawberry cake tea. The girls waited on us pensioners then we had a look round the grounds.

Wednesday 27th June 1990 – Went to the Buff Lodge at 8pm. Visit from the East Cotswold Provincial Grand Lodge. Four Officers attended. Our Order is shrinking in this modern age. The young men do not join these benevolent societies like the Cirencester Benefit Society – it has had a struggle with membership since the Welfare State started.

Tuesday 3rd July 1990 – Meet Mr Mervyn Bayliss at 2pm at the saw shed at Glebe Farm. With a bogie cart we wheel the long carved De Mauley pew section out of the saw shed and into a lower carpenter's shed, which has the gate pickling pit in and collect all the parts of the pew seats and other oak sections together so that the Church Council can see them tomorrow evening and decide what is to be done with this oak timber.

Wednesday July 4th 1990 – Go to PCC Meeting at Glebe Farm at 7.30pm. Lots of council members there, more than I see in church. I called the meeting to get the tower slates put in and the De Mauley pews which we piled together yesterday in the estate workshops decided upon. The roof tiles had been put in by Mr Hart and Mr Lee Bayliss so that was dealt with. It was decided to offer the pews and seats to another church. The parson, the Rev Derek Cowmeadow, would not have any of it back in church. He wanted the space. It was passed at the meeting to offer it to the other churches. The councillors, most of them had a look at the decorated pews – 14 foot in length – after the meeting. The Rev Derek Cowmeadow did not bother to look at them. He put pressure on the council to get his way. It happened to be the World Cup match with Germany and we wanted to watch the match.

Saturday July 7th 1990 – Go to Williamstrip Cricket Club Fete at Williamstrip House with the Fairford Band and we played on the grass in front of the house. A fair amount of people – we played till 4pm. I saw Jesse Mustow and Ronnie May there. I thought of all the old times we had together, also Chris Moaby. We are all getting older.

• The three generations of the Williamstrip CC cricketing family . . . (l to r) Ken Mustow (son), Jesse, and grandsons Tim Townsend and Keith Mustow at the '50 years' celebration.

Wednesday 11th July 1990 – Have visit from Jesse Mustow, my old school mate, who has returned from farming at Perrott's Brook. He brought me a photo of Coln St Aldwyns Home Guard taken at the Severalls in 1941 at the retirement of Col Gibbs. There are about 25 men and only 8 are alive today. I am so pleased with this picture as Rory O'Connor is on there, who used to lodge at John Winfield's father and mother's house. He worked on Cockrup Farm, later on in the War Agricultural section. He was very good in the Home Guard physical training team under Sgt

The Coln St Aldwyns Home Guard, left to right: Front row sitting: Charlie May, E Reeves, A Winney, Jessie Blackwell, Bert Spreadborough, Fred Kiddle, Bill Keene. 2nd row: C Minchin, John Lander, Jim Hutchins, David Mustow, John Tarrant, Unknown, Frank Sharps, Buster Sharps, E Stephens, Algy Bartlett. 3rd row: John Card, Unknown, Charlie Pollard, Unknown, Jessie Mustow, Rory O'Connor.

Major Austin. When he came over from Ireland earlier this year he asked if I had any photographs. Now I can send him one. Jessie said he wished he had known when he came over here as he would have liked to have seen him. He also said his father talked about a Mustow marrying a Sims years ago – could be right.

Thursday 26th July 1990 – Have a visit from my old friend Molly Mills who is over here from the States with her granddaughter on holiday in England and Scotland. She called here this afternoon with some pictures of Coln, Hatherop and Quenington British Legion darts club and members, also the CHQ Home Guard 1941 of which Charlie Mills was a sergeant. She went to Hatherop School in my time in the thirties and lived in one of the cottages at Williamstrip Farm where Charlie Mills worked on the farm. She was and is a very attractive lady.

Sharrington is being sold – the house where the estate workers were paid by Mrs Radway every fortnight. The house that was built for my grandfather, Reuben Sims in 1888. He carried a small Derringer in his pocket which I destroyed on my father's death. The left-hand side of this house was built in 1907 when Mr Edward Radway came as Estate Agent. My grandfather then moved to the school house, next to Mrs Griffin and her son Joe. When Joe came home drunk and fell in the doorway, my Aunt Beatie told me his mother said: "The Devil had thee father and the Devil will have thee!" Joe was an expert at catching rabbits for a glass of wine or he would pick mushrooms for a glass of homemade wine. He wore a green coat given him by a brother who was a commissioner at a theatre in London. The gardens at this house were tendered by Mr Harry Smith who lived at the Netherton Lodge. Mr Edward Radway lived in top class style managing the Williamstrip, Barrington and Hatherop Estates. He finished with Williamstrip and Barrington Estates after the office boy, Comely, stole money which went on horse racing. Mr Radway had a car which he kept in a garage at Home Farm and rode a bicycle back and forth through the drive of Hatherop Park. His word was law. He was always at the 11 o'clock service in Hatherop Church. Mr Radway was followed by the Hon Patrick Seely in 1937.

Sunday 5th August 1990 – Walk to church. Lady Sally Worsley had opened up and put the lights on. I pulled the Sanctus Bell, fourteen communicants present, including Lady Howard of Dean Farm and Mrs Townsend and her daughter, Mrs Backhouse from South Farm. Mrs Dorothy Wood from Coln and Mrs Bischoff from the Severalls, Mr and Mrs Colby from the Hornbeams and others. Mr Mervyn Bayliss told me Miss Marjorie Brindle who was in Fairford Hospital, had passed over early today, her brother's children were on holiday and had to be contacted. So that is the end of the Brindle family in Hatherop. When I was a boy Dick Brindle was a mason and roofer on Hatherop Estate. Mrs Brindle was a good dressmaker, Kathleen was the school teacher and the best church worker we ever had. Marjorie worked in large private houses and worked a capstan lathe in the wartime at Godwin's Works, Quenington. She is either 85 or 86 years old. I am sad, so many of the old Hatherop people gone.

Monday 6th August 1990 – See Mr John Winfield who came and filled a bottle full of the Artesian water. Years ago there was a force of water that gushed out of the side of the borehole which could never be stopped. Talk to Mrs M Bayliss on the phone and she said that "one of Miss Marjorie Brindle's nieces had come from Bristol and the solicitor had allowed the house to be cleared". Mr Lee Bayliss is having the coal and wood and is loading it on his trailer this evening. Miss Brindle had gone down to four stone in weight when she died in Fairford Hospital although there was plenty of food in the house. This was the last Brindle in Hatherop – I believe they came from Bibury in 1914.

Friday 10th August 1990 – Pat and Bob Hutchings came from Cheltenham and drove me in their Mini car to the New Inn at Coln St Aldwyns which was opened at 6 o'clock after being closed for about two years. A man with a camera took pictures of us all in the roadway with our glasses up. It is very nice inside – Mr Blackwell's kitchen has been included in the main bar. I had the first half pint drawn.

Monday 13th August 1990 – Go to the funeral service of Miss Marjorie Brindle at Hatherop Church at 2pm. Tom Lemon of Coln St Aldwyn, Reuben Sims and the six bearers in the choir stalls. Sir Thomas Bazley, Lady Howard, Mrs Rachel Bennett, Mr and Mrs Mervyn Bayliss who did a great deal for Marjorie Brindle and Mrs Hart, who took the place of Lady Sally Worsley who was on holiday in Scotland, and Jim Brindle's family from Gloucester. Jim was the brother now dead.

Friday 31st August 1990 – Bob and Pat Hutchings came and took me to the Sherbourne Arms at Aldsworth where we had a ploughman's lunch and I had a pint of cider. Then we drove to Northleach and had a good time looking at the old prison. The "House of Correction". All the old wagons and farm machinery that I worked on when I was a boy at Mr Rueben Briggs firm at Fairford by the Railway Inn. The wheel bonding equipment – how well I remember all the bonds on bricks, the smaller ones in the middle, the wood fire, then getting the bonds out and putting on the wood wheels screwed to the platform, then cooling them off with water in the watering cans. What a hot busy time it was. My job was to keep the fire up together, the burning timbers were old wood elevator trough parts etc about 2 feet long which were pulled away when a bond was dragged out of the fire. Fred Parsons, the smith, always had plenty of beer from the Railway Inn that day. We saw the courtroom and the cells. What conditions – the prisoners had plenty of fresh air and also the kitchen where the bread was made, little light in these places. After the visit we went to the Aldsworth Road and picked some sloes for Bob's wife to make some sloe gin. A very good day out.

Sunday 9th September 1990 – A large fete, The Cotswold Games, is being held in Coln St Aldwyns to help pay off the debts of the fight to keep the New Inn open. It was a very costly affair. A large party is being held at the New Inn at 6.30pm – the Chedworth Band is playing in the Park.

Cotswold Games.

Wednesday 19th September 1990 – Mrs Sinton of Coln told me John Winfield, our Brother of the Buffalo Order and Chairman of Coln St Aldwyns Parish Council, had passed over – his wife found him dead in bed. I am very sad. He played a great part in keeping Hatherop Club running and was a great supporter of the Steam Engine Rallies and many more things, He fought so hard to keep Coln St Aldwyns Village Hall open when the rest of us at the time did not worry about it.

John Winfield (right) with Peter Hicks Beach 1967.

Have phone call from Mrs Davina Wynne Jones of Arlington Mill, to ask me about the things I gave to the Mill Museum would I mind if they went to the Northleach County Museum. I told her I would like them to go there, except the Woodworker's book of John Sims 1818. I would have that back. I gave various things to the Museum at the Mill including a Galvonometer used by my grandfather Rueben Sims at Hatherop Castle which was one of the first houses with electricity. Also his wooden garden barrow, a gaming board of Nine Men Merels and an old tape measure, a brass blow lamp, maybe other little things. I shall be pleased for it all to go to the Northleach Museum. Go to Buffs in the evening where we talked about the death of our late Brother John Winfield.

Tuesday 25th September 1990 – Mr Mervyn Bayliss drove me to Coln St Aldwyns Church for the funeral of my great friend John Winfield (Ginger) at 2pm. A lot of people there, he was a very popular man, very clever with words and engines and electrical things, I am very sad. A lot of RAOB members came. I read the lesson and we sung the Buffalo anthem. Lots of Buffs stood at the rear of the church by the font. The choir stalls were full. All the Buffs placed ivy leaves in the grave. Mr Ronald Sharps brought me home. It has been a heavy day. John was a great friend of mine. God Bless Him.

Wednesday 26th September 1990 – Have phone call from Mr Leonard Godding of Crabtree, Hatherop Road, Fairford, to say he will call at 3.45pm to pick me up and take me to Kidderminster to go to my friend Stanley Clack's son's wedding on Saturday at 1pm. I have not been away to stay for over twenty years.

Friday 28th September 1990 – Journey to Kidderminster – what a day it has been looking at everything and fixing up clothes. Mrs Linda Cox is looking after my dog for me. Meet my friends Stanley and Beryl Clack at Aggborough Crescent and have a good chat, then to bed.

Saturday 29th September 1990 – We all go by taxi to Chaddesley Corbett to the lovely church there for the service at 1 o'clock. A good organist, good surplice choir of men and boys. Good singing. It starts to rain. The photos were all taken in the church. The bride and Ruth and Stanley's boy, Martin, looked fine. Also the best man and bridesmaids. Stanley looked fine in his gray topper and suit. His wife Beryl was very smart in her green suit and yellow hat. The bride's mother had a blue dress and large blue hat. The reception was held in a large marquee. Plenty of eats and drink and a disco held there in the evening.

Sunday 30th September 1990 – Stanley took us to see the Steam Railway built by the original railway and steam trains working there. Go to a public house called the Fox for lunch – lovely cooked food, I'm all full up. Drive home with Leonard and Mrs Rene Godding about 4 o'clock – get home and see Linda with Trixie who is glad to see me. A very hectic weekend.

Monday 15th October 1990 – Have a talk with Mrs Victor Cox – she said that "her mother told her Canon Kent had a butler and a staff of servants". Mrs Gladys Woodcock [*nee Tombs*] told her that a supper was held for the villages in the school and her father, Mr Tombs, had to give the toast. He got up and said "If life was all that money could buy, the rich would live, the poor would die". Canon Kent said "Sit down Tombs, sit down". Such was the style of life in those days. Few Cotswold working people

Canon Kent

in Hatherop today. Mostly Southern middle-class people, curtains left open at night, so you can see their rooms. Different to Cotswold people who draw blinds as soon as the room light is put on.

Friday 26th October 1990 – Walk to Coln Stores to get a Standard paper and one for Mrs Victor Cox. She told me her mother's room had pictures of Canon Kent and all his staff in their caps and uniform and also her grandfather, a Mr Praetor who lived in the gardener's cottage by Coln Vicarage and worked in the gardens for forty years. All single women who were pregnant were sent to Northleach Workhouse such was the times of those days. The Church of England parsons lived awfully well.

Saturday 27th October 1990 – Walk to Coln St Aldwyns in the afternoon for Mr and Mrs Tom Lemon's 50 years of marriage party at Manor Farmhouse. Mrs Lemon made a lovely cake which stood in the corner by the window, lots of 50 year cards and pots and baskets of flowers. Lovely crowd of people, lots of food and wine. Lady St Aldwyn came and chatted with the guests but she is still shaken at the death of her son Peter. Earl St Aldwyn could not come, he was having oxygen at Williamstrip House. The Manor Farm House has been vacant for about eighteen months.

Tuesday 6th November 1990 – Miss Jill Tugwell took me to the Quenington Chapel at 6.45pm for a film show on Romania, how the secret police are still there and the orphaned children have little food and great shortages in the country. It will take years to get the country to democratic rule.

Friday 16th November 1990 – Michael Heseltine is challenging Maggie for leadership. What a wonderful lady she is, how different the country is since the Labour government of 1979 when we were the sick country of Europe and strikes where people could not bury their dead. Then later the miners try to take control of the country with Arthur Scargill. Share ownership has been introduced, people have bought their council houses and lots of new houses built. People are far more prosperous and do things today that we never dreamed of years gone by. Couples live together and are not married. They would have been turned out of the houses years ago on these estates.

Tuesday 20th November 1990 – Watch TV till 6.30pm when it was announced Mrs Thatcher had not got an overall majority – they will have another ballot, very exciting time. She has been marvellous for our country but it seems that a lot of Tories want to replace her. A great pity. Geoffrey Howe's acid speech started it all. But of course being a lady none of the Members of Parliament could match her in speaking and she used to cut Mr Kinnock down to size many a time.

Thursday 22nd November 1990 – Watch a lot of TV – Mrs Thatcher announced that she would retire from being Prime Minister. Watched her at the dispatch box in the afternoon – how she performed and cut the opposition down to size. The men could not command this lady – how she said "I am enjoying this" was marvellous. What health and strength she has got.

Wednesday 28th November 1990 – Do not go to Buffs this evening. Watch the telly and see John Major our new Prime Minister at Number 10. It has been all politics on the TV lately.

Friday 30th November 1990 – Walk to the church for a Carol Service by the girls of Hatherop Castle School. Very good carol singing and wonderful organ playing and a wonderful lady conductor. Afterwards all the pensioners had tea in the old billiard room in the Castle. Mrs Lucy Thomas thanked the Castle staff and girls for a lovely afternoon. I sat at tea with Mr Frank Sharps who is around eighty-six and we talked about gardening and how there was a show tent in Hatherop Park and how his family had three allotments. Today lots of the cottage gardens are grass. Fourteen allotments remain.

Saturday 8th December 1990 – The Irish yews down the church path are bent down with snow. About 6" deep in the park but lots of drifts. Power off so cook breakfast with the Primus stove. When the electric power goes off everything is finished in modern society. Get the Aladdin lamp ready for the evening but power comes on before dark so can have weather reports on TV.

Tuesday 11th December 1990 – Lots of people caught out in various parts of the country with power and water shortages. Walk to Coln St Aldwyns where Mrs Sinton said her shop has been full of people after goods as they could not get their cars out to go to the towns to shop.

Tuesday 18th December 1990 – Fix my coloured lights in my window to have a little Christmas light in Golden Row.

Tuesday 25th December 1990 – Unlock vestry door for the Deaconess [*Patty Schmiegelow, later Patty Price*] and the ladies pulling the bells. We all sang carols with the lights out in the nave. I walk home, John Iles and his son-in-law were there to take me to Wroughton. Picked up my shaving things and said goodbye to Trixie and away we went. Mrs Linda Cox is looking after my dog. Have a good time with the Iles family, stay the night and come back home the next day at 3 o'clock. Linda came in with some presents for Trixie and a bottle of sherry and cheese for me.

Friday 11th January 1991 – Bob and Pat Hutchings called at twelve noon in their mini car and took me to the Vic Public House at Eastleach for a ploughman's lunch in honour of my birthday. I am sixty-eight years old today, how time flies. The Vic is extended to cater for meals but very few people came in. Drove through the Macaroni Wood where the old RAF camp was in the last war. Some old buildings there and some used for a business venture.

Reuben Sims with Bob and Pat Hutchings.

Thursday 17th January 1991 – The TV is full of the serious trouble in the Gulf, it is a very serious and awful time. The shopkeeper at Coln tells me the war has started with Iraq – it is sad so much poverty in the world, so much money spent on weapons of war, yet so much poverty and hunger in Africa millions of people have not enough to eat. How stupid it all is.

Monday 21st January 1991 – See Mrs Victor Cox by the chestnut tree on Coln green – she said in her mother's day the Malt House was three cottages. When one looks at them one can see it. Walk home and in the evening Mr Eddie Hunt came. He loves retirement, I do not.

Wednesday 23rd January 1991 – Watch more TV on the war in the Gulf. We have lost five Tornado bombers, SCUD missiles are a great threat. Each war brings more deathly weapons.

Saturday 26th January 1991 – I think the lady team of ringers has ended for the moment. Mrs Ruth Mowat is writing to Mr Lou Sly to thank him for all he is done. I'm very sad about it all but I tried to get the team of lady ringers as the men will not do it and it did run a twelve month. When I think back to my boyhood and the ringers and Charlie Barnett, George Mustow and Jim Shephard. George Mustow went on till the 80s. He always said "A good ring and a good sing made his Sunday".

Monday 18th February 1991 – The snowdrops have come up in the churchyard. My little sister said in her last days: "Don't pick the snowdrops Mum". They are so lovely, a sign of spring.

Wednesday 20th February 1991 – Make a good apple tart, busy cooking it in the afternoon when Ron Newport and Dennis Smith drove over to see me. We had a good chat about the crowd at the Fairford Air base where they are watching the B–52 bombers takeoff and also the peace protesters who are there. Dennis said "they are a dirty dishevelled lot". It will be good when this Iraq War is over.

Thursday 21st February 1991 – A dinner was held in Quenington Institute in memory of Bill Cuss the pattern maker at Godwin's [*who left a legacy to the Institute*]. New crockery has been bought for the Institute, also about £40,000 has been invested to help keep the hall running – this was a third of his money after the sale of the two cottages and the gardens attached. Miss Edith Pitt who lived in the smaller cottage, left them both to Bill who lived with his father Bert Cuss, the great staircase maker, and his mother. Edith Pitt laid out over one hundred bodies for burial and was the Post Mistress with a cycle to deliver letters for many years. Miss Pitt's little cottage had a wonderful bread oven in it. Bill left his other money to Fairford Hospital and Blue Cross Dog's Home. His father, Joiner Bert Cuss, always had a dog and said "A dog is always pleased to see you and never likes to see you go".

Edie Pitt at the gate of Yew Tree Cottage.

Thursday 28th February 1991 – Iraq War over thank God.

Friday 1st March 1991 – The house before Coln Post Office is up for sale. Mrs George Moaby and Miss Mace lived there years ago. I used to take a lot of damsons from the Lodge to them from Mum – they made a lot of jam.

Friday 8th March 1991 – Chatted to Mrs Gladys Keene who told me a lot of farmworkers, including her son on the Williamstrip Estate Farms, went to Cheltenham to the funeral, about three weeks ago, of Mr William Jowsey who was the farm manager there for a good number of years. The Legion and RAF flags were brought in. He was one of the youngest pilots in the RAF and a member of the Path Finder Force.

Tuesday 12th March 1991 – Walk to the church in the evening and meet Mrs Davina Wynne Jones who is staying in Miss Marjorie Brindle's house (No 39) while she disposes of Arlington Mill Museum. She has John Sims old Carpenter's book – I am fetching it tomorrow evening, she says it has one of the outside covers off but at least I shall have it back. I did not realise the Mill Museum was going to close when I gave these old things to the Museum.

Wednesday 13th March 1991 – Mr Mervyn Bayliss comes along the church path and said "A man from Hastings came yesterday and fixed a new motor on the clock quarter chimes and started the clock again". But it was stopped at a quarter to five so we both went up the tower and Mr Bayliss worked the chimes around and started the clock at quarter to ten and we both came away again. It is nice to hear the chimes ring out again. Have a look at the new tombstone erected yesterday to Kathleen and Marjorie Brindle. Two fine spinster ladies. Tremendous work done by Miss Kathleen Brindle for Hatherop Parish Church and the Girl Guides in her lifetime. She died alone while on holiday down in the South West, her companion Mrs Prytherch of Fairford, also a schoolteacher, came home and left her there unwell. Mrs Nan Sainsbury and Mrs Stallard of Poulton were driving down to the South-West in a minibus to bring Miss Kathleen Brindle home when they could not contact her but she died in hospital before they started. She went back to private service after the War but said times were different, the householders used to come into the rooms when you are cleaning them, this they did not do before the War. A very quiet and reserved lady, lived very much on her own and in her latter years got up about 10am. Mr and Mrs Bayliss brought her pension. The Coln Stores brought her grocery. She never used the Raeburn, instead for heat she put the electric cooker on in the little kitchen where she lived.

At 5 o'clock I saw Mrs Wynne Jones. She invited me in, there were two small children there. I asked for my old Carpenter's book with "John Sims 1818" wrote in the front pages. The lady fetched the book which had been in Mr Verey's Arlington Mill since about the mid seventies. The covers were torn off with only one board remained. The page with John Sims's name and date on gone, also a page that unfolded, showing sections of the tree trunk. The book was in a shocking state of disrepair. I regret ever giving it to Arlington Mill. It was in good condition when I let it go to the museum. It seems after Mr Verey's death, the daughter ran the museum for six years then got tired of it and now wants to sell it – things were not looked after. One's generosity can be abused. The lady is going to look for the outside cover board that is missing but I think that is the end of that. I will give no more to private museums. Other things I put in will have to stay as I gave it for all time. I'm very sorry about it. Mr Roger King, now living at Quenington, told me he went in and took the stuffed birds in a case he had given. Mr Sidney Jacques of the Quarry, Fairford, put in a lot of Roman coins he had. What will happen to them I do not know. We all thought this museum was going to be there forever. Moral – never give to a private museum.

Friday 15th March 1991 – See Mrs Victor Cox on the way to Coln Stores. She said "What a lot of fuss about our troops and their families after the Gulf War". Her mother in law told her that when her husband came home on leave from France, he went to bed for two days then had to go back to his unit again. Saw Mrs Freda Blackwell in the stores (her name was Cole when they lived at Coln) and she said that "when they were small, they had to curtsy to the old Dowager Countess St Aldwyn when she went by". Not so today. Another thing I have just thought of was how Mr Raymond Cuss, the fitter and Turner at Briggs's, used to say how he shovelled the tonsils on the boiler fire after operations when he stoked the Fairford Cottage Hospital boiler.

Sunday 17th March 1991 – Mr and Mrs Tim Mowat are moving to Fairford, to another house. I'm sorry they are leaving, Tim was a good man on the Church Council and his wife Ruth became a good bell ringer till it all collapsed.

Friday 22nd March 1991 – The furniture van is at Sharrington's again – the Mowats move out today. The Owens move in – it is their first night. They have come from Cross Cottage near the Green at Quenington, previous to that they bought the old nurse's cottage here.

Saturday 30th March 1991 – Meet Mr Mervyn Bayliss and Mr John Plaister of Swindon and we look at the clock which will not keep going with both dials. Hope Public Clocks can sort this out.

Wednesday 3rd April 1991 – Saw Mrs Keene in Coln St Aldwyns, she said Mr and Mrs Peter Murray had left their house on the bank opposite the New Inn and had gone to a home at Shipton under Wychwood. They were nice couple and he was a good preacher.

Went to a Church Meeting at Hatherop C of E School. At the meeting the school teacher of Hatherop Castle School reported how youths come up the back drive to the Club and when going back shouting and swearing goes on under the archway. Sometimes in the day, youths look in at the classroom windows. There is a lot of this kind of thing goes on. The school has school houses for teachers but the teachers prefer to ride away in their cars in the evening. In my day we had a teacher in the School House with a cane and the words "Punctuality is the soul of business" and in my father's day they had Miss Marsden with the words "I'm not afraid of a regiment of soldiers".

Sunday 7th April 1991 – Mr Oliver Puffitt from Meysey Hampton called in the afternoon with a cake from his wife. I was playing Ramona on the piano. We talked about all the old Cotswold barns being made into houses. How the barns used to be full of sheaves of corn, the thresher was pulled into the main doorway and the place full of dust from the threshing. All this has gone now with the combine harvesters. The barns are not used now.

Monday 15th April 1991 – Draw pension at Coln Post Office. We have had a rise, nearly £60 per week now. When the Welfare State came in my mother was on 10s per week and had to pay for a stamp of five shillings a week for ten years to get her old age pension of £2 per week at sixty years old. I never voted Labour again after that.

Thursday 9th May 1991 – Go to Ascension Day Service at Hatherop Church at 4pm. The Deaconess from Coln St Aldwyns gave the chalice with the wine – the Blood of Jesus Christ. I am not quite sure whether I like this or not. Lady Sally Worsley and Rueben Sims the only members from Hatherop present. We went to the Castle for tea in the old billiard room. One of the Castle schoolgirls, Katie, showed me the old servant's hall – the room with the fireplace and high windows where my mother talked about Mr Eborne, the butler, cutting the joint of meat and saying "How much meat for you Miss Upshall?" and she said "Knuckle end please Mr Eborne". We also had a look at the drawing room with its ornate ceiling and large mirror over the fireplace. Mr Ronald Sharps and the men at the Castle have redecorated it and it looks lovely.

Sunday 12th May 1991 – Walk to Coln St Aldwyns to see Mr Tom Lemon about a coach trip to Henley to see the Victorian Museums there. The trip is being organised by Mrs Tugwell of Quenington Chapel – cost £6. See Mr Tom Lemon who will come on the outing. Bill Brindle of Fairford drove here and brought me a book on the Second World War written by A J P Taylor [*Alan John Percival Taylor, Historian*], 'The Diary of a Cotswold Parson" by the Rev Francis Edward Witts edited by David Verey of Barnsley and a pack of reproduction maps and identity cards of the Second World War. It was very nice of him. I gave him my old box camera that I had as a prize at Fairford night school in 1938 presented by Mr Gussie Gardner the Engineering Drawing Master.

Monday 13th May 1991 – Walk to Quenington and see Mrs Tugwell at the Lines and pay £6 for the coach trip to Henley on the 28th May. Walk back up the hill see Stanley Bailey and we talked about the new houses built. How Mr Gordon Timms has built a new house and is selling the old house that Mr Archer lived in who was a relation of Jimmy Strange, landlord of the Earl Grey. Godwin's men were returning to work in nice blue overalls, none of them dirty – different to the War years.

Saturday 18th May 1991 – Walked to the church for the confirmation of the Castle schoolgirls by the Bishop of Tewkesbury. Lady Abel Smith sat in the rear seat by the pillar, known as the Mustow seat. All the Cotswold people I knew gone now – sad. All the girls looked very nice.

Monday 20th May 1991 – Receive a phone call from Mrs Payne of Coln St Aldwyns saying her husband had died and would I speak at his funeral on Wednesday. I said I would come down in the evening and see her. She told me things about him – where he had worked for Major Scott of Williamstrip House [*Major Scott leased Williamstrip House from 1914–1930*] as a groom when he was a boy, also for Herbert Stevens, General Fortescue and Lady Delia Llewellyn as a groom chauffeur. He was at the Dunkirk evacuation of the BEF [*British Expeditionary Force*] in 1940. He served in the North African Campaign and in the Eighth Army under Field Marshall Montgomery till the end of the war, finishing his working life with the PSA at Fairford Air Base. I told Mrs Payne I would do my best.

Wednesday 22nd May 1991 – Walk to Coln St Aldwyns church for the funeral of Dennis Payne at 3pm. The Rev Cowmeadow took the service, Colin Walters played the organ. I gave a little talk on the life of Dennis, or Denny as he was called. We had tea at Mrs Tarrant's after the funeral. Denny had five sons – all grooms like he was, and two daughters.

Saturday May 25th 1991 – Have a visit from Mrs Wynne Jones with my Nine Man Merels board made by my grandfather, also my galvanometer

Denny Payne (right) with Laura Payne in the background.

and a cycle gas lamp my mother used to write by. Frank said Bob Stevens who had had the cycle shop at Fairford where the post office is now, had a drum of carbide behind the door as you went in and he filled your gas lamp with the carbide for 2p. I thanked Mrs Wynne Jones very much for the return of my antiques. She said she was having some difficulty selling the museum as there is not enough money to be made out of it for the buyers.

Tuesday 28th May 1991 – Get on coach at 9am for Windsor. Meet Tom Lemon and we see the display about Queen Victoria and also her GWR engine and coaches on the railway. Also wax figures of her meeting her guests and the Coldstream Guards [*In 1982 British Railways and Madame Tussauds restored Windsor station, creating an exhibition called Royalty and Railways, later renamed Royalty and Empire. The exhibition recalled the Diamond Jubilee of Queen Victoria in 1897, using displays of wax models and an audio-visual show featuring Audio-Anamatronic figures – the first of their kind seen in Europe at that time*]. Then some lunch and then a tour round St George's Chapel, a wonderful building, lots of foreign visitors around. It was a very cold day but I had my thick pullover on.

Tuesday June 11th 1991 – Have a visit from a lady from Smith-Woolley – agents for the Hatherop Estate – who looked round this property and said my rent would go up 25%. I am not too happy about that but everything seems to be going up.

Thursday 4 July 1991 – Mr and Mrs Robert Hutchings arrive about 11 o'clock and we load old toolboxs and cross cut saw and two scythes – he has now a good collection of my grandfather's tools and he will dispose of them at some sale at Cheltenham and I shall be able to get rid of the garage and the cost of same. With the cost of £400 in rent increase, I hope I shall have reduction of rent.

Tuesday 9th July 1991 – Mr Oliver antique dealer of Cheltenham called and took two clocks I had and the chestnut tallboy made by John Sims. I got £100 for it – would have had £150 but it was cut in half when my Uncle Jim and Aunt Minnie Sims moved into the smaller cottage in Down Ampney and they had to get it up the cottage stairs. I also sold the commode my mother bought for ten shillings from the sale at Barrow Elm House when Mrs Forbes left there and came to live in Sharringtons. It was handy for my father in 1941. We had the outside privy, box of ashes, shovel, and newspapers. Mrs Gayfer, mother of David Gayfer – an evacuee boy from Manor Park, London, always lit a cigarette before going into the privy at the Lodge – they had a smell of their own. I had £100 for the commode. My rent is

Reuben and Kate Sims with David Gayfer who came to visit in 1953.

Sims family with evacuee children 1941.

£1,700 a year so I need it. I also sold the Zulu shield and spears which were given me by Bill Smith, my father's friend, who went to South Africa before the 1914 war and served in the South Africa police and made a lot of money. I had £50 for them. All the other shield and spears I gave to the School Club and Canon Lowe at Coln Vicarage were lost. It is not a good thing to give to schools.

Monday 5th August 1991 – See Mr Mervyn Bayliss getting his car out of the garage in the estate yard – we talk about the water pumping station by the iron bridge. He said there must have been piped water before the Bazley family because at Sharringtons where the garden hedge comes against the school playground, a 2 inch main comes out of that garden then drops down – must have been a sunk fence or ha-ha. Then it goes under the school building and across to a water tank in Glebe Farm buildings. Some years ago after soundings by instruments around and in the school, the mains was cut by Sharringtons garden and a new polythene pipe threaded back through the old cast iron pipe to the farm tank. The school was built by the De Mauley's and must be over the old cast iron pipe. What water was pumped I do not know, the Artesian well was bored I believe in the time of the Rev Davies.

Friday 9th August 1991 – Have a visit from a Cirencester Police Officer who said Williamstrip House had been broken into on Monday night and Wednesday night. The thieves got in by using a van through the double doorway down the Williamstrip Road. He was round asking every household if they had heard or seen anything.

Monday 2nd September 1991 – Talk to Mrs Sinton at the Coln Stores about one of the partners in the New Inn drawing his money out. It was a great effort by the Coln St Aldwyns Society to stop the New Inn being taken over by the developers. Hope the owner will carry on. Had a talk with William Ash of Quenington. He said Shepherd Hawkins was a liberal in politics and always tied a yellow ribbon to his dog on polling days. I remember they lived at Barn Ground cottage when I was a boy and he and his wife walked to the old chapel at Quenington, opposite the farm buildings at the bottom, carrying a marrow under his arm – they were strong chapel goers

Sunday 8th Sept 1991 – Walk to the church at 5.30pm. A Funday Fete in Hatherop Park – pony rides etc lots of people there in aid of a scanner appeal at Cheltenham I am told. Sally Worsley comes in to church and we light all the candles. All the flowers look nice, also the onions on the font. When I was a boy bunches of potatoes were at every pew end, also beetroot but the Harvest Service is early. The corn has been gathered, it

Tuesday 29th Oct 1991 – Get ready for the funeral of Rev Peter Murray at Coln St Aldwyns church at 2.30pm. I ride my bicycle there, a lady from London played the organ and her husband gave us all some fine solo singing from the chancel steps. The church was full of people, but very few local people. Lady Abel Smith and Mrs Rachel Bennett were there. We were told you could have a cup of tea and a chat at Bibury Court afterwards but I came home on my bike. Pete Murray was a wonderful person between the Rev Mowat and the Rev Cowmeadow. He walked round Hatherop in his black cassock. George said "He always had a smile on his face." He had to go into a home and had great trials with a bad hip and deafness. The Lord will give him eternal life.

Wednesday 30th Oct 1991 – Mr and Mrs Robert Hutchings called from Cheltenham and took me to the Shaven Crown at Shipton under Wychwood where we had a ploughman's lunch and I had a pint of cider. Robert told me he had sold my great grandfather and grandfather's wood working tools. I was sad they are gone – two large chests full but I could not keep them here now I have given up the garage. He gave me £100 for them and said he did not lose on them.

Saturday 2nd Nov 1991 – Still getting over Mr Robert Hutchings of Cheltenham selling my ancestors' wood working tools. Of course he bought them and had every right to do so but if I could have afforded the £2.50 per week for the garage it would not have happened. Frank Blackwell rode up from Fairford, brought me some beetroot and tomatoes, Bill Brindle drove up in his car and we all had a good chat and a good laugh – two pots of tea and biscuits. We are all bachelors and we talked about all the scroungers of society who draw benefits off the social security and the person who saves money is penalised. Socialism has some bad faults.

Sunday 10th Nov 1991 – Walk to church at 9.45am. Helga Perry the conductor came in with three girls: the tenor player, soprano player and the cornet player Kim – she is fourteen years old – played the hymns on the solo cornet. So we were a small band but enough and played in the area in front of the chapel. An ex-army officer, General Bowring, from Coln Manor read the names of the fallen and Kim sounded the bugle call from the back of the church. The Rev Cowmeadow preached a short sermon, the ex-officer hung the wreath on the War Memorial. The service ended with the blessing, the Castle School Girls stayed behind while we played while the congregation went out. They were very interested in the band. Not too many at the service from the three Parishes. Time has gone by and the ex-servicemen are a lot less. 45 years of peace, the young generations do not know of the six years of struggle. Mr Gerald Hartshorn's two sons were playing golf on the football pitch. That's what the Wars were fought for. Had a sleep in the chair in the afternoon and the Castle girls came to see me and said how they enjoyed the Service. Saw the Vera Lynn programme late in the evening, what a lady she was abroad for the troops in the Second World War.

Friday 15th Nov 1991 – I rode to Fairford on my cycle. Saw Mr Alec Iles from Quenington. We talked about Fairford, how things have changed – The George is now a betting shop – he said how he saw the film "A Bridge Too Far" and how he was there with the gliders all smashed up around one of the villages – a pile of rubble. How a frogman blew a hole in the Nijmegen Bridge and how one of the men said they took off from Fairford. He said to him "I bet you were in the Bull" the officer said "Yes, I was." "Well," he said "That's my home town". How strange things happen and the [*bomb*] panniers were filled in Hatherop Park and took to Fairford air base to be dropped over there. One soldier, a Mr Hudson, told me the flak came through the bottom of the aircraft while they were dropping the panniers. A long time ago but so very real.

Tuesday 19th Nov 1991 – Ring Mrs John Akers of Dean Row in the afternoon after seeing on TV the coming home of Terry Waite after five years of captivity in the middle east and the request from the church leaders that the church bells should be rung at 7pm. She will see who she can get to help ring. I walk to the tower at 6.45pm and put on lights. Mrs Akers arrived and Mr John Akers. We pulled the first three bells for half an hour. We did our bit at Hatherop Tower.

Doug Coates

Wednesday 20th Nov 1991 – [*In the evening*] walk to Buffs in the caravan in Mr Bartlett's yard. Mr Roger King told me the news that Mr Bartlett had sold his piece of land there and has to be out in a week's time. So the Buffs will meet in my little room at No 17 Golden Row next week. We will hang the Dispensation on my walls.

Sunday 24th Nov 1991 – Walk to church at 7.40am. Lady Howard, her daughter Mrs Vicary, her daughter Juliet and Mr Gwyn Palmer who she is marrying on the 21st December. The Rev Cowmeadow read out the banns for the first time. Prayers were said for Evelyn Lemon and Douglas Coates in Paternoster the great footballer and cricketer in his day, who is now in a poor way after he lost his wife.

Walked to the Lodge No 45 – James Hart was there and invited me in to look around. I hardly recognised the old house. The large new room and wonderful fireplace of Farmington Stone, lovely stone mullion windows. He told me about £9,000 of Cotswold slates were stolen, very sad. A fine new staircase made by Oaklands in Yells Yard. The old kitchen all gutted out, big oil fired stove there, you would never recognise where the old copper used to be in the east corner years ago before the alterations in 1967. The new modern grate has been taken out of the front room – my big mistake getting Hatherall to smash out the Victorian grate put in by Miss Clarke the school teacher before we went there in May 7th 1927. It was very hot when Ted Griffin and Ernest Sharps, the carters with the horses, got drunk on home-made wine bringing us up the park from the house at the top of the hill at Netherton, now made into a large mansion type house. My thoughts went back to the days my sister sat in a chair there facing the fire and the bed by the east window. How things have changed these last twenty odd years.

Wednesday 27th Nov 1991 – Have the Buffaloes Order Meeting in my little room (they used to be bedrooms in the old days) at 8.15pm. Brother Roger King, Brother Wilfred Franklin and Brother Ronald Ellis, arrived. We had the meeting, a cup of coffee and a good chat.

Saturday 30th Nov 1991 – See Eileen Bartlett, daughter of Blacksmith Bartlett. She said she had not seen me since my sister died in 1950. She is helping clear out the old blacksmith yard. She said tempers are getting frayed as it is a big ordeal for them all. I remember when Blacksmith Bartlett first came after Blacksmith Walter Dunn retired and went to live at Poulton. Both of them fine craftsmen. I was at the allotments with my father when Blacksmith Bartlett had cart loads of manure taken there and Mrs Bartlett used to help dig the allotments. Blacksmith Dunn before him helped – used to dig a sack of potatoes and wheel them home lodged in the frame of an old lady's cycle. This was around the 1938 time when fifty allotments were in use. Some large families had two: one for greens, one for potatoes.

Saturday 7th Dec 1991 – Walk to the church for a Castle School carol service with the Castle School girls and boys. Good tea afterwards in the Billiard Room at the Castle. Sat at the tea table with Mrs Ellen Townsend, Mrs Rose Bailey, and Keeper Smith's wife from Williamstrip. John and Joan Collett reminded me of when I drove my mother on my motor cycle to Cirencester and met up with them on Miller's Coaches and drove to

Blackpool to see the lights. John had his mother with him also. We stayed at Norbreck Hydro Hotel on the north shore. There were pensioners from Bibury and Eastleach as well as these three villages at this carol service. Joan Collett said "Next February will be fifty years since the plane knocked that car over when they were going to Eastleach after the dance at Palmer Hall. Nancy Peachy was killed, also her boyfriend Arthur Smith. How time flies. Nancy Peachy played the piano in the Dance Band; Arthur Smith played the trumpet.

Monday 9th Dec 1991 – See Mrs Cox at Park Lodge – she is full of the scandal of the Maxwell newspaper empire. Walk up Coln Hill into Coln. On the left diggers are making a road way to the pair of cottages facing the children's playing fields. Years ago Herby Card, an estate worker, lived up the far one and Gladys Tombs, later Mrs Woodcock, lived with her father in the one near the road. A proper country character and a great friend of my mother.

Wednesday 11th Dec 1991 – Walk to Coln. See Peter Moaby of Quenington who works for Sidney Bayliss altering the wall at the end of the two cottages by the children's playing fields going into Coln St Aldwyns. He said the cottages are being made into one house. Agg Bros of Burford are doing the work. So many of our country cottages are being made into one house, not good for village life

Saturday 14th Dec 1991 – The flood lights are on at Church Mead, now Severalls. All the front lawns and all the trees show up with all the hoar frost on them – quite a show, also the Christmas lights above the front door. Different to the days when I was a boy and Colonel Conley was there who used to say "When I was in the Army I said to my servant 'do this' and he doeth it. Now it is 'wait a minute'."

Monday 16th Dec 1991 – Have found a way of keeping this room warmer with lighting the Aladdin mantle lamp. Helps this Parkray Stove which is pathetic.

Saturday 21st Dec 1991 – Get ready for the wedding of Juliet Van Oss to Mr Robert Gwen Palmer. Open tower at 3.15pm and wait for Mr Sly and the ringers to arrive. Mrs Joan Akers of Dean Row came, the only Hatherop Ringer; a man and wife and their daughter came from Fairford; Mr Sly and a Bibury Ringer came so we had enough. I had a pull and then the bells were rung from 3.30pm till the 4pm service. All the candles in the windows with the holly and all the white flowers on the candlesticks with holly – it all looked very nice. Two parsons greeted the bride at the church door after she had walked through the canopy from the Castle steps.

Edward Bennett played the organ, the oboe players sat in the choir stalls by the organ. The visiting parson gave an address from the pulpit. The white lights were on the Christmas tree and only the altar electric lights were on. It was warm in the old church with the heating being on since Thursday and all the candles burning. At the blessing the ringers went back up the tower and rung for a quarter of an hour. In the Castle a large fire was in the hall fire place, four violinists were playing in the hall, hats and coats were placed in the old dining room then we waited to greet the wedding couple. Plenty of champagne also orange juice, I drank plenty, lots of lovely eats, ladies round all the time with them, sausages on sticks, the corridor lined with eats, the old dining room packed with people. I walked home when it was dark. Fireworks went off later but I was relaxing asleep in my chair by the fire.

Juliet Van Oss's wedding to Mr Robert Gwyn Palmer.

Wednesday 25th Dec 1991 – All quiet in the village. Walk to the church for carols and readings at 11am. The Deaconess came in, Sally Worsley and others all light the candles. Mr Tim Morris played the organ, a good church full of people. Mr Christopher Kinch and his wife brought Mrs Kinch, his mother, who was my school teacher at Hatherop in my early days in the infant room. She will be ninety next year. It was wonderful to see her and we had a long chat after the service.

Thursday 26th Dec 1991 – Walk Trixie round churchyard and she attacked Mr Colby's dog. He broke his walking stick warding her off. I found it in the church path and went round to the Hornbeams with the broken piece. I offered to get it repaired but he said it was all right he could repair it. Had a whisky and told them about the old estate days, years ago, also about the book 'Spark and Flame' by Muus [*"The Spark and the Flame" by Flemming B Muus – the memoirs of a Dane who went from Liberia to Britain to fight the Nazis after the invasion of his country and is parachuted back into Denmark as a spy*].

Saturday 28th Dec 1991 – Walk to Coln Stores and see a large sign board put up in the piece of land sold from the blacksmith's shop advertising a four bedroom house to be built for sale. The changes one sees in one's lifetime. The Meet is at Williamstrip House today and they are going to Williamstrip House through the gate by Mrs Cox's Lodge this morning not the main drive in Hatherop. Have a chat with Mr John Whiteman who has some friends driving to the meet. We talked of the old times of Mr Reuben Briggs works at Fairford by the Railway Inn and of Fred Parsons the blacksmith who always went to the Railway Inn and had two or three pints of beer every day, then came back to the blacksmith's shop and worked terrific.

On reflection: The men at Reuben Briggs Engineers, Fairford in 1937
Mervyn Groves – Office Boy
Fred Parsons – Blacksmith
John Kemble – Striker
Bert Ayres – Agricultural fitter, smith and gas welder mate
R Sims – Agricultural fitter, plumber and sheet metal worker

Reuben Sims working at East Gloucestershire Engineering.

Raymond Cuss – Senior agricultural fitter, turner and plumber
Ray Cuss JR – a very clever man could also do electrical work and mend watches and clocks.
Jeffrey Hatton – Agricultural fitter and mechanic
Fred Hopkins – Agricultural fitter
Van MR 5252 drivers: Ray Cuss Junior and Fred Spencer
Reuben Briggs the boss – steam specialist, good on boilers and traction engines, would have no Sunday work, only a few times in the Second War. His stock phrase for farmers was "Damn um, let um sweat".

Monday 6th Jan 1992 – Walked Trixie in Grandage and saw the old fishing hut with its thatched roof has been taken down. I am told there are sizes of fish etc. marked on some of its woodwork. This is the hut where Commander Cadogan did his fishing with his friends before the last war.

Wednesday 8th Jan 1992 – Walk to Coln St Aldwyns at 2.30pm. I got ready to take the names of the people who came in to George Jones's funeral. The Rev Cowmeadow said "he had no organist to play the hymn "Oh Jesus I Have Promised" so I said I would play and Mr Slade the funeral director came in and took the names. George was a Coln St Aldwyns Buff for 46 years, never rose to high honours but always there, even when he moved from Coln St Aldwyns to Cirencester. I played the organ for the hymn, said a little address about the life of George how he played football and cricket, was umpire at Williamstrip Club for many years. Remembered the old Coln Feast in the paddock opposite Cockrup Farm where the swinging boats were, also a little set of children's roundabouts, turned by a man on the handle in the centre. George said that man was John Winfield's grandfather, a small pig was greased and set free for the ladies to catch for a dinner. This was fine fun. George worked for Lady Susan Hicks Beach at the farm for twenty five years. One day she took him to Lechlade in the side car of her motor cycle and speeding down the Lechlade Road, with the side car bumping up and down Lady Susan shouted, "You all right Jones?", George replied "Yes Ma'am, where you go, I go". George wound the church clock for many years. As he said "To wind the Coln Church clock you had to take your jacket off when you got on the handle." I played "Abide with Me" after we had formed a broken line round the casket of George Jones in the chancel of Coln Church and the mourners went out and stood in the burial site behind Coln Village Hall. The Buffs sung their anthem then came away.

George, Violet and Tony Jones.

Monday 13th Jan 1992 – Walk to Coln St Aldwyns. Talk to workman from Burford doing the walling for the entrance to the children's playing field and the drive way for the two cottages being converted into one house, the garden gate entrance on to the pavement walled up. Go and see Mrs Lemon in the cottage by the old school as was and walk round Coln St Aldwyns churchyard and see the flowers on George Jones grave. His casket was buried in his father's grave behind the old village hall standing quiet with the memories of joyful years.

Friday 17th Jan 1992 – As I walked down Hatherop Hill, Harvey's Coach was bringing the young to Hatherop School and lots of private cars bringing in their children to the school also Hatherop Castle School. I had to keep Trixie on a tight lead. I arrive early at Coln Post Office so walk Trixie past the Vicarage to the cottage next to the Village Hall, the drive way is still open to the rear of the cottage. A stable box has been erected at the south end of hall. I looked at it and thought of all the entertainment held there, long before the three village centre idea. Mr Baden Powell bought the Coln School and School House from Earl St Aldwyn. Jobbins of Poulton built part of the school into the school house and Mr Powell sold the rest of the school for a private house. The owners of that then had the one large beech tree left in the playground felled – another place that would have made a good hall for Coln Church instead of PCC meetings in the church.

Wednesday 29th Jan 1992 – Heard that Earl St Aldwyn had died around mid morning, he had been ill for many months.

Tuesday 4th Feb 1992 – Walk to Coln St Aldwyns at 1.30pm for the funeral of Lord St Aldwyn. Call on Tom Lemon and we both went to the church together. The coffin was on trestles in the chancel – lots of flowers at the end of the coffin and on the top. The choir pew ends were decorated with evergreen and on top of the oak panelling were bunches of laurel and white flowers and pyramids of pink flowers each side of the altar. The estate workmen sat in the choir stalls on the organ side. Other past and present employees sat in the opposite side. Tim Morris played the organ, his wife with him telling him when it was time to play. Tom Lemon and R Sims sat in the little pew by the organ. The new keeper was one of the ushers. The Rev Derek Cowmeadow took the service. Mr and Mrs Ducker and Mrs Smith, Church Warden were there also. Mrs Wood, Mr and Mrs Townsend, Mrs John Winfield were in chairs at the front of the right hand pews, lots of chairs for people at the back. The St Aldwyn family sat in their family pews. The address was given by the Estate Agent Martin Whitaker and an amplifier was placed by the Eagle Lectern. The hymns "We Plough the Fields and Scatter" "God be in my Head" and "Fight the Good Fight" ended the service. The bearers Bill Keene, John Akers and the Hayward boys carried the Earl to his resting place with his family graves. Everyone was invited to Williamstrip House after the service.

Tuesday 18th Feb 1992 – Have a visit in the afternoon from a Mr Wearing of Banbury who wanted to fill in gaps in his family history. His grandfather or great grandfather had the Stores at Coln St Aldwyns. This was in my grandfather's time – he [*Wearing*] is pictured in the photo of George and Levi Cox and Blacksmith Stone which is around and is in a large picture at Northleach Museum. Wearing is in the horse and trap coming round the bend by the Lodge now enlarged and called the Pump House. Told him about the book "When I Looked Right' by Elizabeth Clark and 'Northern Lights' which deals about Hatherop Castle. [*These two books may be "I Looked Right" by Elizabeth Denham – The hair-raising adventures of an English girl on secret work for the British in occupied France, and "Northern Lights – The Story of Lord Derwentwater" by Ralph Arnold, published by Constable 1959. The book chronicles that Anna Maria, the daughter of Sir John Webb, 2nd Baronet, married James Ratcliffe the Earl of Derwentwater in 1712. The terms of the marriage settlement required the couple to live at Hatherop Castle for two years. A Jacobite sympathiser, he left to join the Rising and was eventually executed at Tower Hill in 1716. Rumour has it that the decapitated skeleton found at Hatherop 150 years later when the house was being rebuilt was that of James Ratcliffe.*]

The Old Forge, Hatherop Hill. The trap, driven by Mr Wearing, was owned by Coln Stores. In front of the Forge are George Cox, Levi Cox, and George Stow. Mrs Maskin is at the gate of the Lodge.

Wednesday 19th Feb 1992 – Mr Lipscombe of Fairford took me to Eastleach Church for the burial service of my friend Mr Ronald Newport who died after a stroke in Cirencester Hospital. I worked with him at the RAF in Fairford – about fifteen of Ron's mates at the RAF Camp were there. I gave a short address about Ron. He was a quiet unassuming man who lived on his own in a cottage just above Causey Barn. I shall miss Ron as he used to come and see me and we had lovely chats over a pot of tea and biscuits.

Tuesday 25th Feb 1992 – Walk Trixie to Coln Stores for some shopping and see the two houses on the left hand side going into Coln St Aldwyns and being converted by Agg builders of Burford is still going on. The hedges round the garden are being pulled out with a digger and a new stone chimney is being built at the rear of the building. There are three old lavatories at this property. It may have been three small cottages many years ago. An oil fuel tank has been placed in one of the old lavatories near the end of the house. When the cottages were small they had the heat in. Today it does not matter with central heating. Mr Reuben Briggs of East Glos Engineers put the central heating in Ravenshill of Eastleach in 1938. I used to ride there on my cycle each day. There was talk of Hitler and the Second War then. Williamstrip House was fitted with central heating around 1933–35 by Ardens the heating firm at Bristol.

Wednesday 4th March 1992 – The Provincial Grand Lodge of the East Cotswold Province of the RAOB came and consecrated this little room at No 17 Hatherop as an RAOB Lodge room. Brother Wilfred Franklin brought a plate of eats.

Friday 6th March 1992 – Saw Mr Dennis Bartlett who told me Tom Lemon had a chip pan ablaze and had to have two fire engines out. I called at Tom's house by the old school, all quiet, the electric cooker was outside badly burnt and a wooden chair also. Tom and his wife must have been taken somewhere away from it all. Tom is eighty four years old, his wife around that age.

Saturday 7th March 1992 – Rang the Rev Cowmeadow in the evening. He said everyone helped Tom Lemon and his wife move into bungalow No 3 and they stayed at the Vicarage after the fire. One of the Hayward boys saved Tom's house by having a fire extinguisher and damped the fire down till the fire engine arrived after about three minutes from Fairford.

Wednesday 18th Mar 1992 – Mrs Sharps of Coln St Aldwyns drove me to Coln House School at Fairford. It used to be an old asylum years ago and I told the pupils at assembly how I walked to Coln School and then to Hatherop at seven years old around 1929. I made them laugh how Mr Garner the headmaster always said "Punctuality is the soul of business" when he wound up the school clock once a week. The school sung a hymn, the head master Mr Davis played his guitar.

Monday 23rd March 1992 – Signs are up at Mr Weston's house in Coln for the Liberal Democrats. He is the candidate. Have a good rest – lots of election on TV. Hope the Conservatives get back in but the Socialists are making a strong challenge – they do throw so much money around.

Tuesday 31st March 1992 – Trixie gets a mutton bone jammed in her throat so Mr Ian Patheyjohns took me and her to Mr Baxter the vet at Lechlade. A Danish girl vet got the bone out with a pair of forceps then gave Trixie an injection against infection £10. I was so pleased to get that done, no more bones for Trixie.

Friday 3rd April 1992 – Mr and Mrs Ken Clements pick me up at 10.30am and drive me to Acton Turville to the funeral service of Mrs Dennis [*Ethel*] Gulwell. Ethel Burge was my mother's great friend who was housemaid with Mum at Hatherop Castle. Mum talked of her often. Mum and me went to her daughter's wedding in 1954 at Badminton Church attached to Badminton House. I shed a tear at mother's great friend passing. It is not easy, living on your own.

Monday 6th April 1992 – See Tom Lemon who lives with his wife in the old people's bungalow since he had the chip pan fire. He said he and his wife will be glad to get back to their own home again when it is repaired. There is no garden or sheds for him at the bungalows – they are places to die in. I thought he would have liked the bungalows but apparently not.

Friday 10th April 1992 – Arise at 7am and put on TV – all election talk. Mr Major has won the election in spite of the recession and poll tax. Late in the day saw Mr Kinnock give his speech acknowledging defeat with his wife by his side. He and his wife were very dejected.

Sunday 19th April 1992 Easter Sunday – 6pm – A new organist arrives from Coln St Aldwyns who has come to live in the Rev Murrey's house on the bank opposite the New Inn. He is very good and we sing the Easter Hymns. The Rev Derek Cowmeadow takes the service, seven communicants. The evening Easter Service which used to be so well supported, better than Matins, is the other way round now. With cars and people better off, they are out and away. We shall have to alter our patterns of services I am sure.

Friday 8th May 1992 – Stopped by a Standard Newspaper man who wanted a picture of me for the Standard paper as one of the old inhabitants of Hatherop. So, playing in Fairford Band and being Church Warden of Hatherop Church for 40 years or near enough, he took me to the church with my E flat bass.

Sunday 17th May 1992 – Picked up by Mr Derek Musty of Lechlade and taken to Coln House School Fete at 2pm. We played under a canopy, it was rather cool with a strong wind blowing, lots of stalls, a traction engine and Majorettes gave displays. Our parson does not agree with Sunday fêtes. Some of the band members said how they saw my photo with my E flat bass outside Hatherop Church taken by the Standard reporter.

Tuesday 26th May 1992 – Went to Mrs Sinton's shop at Coln Stores. The residents [*Philip and Ana Evans*] have moved into the two cottages made into one house on the left going up the hill into Coln.

Ana and Philip Evans with Nickleby and Romina.

Saturday 30th May 1992 – Have taken Trixie round the park, the sun is shining on the old people's bungalows. I think of the days when I was a boy and all the cottages painted with cream paint. Most of the allotments were worked, the little piece with the well in at the end. The bells at the Church always chimed or rung for the services. Sunday School in the afternoon. Evensong was the dominant service. No one walked up and down the Castle steps except those working at the Castle. The Bazley family always in the Bazley pews. Mr Garner and Commander Cadogan read the Lessons. The ringers in the choir and us boys in the pews in the chancel – all of us in cassocks and white surplices. The parson in his black stole. Lots of the young men in the far aisle behind the Harold Wheeler family, Mr Savage the school attendance officer played the organ. The oil lamps in winter lit and blown out by John Westall who stood in the pew seats and used a tube with a mouth piece now been stolen many years ago. Bernard Iles, killed in the North Africa campaign, pumped the bellows in the little place behind the pulpit watching the weight to keep the bellows full. Mr Fred Ford and Mr George Moulden, the two head gardeners, took the collection. Lots of the congregation carried their common prayer book to church. Sunday was a day of rest and church services. The young men gathered by the old pump house which had a stone trough in it and a large cast iron pump with a handle. The parson visited the elderly in the parish. The farm workers and estate workers needed rest on Sunday. We all knew one another and no one had a car, only the Barton family at the farm, the School Master, the Estate Manager, Mr Radway (who was King) and Mr Savage the organist. Our aspirations were very little, all local. The end of an era.

Times Remembered: Hatherop Choir 1930–1939

Left hand choir stalls:
Oliver Puffitt
Jim Shepherd
Mr. Savage: Organ
Bernard Iles: Organ Blower
(killed Tunisia WW2)
George Mustow
Charles Barnett
Norman Westall
Bill and George Dixon
Desmond Jones
Desmond Westall
Reuben Sims

Right hand choir stalls:
Edwin Griffin
Mr Miles: Quenington
Miss Moot: School Teacher
Miss Evans: School Teacher
Kathleen Brindle: School Teacher
Ernest Stevens
Elsie Puffitt
Meg Ferriman
Helen Jones
Barbara Rixon
John Westall: lamp lighter and
blower out of lamps

The laundry girls: Annie Weston and Queenie Ackland who took Sunday School in the afternoon.

As ringers came down from tower, they donned surplices and with the boys in front, walked from choir vestry to the choir stalls. The prayer from the Rev Callander before starting out of vestry was: "Go before us O Lord, With Thy most gracious favour and further us with Thy continuing help that all our works begin, continue and ending in Thee, we may glorify Thy Holy Name through Christ our Lord." All said "Amen". A shorter prayer was said at the end of the service. Jim Shepherd, Charlie Barnett and George Mustow remained in the choir until the end of their days. George Mustow remained in choir till he died in 1984. He was born in 1900 and was in the choir at seven years old. Mrs Charlie Barnett washed the surplices in Hatherop laundry. Wonderful times – gone in this new society.

Tuesday 9th June 1992 – Lady St Aldwyn is in hospital in London, she has not got over the loss of Earl St Aldwyn.

Wednesday 10th June 1992 – Mona comes and gets some cheese and sausages for me from the butcher's at Fairford. We talk about Jim Day of Quenington dying. Jim was a wonderful cheerful chap, a carpenter and plumber for Baldwin's, the builders of Fairford, for many years. For many years he cycled with his tool bag on his cycle to jobs with his companion, Eddie Hunt, before vans were used. He was on the Quenington Parish Council and was a member of RAOB but has not been to meetings for some years.

Friday 12th June 1992 – Walk to church, get the Crimond cards from parson's vestry to take to Coln St Aldwyns to give to Tom Lemon who rang me up yesterday to say his dear wife had died. She had been ill for some time. It is a very sad and difficult time for him. Their dog knows something is wrong.

Monday 15th June 1992 – Have finished a book loaned to me by Mr Dennis Bartlett called "A Country Camera" by Gordon Winter. It is full of old time photographs and very good reading. States how everything changed at the 1914 War. The days of the house servants in the gardens and estate workers like my father, a carpenter, were coming to a close. Today Coln Estate gardens have three houses built there and the gardener's cottage sold. Half of Hatherop Castle gardens sold and a tennis court built. The estate workmen gone – only Mr Gerald Hartshorn, foreman carpenter, left. Such are the times since the Second World War. Half the estate cottages, including the Reading Room, sold and gardens put to lawns and shrubs. After paying bills at Coln Stores I walk round to Tom Lemon and chat with him. At 84 years he misses his wife very much. He has lots of cards on his sideboard. I tell Tom I will be at his wife's burial service on Thursday at 2pm. A lovely lady.

Thursday 18th June 1992 – Walk to Coln Church for the burial service of Tom Lemon's wife. Give an address at the service about Mrs Lemon, how she loved animals and gave lots of money to the RSPCA and made wonderful cakes for people for birthdays and wedding cakes. A lady who always gave a welcome to everyone. A lot of people present. Tom and his wife came here in 1942.

Saturday 20th June 1992 – Bells rung up for the Bayliss wedding at 1pm. Katie Kimberley came and said goodbye to me after the Castle School speech day – give her a box of sweets. This is a sad day as all the boarders at the school are leaving and it will be a day school for young pupils. Am changed for a Fairford Band engagement with a little march at Fairford Primary School at 2pm. When I get home, confetti by the iron churchyard gates where the marriage of Mr Lee Bayliss's daughter had taken place. Lovely flowers in the church and the blue and yellow rosettes on the pew heads.

Wednesday 24th June 1992 – Hold last Buff Lodge meeting in my small room. Next meeting will be at Quenington Institute as we can rent it for one night a week. It is difficult to rent places today, the publicans want so much money. Coln Hall is closed and Hatherop Reading Room is a bungalow. Mr Wilfred Franklin brought a plate of sandwiches. R Sims made coffee. Present were Bro Ron Ellis, Bro Roger King, Bro Wilfred Franklin.

Friday June 26th 1992 – A warm day, walk Trixie to Coln Stores. See Tom Lemon and have photo taken with him sat on wall by chestnut tree by Mr Weston.

Reuben Sims with Tom Lemon under the horse chestnut tree in Coln St Aldwyns.

The Earl and Countess St Aldwyn 1948.

Monday July 13th 1992 – See Mrs Cox who tells me Countess St Aldwyn has died.

Friday 17th July 1992 – Have a phone call from Tom Lemon who wants me to sit with him in the little pew by the organ in Coln St Aldwyns Church for the funeral of Countess St Aldwyn. Mr Hart picks me up, as he picks up Mr and Mrs Blakeney from the Old Rectory which he owns and rents to them and takes them and his wife and me to Coln. Mr Hart has the Bach music for Tim Morris to play on the organ. He is a lovely organist. Have to park by the cottage opposite Coln Stores, so many cars arriving. Walk into church and sit with Tom, people coming in all the time. A large canopy and chairs outside the east end of church for extra mourners. The estate workmen dug the grave but could only go down so far because they came across other slab stones. Lilies were placed each side of altar and beside coffin in chancel. The estate bearers sat in choir stalls, also other mourners and members of Trotman and Hughes the undertakers of Northleach. After the service Tom and I went round to the grave and paid our last respects. The mourners went to Williamstrip House for tea. I went to Tom Lemon's house by the school and had a cup of tea with him.

Monday 20th July 1992 – Get ready for Mrs Maurice Moulden's funeral at Hatherop Church 2pm. The church is beautifully decorated from the Reeve's wedding on Saturday – still confetti by the south doorway. The Rev Cowmeadow took the service. The coffin is on trestles in the church. Mrs Moulden was ninety five years old. My parents' generation, she knew Harry Rogers the gamekeeper; Bill Sims the carpenter; Arthur Iles the gardener; George Walley the shoe maker; Dick Brindle the slatter; George Mustow, groom and gardener; Ernie Smith the shopkeeper; Joe Mills the tractor driver and chimney sweep; Ted Griffin the estate carter; Bill Puffitt the mason; Jim Shepherd and Charlie Barnett – gardeners. Cowman Westall who called the cows in for milking on the Glebe at five o'clock in the morning and Colonel Gibbs who used to call up at Fred Ford's bedroom window in 1940 invasion time, all now gone, a changed society. In Mrs Moulden's time everyone knew everyone else. Not so today. There are now very few of us Cotswold people left.

Tuesday 28th July 1992 – Get on cycle and ride to Coln Church for the funeral of Douglas Coates. A fine sportsman, good at football, a superb cricketer, had a trial for the county. Saw Ron May who said he bowled out all the team at Cricklade. I was in the team when we went to Eastleach with

The New Inn Darts Team 1950. Back row from left: Ted Twining, John 'Pat' Patheyjohns, Tom Lawrence, Frank Sharps, Ernie Tarrant. Front Row: Charlie Winstone, George Winfield, Doug Coates, Sandy Moaby

Bill Smith of Quenington in his swallow car – Douglas hitched his flannels in the door of the car when I got in at the Lodge, Douglas said: "I will bowl the Eastleach team out and make a century." That is just what he did. It came on fine rain as he was bowling the Eastleach team out but we carried on to the end and dried ourselves in front of a log fire at the Victoria Public House. Douglas was a good darts player and good at bowling skittles. He was in the Coldstream Guards in the Second World War. Jack Parry of Fairford laid a British Legion Wreath in front of the coffin in the chancel. The coffin was decorated with lovely flowers. The church was full of people. We sung "The Old Rugged Cross" and "The Day Thou Gavest Lord is Ended." He was buried in the cemetery. I feel very sad. Our Cotswold people are slowly departing.

Thursday 30th July 1992 – Mr Gerald Hartshorn is helping his son clear up after leaving No 18 Golden Row. He told me he saw a lady at the estate yard about a month ago enquiring if she could look at Hatherop Castle. He told her he did not think anyone would mind – she said she was the daughter of Sgt Major Austin who was the physical training instructor at the Castle during the Second War when the secret service unit was there. She wanted to see where he was. Gerald said she was evacuated to Mr and Mrs Robinson's at the Mill, Quenington during the war, I did not know that. She also saw Mr Jack Harris in the old people's bungalow at Quenington who kept the Keeper's Arms where the troops went for a drink and the old piano going all the evening. Sgt Major Austin was a fit man. Every week in Coln Village Hall the shout "Touch four walls and back" and "Start running round." The vaulting horse from the Castle brought in a sheeted-down truck – the long pole to throw from one row of men to the other.

Monday 3rd Aug 1992 – Work is going on at the house being built where the old blacksmith's shop used to stand. Two courses of bricks have been laid, and filling in the centre. Have a chat with Mr Bill Keene about the changing times. He said "The old Mill into flats, also the old saw Mill, two of the people's bungalows taken over by the New Inn for staff cottages, two turned into one house, very few working class people left to run a fete or other social function like years gone by when fêtes stayed open until seven or eight o'clock in the evening, now they are over by four o'clock.

Monday 7th Sept 1992 – Make appointment to see doctor, do not feel well.

Tuesday 8th Sept 1992 – Cycle to Fairford to see doctor, collapse in waiting room, taken to Fairford Hospital. Trixie taken to Blue Cross Kennels at Burford.

NO DIARY TO 28th SEPTEMBER 1992

Monday 28th Sept 1992 – Brought back from hospital by Mrs Mona Rixon. She has been a wonderful friend to me and has looked after my house affairs and cleaned it all through and seen to my papers and post affairs.

Tuesday 29th Sept 1992 – Mr Tony Nash of Fairford took me to the Blue Cross Kennels and we brought Trixie home – she was pleased to see me. She has kennel cough but will put it right with Benylin.

Wednesday 30th Sept 1992 – Had a visit from Mr Mervyn Bayliss who said the address I wrote in hospital for Mr John Reeves of Coln St Aldwyns who was buried in Hatherop churchyard yesterday afternoon was well received. It was read by Mr Blakeney who knew John well. Mr and Mrs Blakeney live in the Rectory now, the property of Farmer Hart.

Monday 5th Oct 1992 – Have a health visitor about the sugar diabetes I have. They found it out after my stay in Fairford Hospital. She told me to keep off sugar and will see me in three months time.

Saturday 17th Oct 1992 – Visit Tom Lemon at the Weston's house. Tom is making bread in the kitchen for Mrs Weston and the children. Tom still has the skill to make bread like he did at Coln Stores in the old Co-op days.

Sunday 25th Oct 1992 – Lady Sally Worsley picks me up at 12 noon and takes me to Williamstrip House where we met Michael St Aldwyn, David Hicks Beach and the church wardens of the other 4 churches. We discussed the retirement of the Rev Cowmeadow and getting another parson. Our parish is made up of five parishes and is big enough for a paid priest. Other parishes like Bibury who are not, may merge with other parishes. The changes we are seeing. Have a glass of sherry and a good chat. The members seem to think something for his model railway would be a good parting gift.

Tuesday 3rd Nov 1992 – Eddie Hunt of Quenington drove me to Ready Token and we looked at Coal Owner Jocey's tomb stone in the wood there and copied the verse inscribed on the stone:

When I am dead my dearest sing no sad songs for me,
Plant thou no roses at my head or shady cypress tree
With the green grass o'er me and flowers and dew drops wet
And if thou wilt, remember, and if thou wilt, forget.

My Uncle Jim Sims married a Miller whose father worked for Mr Jocey at Poulton Priory. She used to quote the tombstone verse. We drove on to Poulton Church to plant some crocuses and hyacinths on Jim and Minnie Sims grave, but a funeral was in progress so we drove on to Down Ampney Church and planted some crocuses and a hyacinth on my

Aunt Beatie Humphry's grave. We drive back to Poulton Church where my Uncle Jim Sims married Minnie Miller in 1912. I plant two hyacinth bulbs and twenty-five crocuses. They were good people. I am very pleased with the morning out with Eddie.

Thursday 5th Nov 1992 – Miss Hobbs is representing me at Mrs Keene's funeral. She was head of Coln Laundry at one time and her husband used to see to the boiler there.

Coln Laundry Ladies – Sitting: Mrs Hampton and Emma May. Standing from left: Mary Sharps, Mrs Healey, Unknown, Gladys Keene, Mrs Brogden, Dorothy Sharps, Eva Broderick, Mrs Herbert.

Wednesday 11th Nov 1992 – Walk to church about 5pm and meet Bill Keene coming away from his parent's grave. The ashes of his mother Mrs Keene had been placed there this afternoon. We had a chat, his mother was in her eighties. Bill has a job on his hands looking after himself. I have done it for 25 years.

Tuesday 17th Nov 1992 – Mr Hart takes me to a Coln Society meeting at the Malt House. We meet at 7.30pm in what used to be the Coln Reading Room but Mr Weston, the present owner with plenty of money, has taken out the ceiling and exposed the roof rafters and timbers and had paintings of book shelves full of books on the walls. Have a good chat but most of the people are new here and know nothing of Cotswold life in days gone by. I drank three glasses of wine.

Wednesday 18th Nov 1992 – Catch service bus to Cirencester at 9.30am. I am the only person that catches this bus, they all have cars here. We are in a recession but the pensioners in the old people bungalows all have cars, quite remarkable. Arrive home 12.30pm. Have dinner, rest and then get ready for journey to Eastleach Village Hall at 6.45pm for a meeting with the Rev Lewis, Archdeacon. Farmer Hart takes Miss Hobbs, Mr Robinson of Barn Ground Cottages and myself. A lot has been done to Eastleach Hall since the parish had it from the Bazley Family when I cycled with my friends to dances there in 1943–1945 time. A store was in the centre with a wire guard round. Food was rationed but you could buy a cake at a dance for one shilling. On the wall were pictures of old Sir Thomas Bazley. On the east end wall was a large notice, about 3' x 3' with big letters, it told you beer was 2p a pint. This amount saved over ten years invested in the Post Office gave you round about £300 pounds – these figures were painted in red. We had some wonderful nights there during the war with a band of piano and drums and banjo at the west end. We have our meeting with the Archdeacon, about thirty odd people there, I know very few of these people who have come here in recent years. But monied and well educated – should be a benefit to the five parishes.

Sunday 29th Nov 1992 – Walk to church for 10.30am Holy Eucharist service with all five parishes. Mrs Susan Vicary has lit all the candles, Colin is playing the organ. Mrs Mandy Weston has brought Tom Lemon from Coln and we all sit in the choir stalls by the organ. We sing well, about forty communicants and about ten boys of Hatherop Castle School in their blue blazers with red trimmings with one of their male teachers.

Wednesday 2nd Dec 1992 – Catch bus for Cirencester – have a cup of coffee in the church shop in Dollar Street. 50p too dear shall not walk all that way again when I can get a cup at 20p at the pop-in on the road which leads off the police station.

Saturday 19th Dec 1992 – Mr Voaden takes me to Fairford and the band plays carols round the Christmas Tree in the Market Place. A band of about a dozen carol singers join us and we play plenty of carols. Mr Maurice Jones, the Town Crier, is there with his bell – lots of people around.

Friday 25th Dec 1992 – Walk to Church at 7.15am and put on the lights. The Christmas Tree behind the parson's pew looks lovely. Sally Worsley and Frazer Hart come in and we light all the candles and bring out the brass candle sticks and brass cross for today. R Sims pulled the Sanctus Bell, it is eight o'clock and the Rev Derek Cowmeadow takes his last Christmas Holy Eucharist at Hatherop. 22 people present.

Wednesday 30th Dec 1992 – I walked to Coln St Aldwyns and had tea at the Malt house in the old Reading Room with Tom Lemon, Mrs Lily

Reeves, Mr Reg Mustow, Mrs Ellen Townsend, and others at the invitation of Mr and Mrs Weston. We all had a good tea, crackers and a glass of sherry. Mrs Weston brought me home afterwards. A good time had by all. The two candelabra made by Dennis Bartlett looked fine. We had a look at the sheep in the old Rifle Range afterwards. Think of past days in the forties and before, when we danced the old year out and the New Year in.

Sunday 10th Jan 1993 – After a very wet night do not feel well. Giddy and unwell so do not go to 'Together at Ten' at Hatherop Church. Cook my half shoulder of lamb, potatoes and curly greens from my garden. Ring Tom Lemon and tell him why I was not at Church as Mandy Weston was bringing him up. He was pleased to hear from me, he said they had a good service with the families.

Monday 11th Jan 1993 – Reuben Sims is 70 years old today.

Sunday 24th Jan 1993 – Have the last Eucharist Service by the Rev Derick Cowmeadow at Hatherop Church at 8am.

Sunday 31st Jan 1993 – Walk to Mr and Mrs Blakeney's at the Old Rectory and they drive me to Coln St Aldwyns Church for the last service of Holy Eucharist at Coln Church at 11am. Members of the other parishes: Hatherop, Quenington, Eastleach and Southrop were there. We had five hymns during the service and a full church. Miss Hobbs brought Mrs Bartlett, the late blacksmith's wife aged 93 years. The Rev and Mrs Cowmeadow stood at the main door as we all went out after the service. Then the Blakeneys brought me back to Hatherop Castle for a lunch in the old drawing and billiard rooms. I gave a little speech and presented Mr and Mrs Derek Cowmeadow with a painting of the five churches which Lady Sally Worsley had

painted. It is a sad time to lose a parson of the five parishes after fifteen years, ten with CHQ, then taking on Eastleach and Southrop the last five years. Now we have to carry on till we find a new man. I walk home after the lunch and too much wine.

Wednesday 3rd Feb 1993 – Mr and Mrs Mervyn Bayliss drive me to Lechlade Church for the funeral of Mrs Tom Lappington at 11am. Lechlade Church is a fine large building. Mrs Lappington was Vera Packer in single life – the sister of John Packer who played right back for Hatherop Football team when I was a boy. His mother married Ted Griffin the bell ringer and choir man at Hatherop Church. She died about the same time as my father in 1943. She used to say "Bill and I are going home together". Dorothy Westall her sister was there and also her family. Mr Derek Musty was there, his aunt married John Packer. The cortège went to the cemetery and Mr Bayliss drove us back to Fairford where we did some shopping then came home.

Tuesday 16th Feb 1993 – Have a phone call from Sally Worsley to say a lady has died in Oxford, a relation of the Day Family – must be of Dean Farm, and wishes to be buried in Hatherop Churchyard. Would I mark a place for a grave? A priest has been found to take the service.

Saturday 20th Feb 1993 – Get ready for the Day funeral at 3.30pm. Walk to church at 3pm, put on lights, put brass candlesticks and cross on altar, you cannot leave any of these things around today or they are stolen. Canon Jeffries arrives from Ampney St Peter, lovely man, also the organist. The cortège arrives of about forty people from Oxford. Mr and Mrs Charles Pollard are there, they are relatives. We have two hymns 'Praise my Soul' and 'The Day Thou Gavest'.

Thursday 25th Feb 1993 – Weed-kill Mr and Mrs Bush and their daughter Mary's grave. £100 is left for the upkeep of the grave but no one knows them here now and the £8 interest per year goes into the church account. Mr Bush, a short man in boots and gaiters, milked the Jersey cows at Home Farm. My dad shot the fantailed pigeons for him with an airgun when they got too many. Mrs Bush, a plump lady with rosy cheeks, patted up the butter and separated the cream which was took to Hatherop Castle along the milk walk which is now long gone across the park. Mary Bush was never strong, had consumption and went to Standish Hospital. All the villages used to walk down and get their milk. Then Mr Herbert Stevens of Coln St Aldwyns sent round a milk trap with churn and horse and you put your milk jug on the doorstep. Charlie Herbert of Coln St Aldwyns was the driver.

Saturday 6th March 1993 – Ring up Tom Lemon of Coln St Aldwyns in the evening, he lives on his own, has seen no one all day, he was glad of a chat, he is eighty four years old.

Saturday 17th April 1993 – Go to the Church Tower at 2pm. Meet Mr John Reeves, his son in law Mr Gibbs, Mrs Ruth Mowat, Mrs Joan Akers and Mrs Lindsay Sharpes. Together we rang the Church Bells till the bride came for the Tufnell wedding at 2pm. The church was full of lovely white flowers, also all the candelabra. Visitors in Morning Dress. We rang the bells when the service ended and the bride and bridegroom and guests all went away to the reception.

Tuesday 20th April 1993 – Walk to Coln Post Office, draw some money out of my Savings Account. You need an awful lot of money to live today, everything is expensive. See Mr Mervyn Bayliss who said the chimes have jumped again. We have had more trouble with the clock since it has been wound electronically than ever we had in the old hand-wind days.

Friday 7th May 1993 – Talked to a fisherman on the bridge about the Windmill firm of Godwin's before the Second War and Reuben Briggs of Fairford who started me on 5/– per week. I asked him for some more money after twelve months, he said "was I worth more?" I said "Yes" and he said nothing but gave me ten shillings the next day. My job was to see to the wood fire when they got the bonds out of the fire and put them on the wooden wagon and cart wheels on the cast iron bonding platform. I cooled the bond down with water – we all worked and sweated like demons. Fred Parson the blacksmith always had too much to drink from the Railway Inn on bonding day. He always had a pint there every day but Mr Briggs did not mind, he was such a worker. The sparks from the forge used to singe the hairs on his chest and arms but he still carried on and made the cart horse shoes and hunter shoes. It was quite a performance shoeing all these horses from Fairford Park House and all the local houses who used horses for hunting or traps. All the local farmers brought their cart horses to be shod. I remember Billy Heath coming to the blacksmith shop door and saying "I will bring a horse tomorrow Fred, at half past three" and Fred saying "Bring him when he's tired Bill." Such were the days so long ago before big tractors with cabs on and all large equipment took their place.

Thursday 20th May – Go with Sally Worsley to Fairford Church for the Church Wardens' swearing in – I rang her – she had forgotten all about it. We go down the Fairford road at sixty miles an hour. We go into the church for the swearing in and find there is a communion service on in the chapel on the left. We join in. The swearing in must have been at Cirencester.

Saturday 22nd May 1993 – Get a ring from Sally to say the Archdeacon will induct us as church wardens at Quenington Chapel after the service on (D Day) 6th June, it will take about three minutes. The swearing in service at Fairford for many years was so lovely from 1950 with Mr Fowler with his wig on. Then his son took over and we paid the £1.1s at the Bull afterwards. All that has now gone. Now it is done at Cirencester.

Saturday 5th June 1993 – Dress up and walk to Coln St Aldwyns to sing at the wedding of Major General Bowring's daughter at 3pm. Church decorated. Tom Lemon and Reuben Sims in surpluses in choir. Dr Henderson played the organ. The bride's mother and relatives sat in the choir stalls. Canon Jeffries conducted the service. We sung three hymns, "He Who Would Valiant Be" "Fight the Good Fight" and "Guide Me O Thou Great Redeemer". The Roman Catholic Priest from Horcott gave the blessing afterwards, then champagne and peach wine and lots of food. I had enough to drink in a large marquee on the Manor lawn. Lots of people there, men in morning coats, ladies in tight shirts and large hats. Mrs Bowring the bride's mother the best dressed lady there.

Sunday 6th June 1993 – Did not get up in time for Communion at 9.30am – too grand a time yesterday. Lady Sally Worsley picks me up and we go to Quenington Church to be sworn in as Church Wardens by the Arch Deacon, the Rev Lewis after the morning service.

Tuesday 15th June 1993 – Leslie Cuss of Mount Street, Cirencester arrives in his car and we have a good chat about this modern world in which we live, the attacks on people in the street, the break in of houses, the putting of the cross and candlesticks in our church under lock and key when not used for services, the lack of religion, how people of our age, 70 years, are glad they were born when they were. Divorce and people living together not married. We have a good afternoon. Had a phone call from Tom Lemon of Coln St Aldwyns at 9.30pm. He was in bed. He has two phones put in by social security, someone to clean his house and pay his rent. I'm afraid I cannot get that treatment.

Sunday 4th July 1993 – Have a chat with Mrs Mervyn Bayliss who told me Mrs Malet, at the Walled House, nearly went down a well on the edge of her property. There was ten feet of water in the well. Mervyn said it must have been the well that fed the pump in the Pump House. I remember the stone trough and the long handled pump standing on the right hand side of the Pump House. This was before my father and Leonard Miles made the seat which is there today. This was always the place where the lads of the village gathered for a chat nights and Sunday afternoon.

Saturday 10th July 1993 – Walk to Williamstrip House in the evening for drinks at 6.30pm in honour of David Hicks Beach's wedding to Miss Henriquez of Winson. A fine party. Drinks and eats and a steel band finished off the evening. Lord and Lady St Aldwyn greeted us in.

Tuesday 20th July 1993 – Ring Mrs Bennett at Lady Lucy Cottage – tell her I have pictures and writings of Hatherop for her to see. She comes in the afternoon and I gave her the records compiled by Rev Douglas. Mrs Bennett and me had a long chat about the old days and she took the records and a lot of newspaper cuttings my mother had saved. She is compiling some records herself.

Monday 26th July 1993 – Walk to Coln St Aldwyns Post Offcie, draw pension and shake hand with Brian our postmaster. This is the last week here at the Post Office – next week it will be moved to Coln Stores. The counter has been fixed there. Walk round to Lady Lucy Cottage with a photo of Williamstrip Rifle Club at Seven Springs, Cheltenham. Show Mrs Rachel Bennett 'Butler Ebourn' who is in the photo with my Dad and Fred Ford.

Williamstrip Rifle Club 1910. Back row from left: 1st William Sims, 4th Butler Ebourn from Hatherop Castle, 5th Charlie Mustow. Middle row from left: 2nd Fred Ford - Gardener Hatherop Castle, 3rd Jessie Miles – Williamstrip Estate Foreman, 6th Mr Quick, Coln School Headmaster. Front row (middle) Walter Claridge – Haulier.

Monday 2nd Aug 1993 – Walk to Coln Stores to get my pension. The Post Office is closed and the post work is at Coln Stores but the counter is not finished so cannot get pension today so cannot pay bills for groceries. Walk round to Lady Lucy Cottage, and see Mrs R Bennett and give her back the obituary on old Sir Thomas Bazley who owned the cotton mills in Manchester employing 1,800 people. Also gave her the name of the book which says the Hatherop Dent Clock was for the Castle not the church – "E J Dent and His Successors" by Valdre Merser. She is very pleased and showed me the Dent wall clock which used to be by the kitchen in Hatherop Castle and she bought it for ten shillings at the three day sale held after the Second War. My mother must have looked at that clock often when she was housemaid there in the 1914–18 War. Walked on to see Tom Lemon in his cottage and wished him Happy Birthday. He is 85 years old today.

Saturday 7th August 1993 – A notice from the Council pinned to the Memorial Gate states that a strip of land by the football pitch is to be used as a children's playground. A swing and see saw is erected now by the beech tree but the ladies want a slide and other amusements for their children.

Sunday 15th Aug 1993 – Have a walk round the school. Building where the kitchen was has been gutted – no more meals cooked at Hatherop School. Meals to come by taxi from Cirencester – part of the cutbacks in education. Also all the toilet flush boxes are flung outside. In a recession the Council wastes money.

Tuesday 24th August 1993 – Walk to postbox and post a letter back to the Church Youth Leader at Gloucester who wants to know what the youth are doing for my Parish Church. I fill in the form and tell him they are doing nothing.

Saturday 4th September 1993 – Lot of young Dads and Mums at the play area fixing the swings and a play hut and see-saw and cementing in the posts and spreading the wood chippings. Work started at 9am and finished at 6pm. The holes where the swings and see-saw were under the beech tree were filled in and the wood railings around the play area nailed up.

At eleven o'clock this morning walked to Williamstrip House for a meeting with the clergyman chaplain in the Royal Navy as a Parson for these five Parishes [*Tony Ross*]. The young Earl St Aldwyn took the chair. The Parson from Fairford and the new Rural Dean were there. The meeting was called by the gentleman who lives in old Mr Godwin's house [*Mick Barham*] at Quenington. Our Parishes have been without a Parson for around 7 months. It appears the Bishop and Arch Deacon do not agree with this meeting because it has not their authority. Had a nice cup of coffee and biscuits before the meeting with the Earl St Aldwyn and the Countess. After the Parson had answered all our questions we went to a wonderful lunch at the Hatherop Barn ground building. The old barn has been converted to a wonderful house by the previous owner. Far different from the days when Mr Ash who lived in one of the cottages nearby, now made into a single house, used to pump water at the old barn for the cattle there. The gentleman and his wife with his two sons who own it, is a lay reader. [*Hamner and Lucille Webb Peploe*] A marvellous lunch of soup, meat and salad, wine or beer and ice-cream etc. I had a wonderful time. Lady Sally Worsley drove me there in her car and brought me home. Rested all day after that. The gentleman that owns the house has seen me many times in Hatherop Church but I do not know him. I see so many new people round here now.

Thursday 23rd September 1993 – See Mr and Mrs Bunce in churchyard. Mrs Bunce is Mary Stephens, daughter of Ernest and Florence Stephens. Mrs Stephen's was the daughter of Ted (Edwin) Griffin whose family is supposed to have lived four hundred years in Hatherop. Mary wants a copy of the bell ringers outing of 1931 which is in Hatherop Tower and that I have to get copies for the Griffins of Manchester and the Parson Griffin of USA.

Saturday 25th September 1993 – Cherry Malet picked up Miss Hobbs and me and took us to the Parish Harvest Supper in the big barn at Mawley House, Quenington. About 70 people there. Sally Worsley sat opposite me, I sat next to Cherry Malet and Mrs Paul Nixon-Lee. We had a good meal (no grace). The young Earl St Aldwyn gave a speech on the harvest.

Monday 27th September 1993 – Walk to Coln and walk round to Tom Lemon and we both had a walk to the Vicarage and about the grounds which have many trees and shrubs. Saw Lady Blunt in the garden of the old Vicarage Cottage. She wants the laburnum in the vicarage grounds cut down because it shades her dining room window but wants the other hawthorn shrubs left because it shields her Cottage from being looked over by the Vicarage windows. She also said she tried to buy the Vicarage grounds her side of The Vicarage drive but the church authorities would not do that. Mrs Spreadborough, a widow, lived in the church cottage. Her husband was a painter for Baldwin's and was killed cycling to work on the Aldsworth road one foggy morning. The cottage was not modernised and the cottage was sold in the time of the Rev Mowat together with the old coach houses used as a garage which were built in the side up the house. Mrs Spreadborough had to move into the old people's bungalows. Her daughter, Mr Jack Gaiger's wife, was not pleased. What a gain it would have been if the cottage still belonged to the church in this day and age. Builders are redecorating the Vicarage and doing something about the bathrooms. A lot of money being spent but it is a lovely old vicarage.

Mrs Spreadborough (centre) with her two daughters, Jean Pinnock (left) and Dorothy Gaiger (right) and her father, Tom Clements (sitting) outside The Vicarage Cottage.

Wednesday 29th Sept 1993 – Catch bus for Cirencester at 9.15am. A council lady on the bus asks us when we travel on bus and do we use it for shopping? We all said once a week and shopping. Come home at 12.30pm, have a sleep in chair. Mr Hart calls about Church Meeting tonight at the Firs – Sally Worsley's house. Go to church meeting at 7.30pm, have a glass of sherry. I take a bottle of wheat wine. I read out the log book of events then we discuss about the new Rector coming. Mr Webb-Peploe came late, he had not been elected but took the prayers at beginning and end of the meeting. Mr Hart said Bibury and Ablington may have to come in with us. Lots of changes coming about now with more parishes under one parson.

Monday 18th Oct 1993 – Walk to Lady Lucy Cottage to see Mrs Bennett – take her some photos of Frances Bazley's wedding to Mr Hughes when I was a Wolf Cub and a Choir Boy. Told her about when Christopher Cadogan came round with champagne for us boys and Nannie Taylor, the housekeeper, stopped him coming round again – this was in the servant's hall.

Miss Frances Bazley's wedding to the author Mr Richard Hughes 1932.

Saturday 23rd October 1993 – Mr Hart called and brought me the invitation from Williamstrip Estate Office for the installation of the new Rector, the Rev Anthony Ross OBE, on Thursday 11th November at Coln St Aldwyns Church at 7.30pm.

The Sunbeam taking Mr and Mrs Richard Hughes away after their wedding.

Thursday 28th Oct 1993 – Go to Mr and Mrs Frazer Hart's drinks party at the Glebe Farm Barn in the evening at 6.30pm. Marquee put up at Glebe Farm Barn entrances. Three large flower baskets hanging from the barn beams. The barn roof looks fine, the flowers look marvellous. Mrs Hart said the box and other greenery came from Williamstrip Park. Two more hanging baskets were in the marquee where a jazz band of trumpeter, bass, trombone, mandolin and drums was playing for dancing and wine was being brought round. I leave at 7.15pm with wine for the bell ringers who are practising ringing in Hatherop Church Tower. Have a good practice and came away. I could have gone back to the party but was tired.

Saturday 30th Oct 1993 – Walk to church at 3pm [*for James Hart's wedding to Philippa Bently*]. Unlock belfry door. Mrs Akers, Mrs Mowat, Mrs Lindsay Sharps arrive, then Mr Mike Adams, Mr David Gibbs and Mr John Reeves. We get the bells up. Ring from 2.40pm to 3pm when the bride arrives from the Castle steps all in white with a long train, two bearers, a little girl and a little boy in a brown waistcoat. Lots of cine cameras in action. Mr Morris is at the organ. A Trumpet Player does some playing, Ave Maria is sung by Miss Hart, the church is full. The main lights are dimmed with our new dimming switch, all the candles are lit. We ring the bells as the bride and groom come out. All the guests have gone to the farm for the reception. The ringers and me go into the church and see the lovely flowers and beautiful lilies in the sanctuary. Fireworks light up the sky at 10pm.

James Hart's wedding to Philippa Bently: Back row from left: Mr and Mrs Frazer Hart, James, Philippa, Jamie Roger (best man) Mr and Mrs Leon Bently. Front: Adam and Gina Scott-Avis and Jemma Philips.

Thursday 11th Nov 1993 – [*Induction of the Rev Tony Ross*] A lady with car picks me up with Susan Vicary at 6.50pm. Get to Coln St. Aldwyns – it is packed with cars. Park at Lady Lucy Cottage, the old laundry. Walk to the church – all the church wardens are in seats both sides at the very front. We sing hymns and Bishop Jeremy goes to all parts of the church. I give our new Rector the Bible at the lecturn. The church was full including the choir stalls. After the service we went to Williamstrip House for drinks and sandwiches. Then the ladies drove me home then bed. I had had enough white wine – there was plenty of white and red wine.

Monday 20th Dec 1993 – Walk to the funeral of Ron Sharps at Coln Church at 2pm. This is the first burial service by our new vicar. Ron was a single man, lived on his own in the last cottage on the right hand side of the row on the Bibury Road. He was 60 years old and had looked after his father for many years who had died about twelve months ago. He was found dead in his chair. I had many chats with Ron – he worked in the grounds of Hatherop Castle Girl's School for many years.

Friday 24th Dec 1993 – Mrs Sinton of Coln Stores brought groceries. Played carols at the New Nursing Home, Hyperion House, in the evening in an extension room with fine Malayan hard wood rafters. Tom Lemon, who is recovering from a stroke, was there; also Linda Harris from the bungalows at Quenington Green was there – wife of the late Jack Harris of the Keepers Arms – she was in good health. The band then played some carols in the Bull then we all came away. Walked to Hatherop church at 11pm. The church bells were ringing. I climbed the stairs to the bell ringing chamber and wished the bell ringers under Mr Nipper Reeves a Happy Christmas. Lots of ladies there – Mrs Joan Akers, Mrs Lindsay Sharps and two new ladies – Mrs Owen and another lady from the new house built in the blacksmith's yard. Mr Faulkner of the new houses at the Hornbeams. Mr Gibbs, Mr Mike Adams and a young boy who had come from New Zealand to the Owen Family and wanted to see our tower. The lights were dimmed in the church, the organist played the carols. 118 people were present. I pulled the Sanctus Bell. We had the Rev Tony Ross. To see the church with so many young people was inspiring.

Thursday 30th Dec 1993 – The Rev Ross calls at 10am. We discuss the funeral for Aubrey Puffitt at 2pm. He would like me to say a few words about him. Aubrey was a butcher who lived with his parents. Bill Puffitt was the stone mason on Hatherop Estate in my grandfather's time. He died at Tetbury Hospital, being there eight years, after living with his sister Dorothy for twenty years down by the river at Quenington. Aubrey was a coalman for Mr Crowe, the local coalman. I go to the church at 1.30pm. Lady Sally Worsley is lighting the candles, then goes home – she did not know Aubrey – she has only been here twenty years.

Oliver Puffitt and wife from Meysey Hampton were there and the Barker family. Out of the family of 12 children there are three left. I feel it, a good Cotswold family which was in Hatherop in my grandfather's time when Aubrey's father and my grandfather walked the bounds of Hatherop Estate together in the last century.

Mrs Puffitt and Gladys Tombs (later Mrs Woodcock) 1910.

Friday 31st Dec 1993 – Walk to Coln Stores, pay my bills and wish Mrs Sinton a Happy New Year. Take a New Year card and place it on the ringing table in Hatherop Church tower. Spend the night at home watching the Old Year out and the New Year in on TV. TV programmes poor. Go outside at 12 o'clock and have a look round. No one around – we used to go outside in my mother's day at the Lodge and drink a glass of port.

Friday 21st Jan 1994 – Cycle to Fairford – fit new hearing aid I have bought – hearing better but far from perfect – awfully expensive at £450. Ride around and see all the new building down East End – everywhere in Fairford new buildings. Fairlight Grange by the Lover's Walk has completely altered the Hatherop Road area since I knew it, with pasture fields and Lea Garage on the main road at the corner by the Hatherop Road and main road junction. Mr Reuben Briggs had the eight acre piece, now filled with houses and called Aldsworth Close.

Wednesday 9th Feb 1994 – Visit from the new Parson the Rev Tony Ross. He wanted to know the numbers of the cottages and who lived there. I don't know myself, so many changes have occurred in recent years.

Sunday 6th March 1994 – Pull Sanctus Bell for 8am Holy Eucharist Service. Mrs Susan Vicary is lighting the choir candles – her great grandfather gave them with the organ in the last century.

Wednesday 9th March 1994 – Another body has been found by police at Cromwell Street, Gloucester making 9. More than the Christie case of 34 Rillington Place, London.

Sunday 13th March 1994 – Walk to church for 'Together at Ten Service'. Lots of new people there with their children. Posies were given around as it was Mother's Day. Tom Lemon was brought from the Nursing Home at the Hyperion House by Mr Edward Weston. He wheeled Tom in a push-chair up the church path, complained to me how overgrown and rough the path was, will have to see if we can do something about it.

Monday 18th April 1994 – Pay the first instalment of the community charge: £29 per month, £34 the next 10 months.

Friday 6th May 1994 – Farmer Hart rings me up to say someone has stolen the brass heads off the churchwarden's staves. So much is stolen out of our churches today. We had these staves when Mrs Fyfe had so many girls confirmed at the school and we had the Bishop come to Hatherop Church. This was in 1950 after my sister died. After that Quenington and Coln got staves. Bishop Hallam came to Coln Church when I was about ten years old and we practised and sung in Coln Church Choir. I bumped my chair against the oak choir stalls on the practice night and Miss Knapp the school teacher told me "If I did that sort of thing at Hatherop, I did not do it at Coln St Aldwyns".

Wednesday 25th May 1994 – Go to the School for a report by the Teachers on the progress of the School – look at the new toilets and the old doorway which has been opened up and provides access to the toilets and cloakrooms. In my day it was a cupboard where the books on Lord Nelson and Shakespeare were kept. The kitchen has been made into a classroom. The old boiler room at the rear of the main building which was sunk down in the ground and you climbed down a ladder to get to it, has been filled in and a door fixed in the side of the small classroom giving access to the rear buildings. A slate in a frame used for writing on has been kept. It was found when the doorway in the main building was reopened. Some slates were in the school when I started school in the twenties. The wood screen partitioning the main room is still there, put when Mr Percy Garner came there as head master in 1929.

Friday 3rd June 1994 – Lots on the TV about the Normandy landings fifty years ago on 6th June. Remember that time well, all the airplanes flying over with their white stripes on. A high price was paid with those men. We could not have done it all without the USA.

Monday 6th June 1994 – Watch the programme of D Day 50 year anniversary.

Thursday 9th June 1994 – Start chopping out our overgrown churchyard path, 150 yards long, no one will do it. Mr Bishoff at the Severalls mows the grass at the side of path and sunk fence.

Friday 10th June 1994 – Big tent put up in park by football pitch for a fete on Sunday afternoon for Hatherop School. I do not agree with a fete for the Church School on a Sunday but that's how things are today.

Sunday 12th June 1994 – The Cirencester Majorettes with their organs and drums came through the village at 2pm for the fete. Village street lined with cars, I counted thirty. Walked to Netherton – lots of work has been done on the cottages where I was born. Trees are growing in a piece of land at the side, where a garage has been built and the old barn has been pulled down. Walk on down the hill and see a new pair of gates has been fitted at Netherton Lodge. Walk home across Grandage. Rev Ross called to see me to read a Lesson tomorrow at Tom Lemon's funeral at Coln. Lord St Aldwyn rung to know some of the works of Tom Lemon as he is giving the address.

Monday 13th June 1994 – Mr Mervyn Bayliss called to take me to Tom Lemon's funeral at Coln St Aldwyns Church at 2pm. A lot of people there. The young Lord St Aldwyn gave the address. His brother David Hick Beach read the First Lesson, I read the Second Lesson. Tom is buried near his dear wife in Coln Cemetery. I have lost a good church going friend.

Sunday 19th June 1994 – HE at Hatherop Church at 8am. The Hon Mrs Malet there putting out the candles and brass but no key to get the chalice out of the safe. She went home and came back with a large chalice like a glass and we had Communion with that. Seventeen of us there with a visiting parson who has been before with his wife.

Tuesday 5th July 1994 – Went to Fairford Hospital with some Lucozade for Ray Bailey of Quenington who is not well in there. His sister Gwen with her son came in to visit him.

Monday 11th July 1994 – This year may be the last Cirencester Carnival as they cannot get a Carnival Queen. How times have changed.

Friday 22nd July 1994 – Mr Mervyn Bayliss picked me up at 12.45pm and we drive to Coln St Aldwyns church for the funeral of Mrs Elizabeth Bartlett, wife of our late blacksmith, Charles Bartlett. Church full of people – service taken by the Rev Tony Ross. We sung "The Day Thou Gavest Lord is Ended" and "Cwm Rhondda" – good singing. I gave the address from some notes Mr Dennis Bartlett wanted me to say as she was a dynamic lady of 94 years, digging the Hatherop allotments when the family moved to Hatherop in 1937. She was in the Land WACs in the 1914–18 War; reared cattle; used the sledge for her husband at the anvil; started work at 13 years old for the Squires family of Southrop; gave 100 donations of blood and had a gold badge for doing the same; supported the Evergreen Club; ran a taxi business; did her last run at the age of 84 years and loved her garden and went to Coln and Hatherop Churches for Communion till her eyesight and legs failed, then had the service at home. A lady with a lovely smile and great dignity. Mr Dennis Bartlett called when I got back home – went to Dean Row and had tea and cakes with the family.

Wednesday 3rd Aug 1994 – Went to Cirencester and shopped at Tesco's – how good this store is to get things – no trader comes round with things anymore. Mr Robert Meade has died and was buried on July 11th, the funeral held at Quenington chapel. Mr Meade was a very good man, always gave you a good welcome at the Chapel. Tom Lemon and me enjoyed some wonderful services in the new Chapel. My mother and sister enjoyed services in the old chapel which is now part of a house on Chapel Corner. Mr Robert Meade was a good organist and preacher and loved a good laugh.

Saturday 6th Aug 1994 – Have visit from Mona who gets me a loaf of bread every Saturday. I have just washed my curtains and re-hung them and hoovered the carpet – she seems amused at my efforts. Have a phone call from Bob Hutchings – he had noted the death and burial of Keeper Smith at Williamstrip who lived in Keepers Lodge. He asked me about Keeper Smith's funeral. I told him I did not know anything about it, or his age, I must find out.

Thursday 25th Aug 1994 – Jim Luce takes me to Band Practice. I take two small bore trombones to give to Mr Musty, which I have bought from a Sheffield firm I buy from, for Fairford Band to teach some new trombone players. The trombone is a sensitive instrument and these instruments will be good for learners.

Monday 29th Aug 1994 – August Bank Holiday – Walk to the Barrow Elm Farm where the buildings are being altered into seven houses. The old galvanised iron Dutch Barn on the north side of the buildings has been pulled down. The walls are still red from the great rick fire there before the Second War when the ricks were burnt and a threshing machine burnt out. Fairford and Cirencester Fire Engines played water on the great barn doors to save the fire spreading; a large crowd of people gathered as it was in the evening. The farm was under the tenancy of Mr Arly Barton. My mother spotted the flames when she went upstairs to draw the bedroom curtains when we were living at the Lodge. I went to the farm with my father. George Burge stayed at the pump turbine all night to keep the maximum water flowing to a large tank in the buildings.

Wednesday 31st Aug 1994 – The IRA are stopping their violence campaign at eleven o'clock tonight – lots about it on TV – hope it holds and the killings will stop after twenty-five years and they will all live in peace at last.

Tuesday 6th Sept 1994 – The Hon Mrs Cherry Malet's son [*Charles*] visits me and I tell him all about agriculture machinery pulled by horses when I went to work for Mr Reuben Briggs at the East Glos in 1937 and how there was only one tractor on the farm pulling three-furrow Ransome ploughs. Two-furrow and one-furrow were pulled by horses. All the harrows and seed drills were pulled by horses and the farm labourer walked behind. Harry Ferguson revolutionised the work with his Ferguson Tractor and hydraulic equipment in the fifties.

Saturday 10th Sept 1994 – Go to church at 9.30am. Meet Lady Sally Worsley and her little dog. She has brought lots of drinks and cakes for the cycle riders who are riding round to various churches on the great Church Cycle Ride which starts at 10am. She leaves me and I write down the times the cyclists come. Mrs Cherry Malet takes over from me at 11am.

Monday 12th Sept 1994 – A memory: The winter of 1963 when Mr Patheyjohns told the Express reporters there were no WCs in the cottages and only the open fire grate mainly in one room. Baths were held at the Reading Room every Friday evening. Soil buckets were in use which were difficult to empty in the gardens during the bitter frosty weather. Sharringtons, The Quest and 3 or 4 cottages had baths and toilets. Sharringtons, The Quest and the School were connected to the sewer pit in the corner of Sims's Field near the oak tree.

Tuesday 13th Sept 1994 – Hoe off the overgrown Church path which has grown over and nearly meets with grass in the middle – it is now a cycle track and not a path to the House of Almighty God. No one will do anything about it and one's shoes get awfully wet and dirty walking to the Church. It also gives a bad influence to those who come to the football matches and the Children's Sports where the Park is mown by the GCC. Mr Hart comes along on his cycle, wants me to have the path narrower but I'm going to have the path near 4'6" as it used to be when John and Desmond Westall, and sometimes George Mustow, used to keep it spaded to its width. There was no payment, no thanks, it was the natural thing to do to keep the path to the House of the Lord open. Now it is tarmac to the club entrance from the First War Memorial Arch. The Church Path is just a cycle track. I want to make the path open so that two people can walk side by side.

Thursday 15th Sept 1994 – See Marchant's bus with a Tesco sign on it – a new journey from Northleach to the new Tesco Store at Kingsmeadow on Monday, Wednesday and Thursdays. Must try one of these trips to the new store.

Tuesday 20th Sept 1994 – Have a letter from Mrs Gwen Twining thanking me for some bulbs I sent her. A lovely lady, we had some wonderful dancing times in Coln Village Hall years ago. She was my heart throb. Had a visit from the telephone engineer to give me a new telephone as Trixie had pulled mine off the table and broke it.

Saturday 15th Oct 1994 – Put a notice in churchyard for cremation plot for Alf Smith who has died in Cirencester. His son Michael who keeps the Golden Cross in Black Jack Street and worked with me in the Smith Shop at the East Glos, Fairford in Jack Arnold's day, rang me up to get my permission as Warden for his father and his mother to be buried there. Alf was the son of Harry Smith and lived at the Lodge at Netherton. Harry was the gardener, after my grandfather, for Edward Radway who was the estate agent and the house Sharringtons, just across the road from me, was enlarged for him about 1980. His son Alf worked at Dean Farm, then Poulton Priory, then Scantlebury in Cirencester. Married his wife in Hatherop Church, she worked at Hatherop Castle, before the Second War. I agreed to the burial as they are an old Hatherop family and it is their wish.

Thursday 27th Oct 1994 – Catch Tesco bus to the new Tesco Store at Kingsmeadow. A free trip every Thursday – a large store, have to get used to where things are – different to the Cirencester Store where I know where things are.

Sunday 6th Nov 1994 – A very foggy morning, walk to Church at 7.45am. Farmer Hart is lighting the choir candles. This seems the habit now. For some years we only lit them for big services after the electricity was put in when I was a boy. Lady Sally Worsley is giving out the books for 1662 Communion. She has just come back from a tour to Palestine – saw Galilee and the Holy City. The Rev Ross in his black cassock is sat in the Bishop's Chair near the vestry door. R Sims pulls the Sanctus Bell. The choir pews fill with communicants among them The Hon Mrs Malet, Mr and Mrs

Colby from the Hornbeams, Mrs and Miss Townsend of South Farm, Lady Howard of Dean Farm and Mr Blakeney of the Rectory – fourteen communicants with the Rector. Three parts of the village are not up.

I am wondering what will happen when the flood water comes up in the winter to the extensions which have been built to the little cottage by the meadow field at Quenington where the sewer pumps are and the willow trees are lining the banks of the River Coln. The little cottage was church property at one time and I believe it was bought by Mr Bert Harding who worked for H J Godwin in Canon Lowe's time. But every flooding time in the winter the garden is always flooded. It will be interesting to see what happens now.

Thursday 1st December 1994 – November has been the mildest November for three hundred years, the roses are in bloom in places, my dahlias are still in bloom. I walk Trixie to Coln Stores for a book of postage stamps and see Mrs Susan Vicary who told me Mrs Bennett is very ill in hospital. I told her I was sad – the last time I saw Mrs Bennett was standing at the Communion Rail in Hatherop Church a little while back taking her communion Bread and Wine. We both had some lovely talks together about the old days and had a good look at photos we both had of occasions long ago in the old Estate Days before Modern Society swept upon us all. I shall always have some happy memories of Mrs Rachel Bennett, who in my mother and father's day, was known as Miss Rachel.

Miss Rachel Bazley's wedding to Mr Ronald Bennett on 26th January 1939.

Sunday 4th Dec 1994 – Rev Tony Ross said at HE Service that Mrs Rachel Bennett had died.

Saturday 10th Dec 1994 – Go to church and two ladies were singing, practising for Mr Frazer Hart's daughter's wedding this afternoon at 2.30pm. Mr Tim Morris at the organ. Church is beautifully decorated. David Hicks Beach's wife [*Kate Henriques*] and Christa Hart singing. Lots of singing and organ playing at the wedding, church full of people, the ladies with lovely hats on. Mr James Hart brought the ringing money, £6 per bell and a bottle of champagne, we rang again when the bride and groom came out to the porch after the service. I came back home and got some glasses and we drank the wine in the tower.

Monday 12th Dec 1994 – Walk to Coln St Aldwyns Church for a Memorial Service to Mrs Rachel Bennett who was Miss Rachel Bazley when my mother worked and lived in at the Hatherop Castle in the old days. Lady Sally Worsley picked me up in her car half way down Hatherop Hill. People get to these Memorial Services half hour before the service or more nowadays. The Rev Tony Ross took the service, the Rev Hughes [*son of the author Richard Hughes who wrote 'A High Wind in Jamaica'*], Mrs Bennett's nephew, gave the address. We had some good hymn singing and the church was full. A gathering for tea was at Mrs R Bennett's home after the service. Vernon Cole of Fairford rang me up to say Chris Kinch, my former employer at the East Glos, had shot himself. I'm very sad.

Sunday 25th Dec 1994 – Could not get a set of ringers for the morning service of carols with the children present. I'm picked up by John Iles and his family, go to Wroughton for Christmas lunch with their family and brought back again around 4pm. Watched TV then went to bed.

Thursday 5th Jan 1995 – Picked up by Miss Jill Tugwell and her mother in their car and took to Fairford Parish Church for a Memorial Service to Christopher John Kinch of Claydon Cottage, Boss of the East Glos Engineering Co who committed suicide. He had a serious back problem through two falls on his back. It was making him double up and must have troubled him greatly. Fairford Church was full of people. Chris was a quiet, likeable man – came to the East Glos when his Uncle and Aunt, Ruth and John Arnold, ran the business in the 60s when I was blacksmithing and welding there. John Arnold was retiring more and Chris was running the business. A sad day, I felt it very much. After the service had a visit from Malcolm Fidler from Marston Meysey who worked there as a boy. I had not seem him for about thirty years. He now works for the water board in Hampshire and is a grandfather. I was very pleased to see him. He was mate to Vernon Cole of Fairford.

Saturday 7th Jan 1995 – Have a visit from Bill Brindle and Frank Blackwell in the afternoon. We had some homemade wine of mine, a pot of tea and some Christmas Cake which I cannot eat because of diabetes and a good chat. Watch a film on the Nazi Death Camps in Poland – showed the Camps fifty years on – a lot of them still there. I remember in Hatherop Reading Room where the Home Guard had its Headquarters, there was a paperback book which told about one of these concentration camps early in the Second War – the starving, beating and killing by the SS but we did not believe it all. After the troops had entered Belsen and a film was shown at the Regal Cinema at Cirencester I remember the deep silence in the cinema all through the film.

Thursday 19th January 1995 – Photo of William Godwin the Quenington builder in the local Standard. The date stone is built into the stone wall around the new properties that were built after his two houses were pulled down. His own house was called Woodside. The little chapel to seat about twenty people was also pulled down, a great pity. The developers said: "They wanted the stone for building at South Cerney".

Portrait of William Joynes Godwin by R Keeble Jowett c. 1887.

Saturday 21st January 1995 – Brother Roger King takes me to Cirencester Parish Church in his car, for the funeral service of Fred Moaby RAOB. Ivy leaves were placed on the coffin as it left the church.

Thursday 26th January 1995 – Walk to Quenington, have a look at Don Collett's garden and poultry then down Main Street to look at the footings to bungalows being built by Sid Bayliss Builders next to the Institute. There is lots of controversy over these dwellings. Walk round to Apple Tree Cottage – two cottages made into one house. Meadow well up with water and swans. Walk on, see the snowdrops out at Netherton Lodge, up the park and home.

Friday 27th January 1995 – Have a chat to Mrs Gwen Twining on the phone about old times when she was fourteen and worked at Coln Manor. It was when Lady Lucy St Aldwyn lived there and how she emptied the hip-bath water, drew the curtains back at 6.30am with biscuits and a glass of hot water for Lady Susan Hicks Beach before she went to Cockrup Farm at 7am. She was an authority on pigs.

Sunday 29th January 1995 – Mr Hart rings up and takes Miss Hobbs and me to Coln Church for a three parish service. Love the church, lovely service. Ring Mrs Tugwell about the photo of her grandfather [*Willam Godwin*] in the Standard. She was pleased with the dates Tarrant built into the new house boundary wall but sad her grandfather's house "Woodside" and the other house have been pulled down as they were in good condition. Her grandfather also built the Chapel of Rest in the Cemetery.

Monday 13th February 1995 – Watch the film on Bomber Harris. Remember when Goering said not a bomb would fall on Berlin. February 13th 1945 was the bombing of Dresden. How the newspapers carried on about the bombing but we had plenty of bombing here and at the time of Coventry we had nothing to stop the bombers with the V1s and V2s and the doodlebugs on London were awful. Our evacuees said those kind of bombs were worse than a normal bombing raid. Hope our people will never see a time like it again.

Monday 20th February 1995 – Took the history books and newspaper cutting of the late Kathleen Brindle to Mr Gerald Hartshorn, Foreman of Hatherop Estate. He is going to take them to Sir Thomas Bazley at Eastleach Downs Farm who is writing a history of events in the three villages.

Wednesday 1st March 1995 St David's Day – Have to go to Coln church tonight for Holy Communion Service at 7.30pm. The Bishop will be there – the Rev David Bentley. Mrs Blakeney at the Old Rectory takes me to the service. She parked her car in Mrs Bellamy's drive at the house in the old Manor garden and we walk to Coln Church. The young Earl St Aldwyn greets us as we go into the church and ushers all the visitors who come in from the five parishes. The Bishop is a very tall man and stood in the porch at our departure with Rev Tony Ross and Mr Webb Peploe. Coln church looks very well, that lovely old brass chandelier was lit with all its candles. Also the big candles on the altar. For a great number of years they were electric candles – it is good to see a proper candle being used.

Sunday 5th March 1995 – Watched 'The Buccaneers' – Edith Wharton's novel. How my mother would have liked it, she was used to working in those large country houses and that style of living. She said she finished making the beds and came down and into Hatherop Church for Matins when the Sanctus Bell was being pulled, the last five minutes before the 11am service, taking her place with the other servants behind the Bazley pews. In my Dad's time at the turn of the century, my Aunt Beatie told me the footman put their cockade hats in the window on the left hand side going into the church.

Wednesday 8th March 1995 – Walk round Coln by Percy Mustow's old Mill. Look at the old Mill building – am always fascinated by the fish weathervane – it is very good. It must have been there many years. We used to get chicken corn and meal there which we used to mix with mashed cooked potatoes for chicken food. Mrs Curteis, Joanna Trollope, who is living at the Mill House by the Stoney Path, has a play "The Choir" on TV on 19th March 1995 – must watch that.

Sunday 12th March 1995 – Walk to the church for a "Together at Ten" service. Mr Frazer Hart has lit the candles, the church fills up for a baptism. Some of the congregation are from Cornwall. Patti Schmiegelow takes the service, she has her film equipment in the nave, reminds me of the old lantern slides we had in the time of Rev Callender when I was a boy, he was a missionary with the Eskimos. We have the baptism, sing a hymn and had a cup of coffee after the service.

Sunday 26th March 1995 – A new barrier has been put in front of the School Memorial Arch. The last barrier was made of oak by my father William Sims and Leonard Miles around 1939.

Tuesday 28th March 1995 – Walk to Glebe Farm for Church Council Meeting chaired by Rev Tony Ross. We all sat round a long table, about fourteen of us. I gave up my office of Church Warden after forty three years. Mr Colby and Lady Sally Worsley were elected for the coming year. It was dark when we came away after 9pm. FORTY THREE WONDERFUL YEARS.

Wednesday 29th March 1995 – Catch the Tesco service bus to Cirencester and when the bus passes through Driffield I think of the time when I drove in Mr Reuben Briggs's car to East End, Fairford, when two bombs were dropped. Rode there on my pushbike with Bob Hutchings on the following Sunday to see two great holes in a field. Bert Ayres and his wife and son were in their home-made shelter when the German bombers dropped a string of bombs along Bell Lane, Poulton. He was shaken when he got to work the next day. Mr Briggs gave him some brandy. My father and Mr Charlie Gaiger and many of us went to see the string of bomb holes across Williamstrip Park starting inside the wall by the Pump House Lodge. They were not so large but I remember when the bombs whistled down when I was in bed at the Lodge and when Churchill broadcast "I can offer you nothing but blood, toil, tears and sweat". It seems a far cry now shopping at Tesco. We were wrong to kick him out after the war was over.

Saturday 1st April 1995 – A party being held at Williamstrip House – we had a letter telling us there would be a lot of noise. Music from the House went on until 3am Sunday morning. Went outside at 1am – all lit up over there – lots of thumping of the bass drum but nothing to interfere with sleeping.

Monday 8th May 1995 – Have a phone call from Stanley Black of Kidderminster saying did I "remember putting out the bunting and flags at the Lodge on VE Day and how my dear mother said we could have some damson wine when we had finished it?" Bob Hutchings from the Keepers Lodge at Williamstrip came and we drank the wine by the back door. We danced all night to a radiogram in a blister hanger at the top of the garden out in the Park. I said "I did and what a happy time for us all it was". Spoke to Stan's wife Beryl on the phone – she is getting better from her brain blood clot. Watch a lot of TV filmed in Hyde Park all day. Vera Lynn sang all the old War songs. Saw all the bonfires at night and the Queen switched on the lights on the Telecom Building. No country can put on shows like the British.

Thursday 18th May 1995 – See Mr Mervyn Bayliss – we talk about the wood panelling Mr Lee Bayliss, his son, put up in the choir vestry last week and the two choir seats in the chancel each side of the organ he repaired and screwed to the chancel wall. It appears they were one pew and cut in half and put there after the organ was fitted in 1868. Catch Tesco bus at the bus shelter – a first-class bus with curtains at each side-window and a television. Have a visit in the evening from Mr Edge-Partington with a copy of the Wilts and Gloucester Standard with a photo of me and his little daughter we took at the back of 17 Golden Row early in the week.

Reuben with Harriet Edge-Partington.

Saturday 20th May 1995 – Go to the First Reunion of old pupils of Hatherop School since the Twenties. Lots of pupils there. Some evacuees of the Second War. Have a good chicken lunch with coffee and a bar. Mrs Kinch from Tetbury (ninety-two years) was there. She was at the school when I started schooling aged four before the three village schools were altered and you went to Quenington, Fairford or Coln until you were seven years. I walked to Coln St Aldwyns for about two years under Miss Birks then came back to Hatherop where a new headmaster Mr Garner came in 1929. Mr Percy Garner came, the late schoolmistress Mrs Avery could not keep order and some of the pupils had to go to Fairford School under Mr Hedges. Mr Garner's two daughters were at the reunion – Joy and Poppy. I had not seen them for some years. The school pupils did a dance in the playgrounds. Saw Mrs Kinch off in her taxi. Also Mrs Beatie Smith of Quenington was there. Beatie brought me home when I was very young after getting my feet wet in the flood water which was always flooding the road in those days. I took my school photo along of 1931, just before Mrs Kinch in those days.

Hatherop School with the Reverend Cheales 1931. Far back row from left: Mary Sharps, John Iles, Reuben Sims, Megan Ferriman. Near back row: 2 unknowns, Harry Ford, Barbara Rixon, Blanche Iles. Middle row sitting: Lily Shepherd, Norman Westall, Joy Garner, Reverend Cheales, Lily Ford, Bernard Iles, Margery Sharps. Front row: D Westhall, John Garner, Ted Iles, Jim Shepherd.

Saturday 27th May 1995 – Visit from Bill Brindle and Frank Blackwell in the afternoon. They say Denis Smith's wife of Fairford Road, Quenington died yesterday. She did a lot of social work around the area in her time. Also Mrs Vincent of Fowler's Hill has died – she was a great supporter of Quenington Chapel, she was around ninety-two years old. When my mother passed away behind the Earl Grey pub in 1967 she came to see me and brought a rose and pot made by her hands. I shall never forget that. My mother had great joy at the Quenington Chapel Meetings.

Thursday1st June 1995 – A large thermometer sign is erected outside Hatherop School by the playground saying £40,000 is needed to alter the school cottages into classrooms. This does not find approval from everyone here.

Saturday 3rd June 1995 – Ringers ring the bells for the wedding of Charlotte Worsley at 11.40am under John Reeves, Ruth Mowatt, Joan Akers, John Reeves's son-in-law and Mick Adams from Lechlade. The congregation arrive, grey toppers etc. Fine singing by Helen Kucharek and Christa Hart. Organist Robert Baggs. Start ringing again as bride and groom come to main door, lots of cine cameras etc. They all go to a large marquee on the Castle South Lawn.

Charlotte Worsley's wedding day – Brigadier Alistair Mitchell, Lady Sally Worsley, Charlotte Worsley.

Monday5th June 1995 – See Lady Sally Worsley who has brought me the order of service, a piece of wedding cake and a large bunch of flowers. She is a very generous lady. Tony Nash of Fairford picks me up at 1pm with his wife and Eddie Hunt and his wife and we go to Bibury Church for the funeral of Denis Smith's wife. A lot of people there, they were married in Bibury Church fifty years ago.

Saturday 17th June 1995 – Get ready to be picked up by Alan Ayres and taken to his sister's house at Crabtree Lane for a birthday party on their mother's ninetieth birthday at 5.30pm. I worked when I was fourteen years old at Rueben Briggs Engineers with her late husband Bert in 1937. Lots of traction engine work then. Her son Alan drove me to Cirencester and we picked up Mrs Alfred Smith at the new council houses going into Cirencester on the right then went left handed to Crabtree Lane to Mrs Bert Ayers daughter's house who is Mrs Janet Bowler and there I met a lot of people from years gone by. Bert Ayers uncle's daughter Molly Lafford – we talked about her father buried in Ampney St Peter's churchyard. Uncle Hubert, a tall man who drove the Marshall Compound Traction Engine DD2007 for Rueben Briggs. The engine still goes to the traction engine rallies. He was a wonderful man. The Bowler family, father and mother of Janet's husband, knew Mr and Mrs Arthur Iles whose son Bernard came through Dunkirk and was killed just before the end of the North Africa campaign [*He was killed the day before he was due to return home*]. He is on the memorial in Kemble Church as the family moved from Hatherop to Kemble during the Second War. I went to school with Bernard. We had plenty of food, a lovely cake made by Pam Ayers. Sang Happy Birthday. Chris Bowler played his guitar we all sang well, a good party. When I worked with her late husband Bert in Brigg's blacksmith shop, the sparks flew, the forges roared and the anvils rang. Plenty of sweating work but we were a happy band of men.

Sunday 9th July 1995 – Pulled the Sanctus Bell for 'Together at Ten Service' taken by Pattie Schmiegelow. A Bishop christens a child belonging to the Owen Family [*Lily*] – the water came from the River Jordan. Hymns sung to a keyboard organ by the pulpit – lots of young people there. Mr Owen cut a large iced cake and coffee was served outside.

Helen Owen with Lily and Mrs Lemon's christening cake.

Thursday 13th July 1995 – Mr Wilfred Franklin brother of the RAOB drove me to Fairford Church for the funeral service of Brother Henry George Morley, eighty-eight years old, a member of the Order before the Second World War. He was the Manager at Gillett's grocer's shop at Lechlade and Fairford for many years. About 26 Buffaloes there, we had the Buffalo Service round the coffin in the chancel.

Thursday 20th July 1995 – A Commander from Gloucester rang me up about a stone of his family. I find the William Edgington stone near the iron railing on south side of the church. It is an upright cross. He died April 4th 1985 aged 58 years so will be able to tell the Commander when he rings again. In my grandfather's wage sheets of the Hatherop Estate 1899 Thomas Edgington's wages were two shillings a day. There were twenty men. Thomas must have been William Edgington's son.

Thursday 5th August 1995 – Another very hot day, Bill Brindle and Frank Blackwell come in the afternoon. Bill Brindle works on this greenhouse I have bought with Perspex windows. I want him to come and sit and have a chat but he will work on, then we all get at it. Bill Brindle said that the police had to open six cars at the air tattoo at Fairford because people had let their dogs suffer in the heat.

Wednesday 13th September 1995 – Go to churchyard to put some snowdrops on Kathleen and Marjorie Brindle's graves – should be nice in spring. Also George Mustow's and his brother's grave. Put some Glory of the Snow bulbs on Alice Griffin's grave – she used to live the road end of Pudding Row – her people did washing and my Aunt Beatie used to carry the washing in a basket together with Alice to Farmer Stanley Barton's at Williamstrip Farm every week when they were young.

Sunday 17th September 1995 – Have a good cold. Service at Coln Church for Harvest Festival. Rev Ross inducted as Parish Priest of the Five Parishes here by the Arch Deacon Lewis of Cheltenham. There was a lunch at Glebe Farm Hatherop for £5 for African farmers in the Glebe Barn. Two courses, one glass of wine free. I'm sorry I missed it with this cold. I counted thirty-nine cars going by from Coln to Hatherop after the Harvest Service at Coln St Aldwyns.

Saturday 23rd September 1995 – Trixie is getting old and does not want the long walks now. Likes plenty of sleep in her chair. The £40,000 for the school alterations has been reached.

Sunday 24th September 1995 – Jack Gaiger of Quenington rings me to say Vernon Cole of Top End, Fairford has passed away in his sleep. He must have been the last employee of Rueben Briggs at the East Glos, Fairford before John Arnold had the business, besides me. He worked for years with two valves in his heart, a very clever fitter and mechanic. He was around sixty-five years.

Saturday 30th September 1995 – Bill Brindle and Frank Blackwell come in the afternoon. Have whisky, tea and biscuits. We talk about everything. The new people at the Gardener's cottage of Williamstrip Estate have had the railings removed on the right hand side of the cottage as an extension is going to be built on the house. For some years after the last war Mr and Mrs Bullimore lived there when Mr Bullimore was gardener, then he moved to Coln St Aldwyns. Mrs Bullimore has died and been buried at

Quenington Cemetery. At a big fancy dress dance at Coln Village Hall in the last War she and Sybil Lander dressed up as two little girls in blue. That was when Charles Rixon dressed up in my old Victorian dress and I dressed up in my mother's fancy dress of Weldon's Fashions she made for a Fairford Carnival when I was a boy. A great night, Gwen Bailey was a Charmer and Rosie Day was Bo Peep.

Tuesday 10th October 1995 – Number 10 is for sale. These last owners have only lived in it about twelve months – Price £169,000.

Sunday 15th October 1995 – Did not go to the 'Together at Ten' service. Mona brought me an apple pie she had made out of the Bramley apples I gave her yesterday. Cooked a good lunch – good pork chops from Tesco. Made pint of custard for apple tart. Hymn singing from Coventry Cathedral in the evening on TV.

Monday 23rd October 1995 – See Jeff Telling coming out of Williamstrip House entrance. He is doing a lot of walls on the old Williamstrip Estate as the grants come through. My Aunt Beatrice and Uncle Jim Sims and his wife Minnie liked Jeff a lot. He spent a lot of time with them when they lived at Down Ampney. He said he keeps their graves up. I am pleased.

Thursday 26th October 1995 – Mrs Sinton at Coln Stores has talked me into going on a plane flight from Brize Norton in December. A trip sponsored by the Coln St Aldwyns Society. Never been up in a plane – did not go when the Home Guard were taken up in the gliders at Fairford Air Base. They had rough rides, a lot was sick. That was over fifty years ago at Arnhem time.

Monday 30th October 1995 – Have invitation to go on a plane trip by the Coln St Aldwyns Association on November 16th 1995. Plane goes from Carterton Aerodrome.

Thursday 16th November 1995 – Mrs John Winfield picks me up at 8.40am and takes me to Brize Norton together with Mrs Coates and Mrs Jock Reeves. We have a flight to the Isles north of Scotland and fly over the Isle of Mann. Have a good lunch on the plane – ham, apricots, potatoes, yoghurt, orange juice, tea, biscuits, cheese, tomato and lettuce – very nice. We fly above the clouds in the sunshine, about 200 of us.

Tuesday 21st November 1995 – Buy two newspapers to read about Princess Diana and her talk on television last night about her marriage breakup with Prince Charles.

Wednesday 22nd November 1995 – Catch Tesco bus at 9.50am. Shop at the large Tesco, not so many customers, only half the cash desks are working, the girl at the desk I went to said "they are always like this on a Wednesday" – later in the week and Sunday is a very busy day. Arrive home at 12.30pm have roast chicken for lunch – Trixie loves it. Watch football, our team against the Russians in Moscow in the cold weather, the Russian team won – good players. See the results of the West murder trial on TV.

Friday 1st December 1995 – Rosie Bailey (nee Day) rang me up at 6.30pm to tell me that Gwen had passed away. I am very sad – Gwen was a tall, lovely girl. She had a blood condition but her son has been good to her. God Bless them. She worked at Coln Manor in the time of the old Countess.

Saturday 2nd December 1995 – Bill Brindle, Frank Blackwell and Eddie Hunt arrive in the afternoon. Eddie brought a photograph of Quenington with the old factory chimney of the Rag Hill Paper Factory standing. I remember when it was felled in the 1930s before the Second War. They say it made all the frogs croak in that area. Photographs of its felling were for sale in Powell's paper shop at Fairford at the time.

The felling of the old chimney at Knight's Mill at the bottom of Rag Hill, Quenington.

Also Eddie said that they laid a sewer from the Castle sewer on the Castle bank down and across the Grandage by the old swimming pool to the covert out in the Grandage. One of the sewer inspection covers can still be seen by the old swimming pool.

Tuesday 5th December 1995 – The county council workmen with a crane on a lorry have taken our red telephone box away from its position in the centre of the village, where Mr Reece, then Mr and Mrs Charlie Rixon kept a shop and post office. Now the estate has sold the property, the owners want the red telephone box moved. It is going to be placed opposite the village school by the bus shelter.

Saturday 9th December 1995 – Trixie staggers around – call the vet out from Lechlade. He said she has arthritis in her back legs and maybe her kidneys are failing – she is fourteen years old. Have to take her to the surgery at Lechlade on Monday morning.

Monday 11th December 1995 – Ian Patheyjohns takes me and Trixie to the vet at Lechlade. He takes a blood sample and will let me know what her condition is. Come home and see a car is turned upside down on the side of the Lechlade Road by the Hatherop Downs crossroad. Sandwiches are by the side of the car, the windows are smashed, no one in the car. Phone Mr Davies at 4.30pm – Trixie has a kidney complaint and arthritis in her back legs. He will post me some tablets but cannot do much owing to her age.

Friday 15th December 1995 – Trixie better on her legs. Watched the TV a lot. I am very deaf – use the deaf aid but it is a very mechanical sound.

Thursday 21st December 1995 – Have visit from Mr Hart who wants me to come to the Farm House at 6.30pm tomorrow evening to hear the children sing the carols and have glass of wine. Evening news full of the Prince of Wales divorce.

Sunday 24th December 1995 – Christmas Eve, midnight service at Coln St Aldwyns church. No service at Hatherop Church, never known it before. Had a Christmas present from Mrs Susan Vicary at this morning's service – she was there with Lady Howard. A cold day, staying with Trixie who is not well, getting weaker. I stayed up to see the singers at the Beaulieu Abbey and the dinner in the Great Hall – all that Henry VIII left of the Abbey and the choir boys singing the carols in York Minster at midnight. Carry Trixie upstairs to bed, her back legs all weak. I suppose after Christmas I shall have to have her put to sleep. I dread it.

Christmas Day 25th December 1995 – A frosty morning. Leave Trixie upstairs – she does not want to come down. My friend John Iles and his son-in-law Bert come with their car, they take me to Wroughton and I have a good Christmas Dinner with the family. I'm home again before 4pm. I see Trixie upstairs, bring her down and put her in her chair to see the Queen's Speech and also a tour of Westminster Abbey. When I looked round Trixie had slipped out of the chair and had joined the departed. What a friend she has been to me. On my weekly walks to Coln Stores for my pension, round Hatherop churchyard nearly every day, up the tower steps to the ringing room many times. Always at the door when I returned home after band practice for church services. Thirteen years of pleasure, she was fourteen years old.

Boxing Day 26th December 1995 – A bitter, frosty morning – 5° of frost. Have a job to dig a grave for Trixie by the hedge in my garden – feel great sorrow. She never turned her back on me and was always pleased to see me when I came home. Bury Trixie. Will have to put some crocus bulbs on her grave when the frost has gone. Will always remember this Christmas night. Tell Ian Patheyjohns Trixie has passed to the other world – he is very sorry.

Wednesday 27th December 1995 – Walk to Coln Stores, draw pension, walk back home, missed my old friend Trixie.

Friday 29th December 1995 – Ian Patheyjohns and Elaine take me to Burford Blue Cross centre. Have a look at a lot of stray dogs. None really that suit me – sign up the introduction papers. £50 donation if I have a dog.

Sunday 31st December 1995 – Stay up and watch the New Year in. Do not go much on these pop group shows. Drink a glass of sherry at the back door here at Golden Row at midnight. Did not see anyone all day.

Wednesday 3rd January 1996 – Plant some crocus bulbs on Trixie's grave. Walk to the churchyard and plant a lot of bulbs on my grandfather's grave, should be lovely in the spring.

Thursday 4th January 1996 – Frank Law and his friend Margery visit me in the afternoon. We have some ginger wine and some biscuits. Tell them Trixie has gone and the Blue Cross Dog's Home want a £50 donation if I have a dog from there, also they must see my house before letting me have a dog. Marge brought me cake and mince pies – I must be careful eating them with my diabetes.

Sunday 7th January 1996 – Communion at Hatherop church at 11am – I did not get up in time. Watch Songs of Praise from Leeds in the evening. Miss Trixie very much.

Thursday 11th January 1996 – Miss Janet Hobbs comes here when I tell her it is my birthday today and brings me a bunch of daffodils the following day. Have five birthday cards – 73 years old – how time flies.

Sunday 28th January 1996 – Have visit from the lady [*Judy Francis*] at Williamstrip Gardener's Cottage who teaches at Hatherop school for me to take the schoolchildren up the church tower tomorrow morning.

Monday 29th January 1996 – Go to the church put all the lights on and meet the children of Hatherop School. Tell them what I know about the church. Take two lots of children up the tower – around twenty in all – show them the ringing room and the clock room. Some had a peep at the bells and touched the clock bell. Quite an ordeal for me.

Monday 5th February 1996 – The railways went back to private ownership yesterday – it has been quite a task, I hope it succeeds. We took them from the private companies fifty years ago and it will take some time to get them running well again. Call from Northleach undertakers – have to meet them in churchyard at 9am tomorrow morning about the burial of someone to do with the Birtles family who have a boy buried on the south side of the church. We are getting short of burial space now.

Tuesday 6th February 1996 – Snowing more or less all day, brought havoc to the roads as everyone has a car now or goes by bus. I walk to the churchyard to meet Mike Gulwell of Norman, Trotman and Hughes to decide on a grave for a relation of the Birtles at the west end [*Frances, Hilary Birtle's sister*]. We have enough graves for about thirty people. Hatherop School has been closed, no teachers come in.

Wednesday 7th February 1996 – Hatherop Schools still closed, never known it before. Temperature has been around freezing all day. Come inside and cook a good lunch, light a good fire, stay by it and watch TV. It was like this in 1942 when my father died and it took eight bearers to carry him through the park gates and across the Park which was his wish. Today 4 inches of snow and there is complete chaos. The Marchant Bus was due for Tesco but did not arrive.

Thursday 8th February 1996 – Plenty of trouble on the roads, so much is carried by large lorries today, plenty come through this little village of Hatherop. Ring Marchant's of Cheltenham – the bus is trying to get to the Tesco store. Wait half an hour in the bus shelter, bus does not arrive. The church was full of mourners for the Birtle's funeral this afternoon, some came from as far away as Hereford.

Sunday 11th February 1996 – Pulled the Sanctus Bell for the 'Together at Ten' service. A baptism service by Mrs Price. Lots of babies in Hatherop now. No-one there I know, all my Cotswold people have gone. The congregation have coffee after the service. The teacher of Hatherop

School [*Judy Francis*] brought me some tobacco in the afternoon for taking the children up the tower. Jack Smith a boy next door to me, brought me a card he had written on behalf of the school, he is a nice lad.

Reuben with the Sanctus Bell in Hatherop Church.

Wednesday 6th March 1996 – Mr F Hart rings me in the evening to say a Miss Cheales had left Hatherop Church £250 and who was she? I told him she must be the daughter of the late Rev Cheales who is buried at either Coln Rogers or Coln St Dennis.

Sunday 10th March 1996 – Do not go to the 'Together at Ten' service, have walk in the churchyard. Watch a good film on a member of the aristocracy who was a pacifist and helped a lot of Jews against Hitler in the last war. Helmut von Moltke, the Nazis killed him but his large family house is now an international meeting place. ['*The Restless Conscience: Resistance to Hitler Within Germany 1933–1945' was a 1992 American documentary film directed by Hava Kohav Beller. It was nominated for an Academy Award for Best Documentary Feature.*]

Thursday 14th March 1996 – Go to Hatherop Church at 1.15pm for the funeral of Gordon Legg, tractor driver on Glebe Farm. He had been ill for some months with blindness from sugar diabetes. His wife had looked after the village club for some years. We had three hymns at the service – Lady Penelope Robson played the organ. I sat in my old choir pew. His family were all present and many others.

Friday 22nd March 1996 – Go to Hatherop School at 1.15pm for a practice class of the school pupils for a parent visit later on to hear their singing. I told them something of my days at school when Mr Garner used the cane and kept us in order. And how my uncle Jim Sims had a cut mark on his forehead where Miss Marsden threw a ruler at a boy who was misbehaving – he ducked and it hit my uncle who was sitting behind. He was also naturally left-handed, so to make him write with the right hand, he had his left hand tied behind his back. Also how Miss Marsden used to walk that large classroom saying "I am not afraid of a regiment of soldiers" and used to hit the boys across the shoulders if she saw them stone throwing at the weekend with a faggot stick from the boiler house which has now gone.

Sunday 14th April 1996 – Have a baptism service during the 11 o'clock Communion Service – one of the Burton family. Mr Nigel Voaden told me the old rack saw bench, the old saws and the old creosote pit at the old saw shed have gone and a concrete floor put in for the new industrial developments. Wonder what my father would have said about that. He used to wind the old rack bench when they sawed down trees from end to end. Joe Thorn, who had a crook on one arm in a traction engine accident, used to drive the old 10 horsepower portable steam engine. It also drove another saw bench across the other side of the shed for cutting across timber. In my time Marine George Hemmings used to drive the portable engine. After him, the lovely old engine with its large flywheel was scrapped and a tractor used. Never the same power and you have to understand steam.

Monday 15th April 1996 – Mr Gerald Hartshorn comes and gets the riddler going on my Parkray stove. I told him I'd heard that the old saw shed had been cleared out. He said "No, the Long Farm sheds have been cleared out and all the stuff put in the saw shed. The sheds have a cement base put in." So my old dad would not be so disappointed after all.

Wednesday 24th April 1996 – Catch Tesco bus at 9.50am. Meet Mrs Lucy Thomas of Quenington – I went to Hatherop School with her in the 30s. Lucy went in the Army in the Second War. We looked for the Memorial to the Jubilee Bonfire in 1935 – George V's Silver Jubilee – in the field at Ready Token when we came back on the bus. Lucy said it must have been moved.

Sunday 28th April 1996 – Walk to Coln St Aldwyns Church at 7.25am. A nice fine morning, plenty of cars in the streets and drives of the properties in Hatherop and Coln St Aldwyns. A good Communion Service at 8am taken by the Rev Tony Ross – about twenty people there. Lovely Communion rails in Coln St Aldwyns Church. David Hicks Beach took the collection. Meet my two friends from the Williams family of Coln St Aldwyns who have come over for seven weeks from Oregon USA. They are staying at number 5 Meadowside. I believe these houses were to do with the malt making years ago.

Wednesday 1st May 1996 – A wet day, catch bus the Kingsmeadow Tesco and do my shopping. See Mr Norman Tarrant in the evening. He has been to Cirencester in the afternoon and brought me a leaflet on Cirencester bus times. We have a very poor public service to Cirencester. Have written to Shire Hall and complained and also written to Clifton Brown our MP. Our village bus service to Cirencester depends on my voting Tory at the next election. So many people drive cars today – unmarried women go to work and they do not need the bus service. Only people like me who cannot drive a car, have no relations and live on their own.

Friday 10th May 1996 – A RAF military funeral of Corporal John Hague killed out in Bosnia. He lived in one of the houses made out of the barns at Barrow Elm. Lots of RAF personnel from Brize Norton present. Wonderful flowers and a firing party.

Sunday 12th May 1996 – Together at Ten service. Mrs Hart played the organ. Patty Price took the service. A young girl from the Hornbeams, Antonia Faulkner, who does a lot in the church with Sally Worsley was baptised. Lots of young people there.

Thursday 16th May 1996 – Talk to Stan and Rose Bailey on the coach to Tesco. Talk about the all-night vigil in Hatherop Church at the death of Anthony Bazley in 1937 just after George VI coronation when we had a dinner in the stable rooms and sports on Williamstrip Cricket Field. In the evening Ian Patheyjohns brings me a lost West Highland Terrier – I'm keeping her all night.

Friday May 17th 1996 – Walk the terrier to Coln Stores, put a notice of lost dog in window, walk home, see lady in car by Williamstrip House entrance who is looking for the terrier. She is lost from Hatherop Castle School. Go to the Castle and take the dog back – see the painting on the stairs and the old oak panelling my father used to repair years ago when it was a private house. The lady thanks me for bringing the dog back. I come back along the yew tree walk – see the old kitchen gardens are grown over with grass and apple trees growing among it. How times have changed.

It is announced in the Standard paper that Mrs Joan Radway died in Cirencester Hospital on the 12th May 1996 – wife of Sid Radway of Fairford. Joan was one of the Malton family that lived in one of the bottom houses at Hatherop Downs. I remember when the system of schools were changed and Eric and Joan walked to Coln St Aldwyns School till they were seven years old. Then back to Hatherop School till fourteen years old. The first morning we started there, Miss Birks the teacher, played the piano and we sung "Tell Me the Old, Old Story". She was 73 years old, same age as me.

Sunday 26th May 1996 – Mona rings me up to say Gladys Wheeler has died in Paternoster House. She was the wife of Harold Wheeler whose people lived in No 45 the Lodge years ago. She has been in poor health for some years. When her husband Harold lived in the semi-detached house near Glebe Farm, he was the carter with the horses. He told me his grandfather said they dug the De Mauley crypt by lantern light. She is 84 years old. What a wonderful pair she and her husband were at the village dances. How she kept their house so spotless and lovely shining brass, when I used to go watch their television for the cup final, when we had no electric at the Lodge.

Tuesday 28th May 1996 – Meet the Rev Tony Ross in Hatherop Churchyard just before lunchtime to find the Wheeler graves where Dot Amer wants Gladys Wheeler to be buried. We try to find a place near where their child is buried. He also comes with me to make his first visit to Hatherop ringing tower and saw the fine church clock in its case and the bells.

Sunday 2nd June 1996 – The plot has been dug for Mr Pat Patheyjohns and Mrs Harold Wheeler. Knock on the door in the afternoon and Janet Bowler has brought her mother to see me in her car, we have a good chat, she will be 92 years old on 18th June.

John "Pat" Patheyjohns 1996.

Monday 3rd June 1996 – Today I was reminded when my father used to tell the tale of when the Rev Davies was walking down Hatherop Hill when the borehole was being bored in the spinney by the pump house. He saw a boy and he asked him: "Who is at the borehole, my boy?" the boy says: "Mr West and Mr Birch, Levi Cox and Salty Church". Mr West was Foreman Carpenter, Mr Birch was on the estate – not the labouring classes. Levi Cox was the blacksmith at the bottom of the hill who used to come to receive instructions from my grandfather about how many gate hinges to make and have a glass of beer. Salty Church was an old sailor. My grandfather had to give up the Foreman's job in favour of Mr Radway of Park Farm, Ampney Crucis because he was not gentleman enough. This was in 1910.

Tuesday 4th June 1996 – See Mona who said she went to the burial of Gladys Wheeler's ashes. She saw Dot Herbert (married name Amer) Gladys's sister and the Hodder Family. What a lovely church couple Harold and Gladys were. The sale notice of what is called Pump House the Lodge at the bottom of the hill still remains, the wing is still being built on, tennis courts, garnishes, a lot of building has been done in these last few years.

Wednesday 19th June 1996 – Catch Tesco bus at bus shelter and do shopping at the Kingsmeadow store. Lots of ladies on the bus talking about the BSE disease with cattle. Mr Lander of Home Farm has had a lot of his dairy cows slaughtered to comply with the Common Market. I voted for the market but do not agree with this federalism. Each nation has its own identity – we certainly have ours. Jack Gaiger of Fowler's Hill Quenington rung me – he would like me to go to the Buffalo Order Meetings at Quenington Institute but I do not feel like being picked up now my hearing is not good.

Thursday 18th July 1996 – Have visit from Mrs Christine Morley of Fairford – daughter of Mrs Barbara Patheyjohns at the village shop here number 12. She has brought her wonderful collection of village photos and she looked at my mother's collection of photos and took some of them to be copied. We spent a long afternoon looking at old photos.

Saturday 20th July 1996 – Mona got my bread this morning and left her car at the Croft [*Fairford*]. Had her car door bashed in – she believes it was Dr Shaw who had backed out of his garage and went away while she was shopping. Had a visit from Mrs Charlie Barnett's niece, I had not seen her since before the War. Her son and daughter-in-law had a walk to the Barnett graves while we had a chat about the old Estate Days. The joint of ham on the bone at Christmas Supper at Barnett's at the Bothy when I was a boy, and the mashed potatoes and the big tart at supper time. Charlie Barnett used to tell my Dad he was on the wheel, so had to stoke the boilers before supper time. How he called his wife Sam and she brought in the food and we all came away about 10pm. Mr Gurney sang Old King Cole – his wife prompted him. Wonderful days.

Sunday 28th July 1996 – Do not feel well so do not go the Communion Service this morning. Thought about the photo I loaned to Mrs Robert [*Christine*] Morley of Fairford of the estate workers at Frances Bazley's wedding at the Castle with Mr and Mrs Harry Smith on it – Robert Morley's grandfather and grandmother. Mrs Smith told my mother and me that when the choir vestry was put up in Hatherop Church made out of the pews with the main door they called it the The Cow Stall. This was so as to

Staff and Estate workers outside Hatherop Castle 1932.

have a group choir which paraded to the choir stalls in the chancel at every morning and evening service as they did in my day. Sadly no choir today.

Monday 5th August 1996 – A gentleman has picked all the gooseberries on the bush growing on top of the Meadow wall going into Coln St Aldwyns. The bush has been there some years.

Tuesday 6th August 1996 – Postman on strike for more money. Their Union leader said they were the only body of men working a six-day week for £10,000 a year. What a carry on.

Monday 12th August 1996 – Have a chat with Mrs Ellen Townsend. She is a little older than me – seventy-four in October. She left school at the half term and I left school the following Easter. She went to work at a big house by Poulton Church with Mrs Lily Reeves. Lived in of course. I asked her where all the silver cups and trays went which used to be in the window of Mrs Clifford's house situated on the top of the hill going down to Percy Mustow's farm at Quenington. She did not know but she said: "There was also a sideboard full of them inside the room which I cleaned when I worked there". In these days they would be stolen. Theft and corruption is the sign of the times today.

Friday 16th August 1996 – See Mrs Dennis Bartlett at Dean Row on my way down to Coln. She said "Buster Sharps's wife had died – she had been ill some time.

Saturday 24th August 1996 – Last weekend in Coln St Aldwyn the cars were stopped going through the street and given a ticket for a cream tea at one of the bottom houses by the River Coln. In return they put money in collecting boxes – they raised £1,000 for the restoration of the Coln Church Bells.

Monday 24th August 26th 1996 – See lady with her family looking at Golden Row. She said she had come from Nottingham and was an evacuee here in the Second World War. She had seen the school where she was educated by Mr Percy Garner and remembered Harry Sharps who played the melodium in the cottage. I told her it is a holiday cottage now. She also remembered riding on the back of the soldiers' motorcycles down Hatherop Hill. She was now going to Quenington to see the Pig and Whistle public house which I told her was now closed but the house is still there. She remembered Desmond Westhall who had diabetes and had injections and lived at the end of this road near the Sharp's Cottages. I told her he was now dead. She went away pleased with her visit. Walk to Glebe Farm in the evening and see Mrs Fraser Hart who told me she would pick me up at 10 o'clock to drive me to Gloucester Cathedral on Wednesday morning for the burial service of the Venerable Eric Evans, Dean of St Paul's London. I had a Christmas card from him every Christmas while he was at St Paul's. He took a gallon of wheat wine away with him when he went back once after we had supper at the Rev Murray's house at Coln St Aldwyns opposite the New Inn. He loved my wheat wine.

Tuesday 27th August 1996 – Ride to Fairford on my cycle to Wilmot and Co. Saw Jim Luce of Lechlade in the Market Place – told him I had finished banding and would not be playing the Eb Bass again so could he pick the instrument up when he was calling this way. I started playing when Fairford Band started again after the Second World War in 1947 when the members had their meeting in the old infant School, now a public library. They brought in their dusty instrument cases and played the March "The First Parade". I started from there with two nights a week practice then with plenty of contests at Oxford and Witney, always playing by King Alfred statue at Wantage on the way to Reading.

Wednesday 28th August 1996 – Mrs Ros Hart takes me, Lord Wigram and Mrs Malet to Gloucester Cathedral for the funeral service of the Venerable Eric Evans. The cathedral was full, the bells rung muffled.

Sunday 1st September 1996 – A fine baptism service at 11 o'clock of James Hart's child – Mr and Mrs Hart's grandchild. Communion during the service, seventy-three communicants.

Monday 16th September 1996 – Mrs Cox's Lodge at Coln St Aldwyns is being cleared out. She has been put in a home – she is ninety-six years old.

Wednesday 18th September 1996 – Talk to Mr Mervyn Bayliss by bus shelter while waiting for Tesco bus. He has got his wife home again from hospital and she is getting better. Have lovely long chats with Mr and Mrs Stan Bailey on the bus. Rose, Stan's wife, shows me some photos of my mother on a coach trip and one in Fairford Market Place. They must be before I was born as we do not know all the people there. This was in the days before holidays. Mrs Lucy Abel Smith is picking me up at 5 o'clock Saturday to meet others to talk about Cotswold people as we are a rare breed now.

Friday 20th September 1996 – See Mr Dennis Bartlett who said was I going to the Rangoon Pub on the Welford Road on Sunday with the Buffalo Order. I told them I was engaged as I was being picked up to go to Mrs Delma Clements at Quenington to lunch, as Peggy, daughter of Ethel Burge, was coming from Chipping Sodbury. My mother was housemaid at Hatherop Castle with Ethel Burge, Gussie Burge and Margery Tucker from Bristol. The Burge Family were the first family she came to know when she came to work at the Castle.

Sunday 22nd September 1996 – Walk to church and pull bell – people come in for service and baptism. Collapsed during the service. Took by ambulance to Cirencester Hospital. Brought home again on Thursday afternoon 26th September.

Friday 27th September 1996 – Mona visits me in the afternoon. She has been very good to me. Saw Peggy and Keith while I was in hospital and also Mrs Delma Clements from Quenington who I was going to have lunch with on Sunday. The collapse put all things out of gear.

Wednesday 16th October 1996 – The old bungalow belonging to Mr and Mrs Dingle, the bus proprietor, has been pulled down and two houses are going to be built on the site – the old petrol pump and all has gone.

Monday 21st October 1996 – Look in at the old Hatherop Castle Gardens. Michael Murby with a digger has levelled the entrance and gravelled it. Mr Grey of No 9 has taken the gardens on from Sir Thomas Bazley but it must be organic. It is very overgrown – lots of people have had these gardens but not made much success. In the old days five or six people worked in the gardens. Little box hedges about 12" high grew round the borders of the patches. It was all dug with garden forks. With modern machinery it could be good again. The large greenhouse is in very poor condition – it will take a lot of work to put that right. A bunch of grapes hangs on a vine against the wall.

Wednesday 23rd October 1996 – Ted Peare rung me to say my old friend Eddie Hunt had died.

Thursday 31st October 1996 – Walk to the churchyard and plant some crocus bulbs on Tom Ambidge's grave. He lived in this Golden Row Cottage with his Mum and Dad years ago. He was a bachelor and worked in Cirencester and at Brize Norton Drome. His money was left to Fairford Hospital but he had no headstone. I put some daffodil bulbs on his grave some years back. Thought I would improve it with crocuses – they are always early in the spring before the mowing season. Think about my old friend Eddie Hunt who I worked with at Fairford Camp. I shall miss his visits to me. He was a good RC – his church was at Horcott at Fairford.

Thursday 7th November 1996 – Funeral of my great friend Eddie Hunt at Kingsdown crematorium, no flowers, only the family. A fine man.

Eddie Hunt.

Friday 8th November 1996 – Go to Sally Worsley's at Fir Tree Cottage at 12.30pm for lunch and the presentation of a glass chalice to Mrs Robinson who was our PCC Secretary for about twenty-five years and now lives at Faringdon. Then fish pie lunch and afters. I took a bottle of white wine from Tesco.

There is an article about the Earl Grey Pub in the local news and how it is going to be turned into a private home. It was the public house where my dad used to go when Jimmy Strange ran it. He drew the beer from the barrel and it was drunk out of clay mugs. I have one of the mugs with me now. A good collection of matchboxes were on a ledge around the walls now long gone. I got a couple of bottles of Garner's beer when my father was ill. Jimmy Strange gave me £1 to give to my mother when my father died in 1942. My father used to sharpen his woodsaws and keep his bar clocks going.

Saturday 9th November 1996 – Give my Eb Bass of Fairford Silver Band back to Cecil Voaden. The band wants it for the Armistice Parade at Fairford. Also my blazer bought from Edmond's shop in Fairford, a lyre, valves springs and felt pads, a new mouthpiece I bought and the instrument strap.

Sunday 10th November 1996 – Hatherop Church at 10.35am – lights all on, Sally Worsley, Farmer Hart, Mr Colby with his bow tie were there. Mr Murray-Walker was the clergyman who took the service. Mr Colby put the wreath on the nail above the War Memorial. R Sims read out the names of the fallen of the three villages. Mr Hart read out "They shall not grow old as we that are left grow old". We sung 'Valiant Hearts' and 'O God our Help in Ages Past'. We had the two-minute silence and the Last Post and Reveille were played on the recorder. The first time I'd ever heard that. The church was well attended and the Bazley pews were empty. I never saw a medal. When I was a boy it was the clink of the metals being worn by the servicemen that took your attention. Times have gone by. But everyone thought a good service.

Sunday 1st December 1996 – Have visit from Mr Fraser Hart with a good plan of Hatherop Church on vellum and some writings I had put with them in 1957. He also brought a plan of the church when De Mauley enlarged it and a plan of Hatherop School before the small classroom was built. Watch a film about the bomb in a suitcase set to kill Hitler in an army hut in Germany after which Rommel took his life. I remember that time. He was given a state funeral.

Sunday 8th December 1996 – Service for families – Together at Ten with preacher Mrs Patty Price. I did not go, stayed in all day and kept fire going. Watched the film "The Longest Day" in the evening – 6th June 1944. I remember the planes flying over here with their white stripes on. We did not have the German Bombers over here at night after that.

Wednesday 11th December 1996 – Mr Hart rung me up about old Farmer Bush's grave which we have interest on a sum of money to keep it up. He thought as times have gone on and there is only my generation left who remembers him, it would be better to put the capital to the Radcliffe Hospital as it states in the will. I agree with him and we will have talk about it in the future when we compile the new churchyard plan. I told him old Farmer Bush wore a cap and leggings and I have seen him winding the separator to get the cream and Mrs Bush, a large lady with a rosy face, patting the butter which was made from the Jersey cows. Mr Bush used to get my father to shoot some of the fan-tailed pigeons when they became too numerous. Mrs Bush went to the almshouses at Eastleach when they finished with Home Farm. At the sale of the farm, the Jersey cow "Hatherop Maid" fetched £8. Their daughter Mary, who used to sing the hymn 'Jerusalem the Golden', had consumption TB and I remember going to see her with my mother when she was in those open air beds at Standish. [*Standish VA Hospital at Stonehouse, Gloucestershire – unusually for a Red Cross auxiliary hospital, Standish remained a hospital after the war and became an important local facility for the next 85 years, specialising first in tuberculosis and later orthopaedic and respiratory care. It was also unusual in that most of the VAD nursing staff were able to live on site. Built around 1830 and originally a private house belonging to Lord Sherborne, the building and its 31 acre grounds became a Tuberculosis Sanatorium in 1921. Despite a long and vigorous campaign by the local community to keep the hospital open, it was closed in 2004 and the site sold off in 2006.*]

Saturday 14th December 1996 – Wait at bus shelter for stagecoach bus to Cirencester at 8.45am but bus does not arrive. This is a poor service to Cirencester now, so many services have been cut off, so many people in the villages have one or two cars. Long gone are the days when Cowman Westall, at 16 Golden Row, milked the cows at Glebe Farm up to the Second War for £1.16s a week, no holidays, only Bank Holidays. But one could walk the streets without fear of being mugged.

Wednesday 18th December 1996 – Have visit from the Rev Tony Ross to see I am all right. Show him my grandmother's family Bible. I keep it on a little round table my father made for my sister. George Mustow said a year's wages in those days bought one of those Bibles.

Monday 23rd December 1996 – Mr Derek Musty comes in the evening with a clock from the Fairford Silver Band for my fifty years of service with the Band and my Christmas cards from the Band. I gave him some cards to take back.

Tuesday 24th December 1996 – Visit from Mona with a Christmas present and a card, go to see Mr Blakeney at the Old Rectory after a phone call about a Christmas present from the younger boys. On my walk to Coln St Aldwyns see Mr Sid Bayliss – he showed me a strip of wood he took out of Williamstrip House bakery with my grandfather's brother's name [*John Sims*] on and a date 1879. He and his wife Julie are buried at the south side of Coln St Aldwyns Church.

Hatherop United Football Club 1908 with John Sims in the front row. Back row from left: William Sims, A Timbrel, W Sharps, John Lander, J Smith, T Pea, W Winstone. Front row from left: Charlie Barnett, John Sims, H White, H Smith, B Wheeler, Fred Kiddle, J Wheeler.

Midnight Mass at Hatherop Church. Farmer Hart is pulling the Sanctus Bell. The church is full of people from the five parishes. I carry on pulling the bell till the Rev Tony Ross, Mr Webb Peploe and a visiting clergyman come out of vestry and start the service. Choir stalls full of people who have not been for a long time. We sing hymns, have a sermon and Communion. A packed church when we came out. In the old days the Tower Bells would have been ringing, perhaps another time. The next day my old friend John Iles sent his son-in-law to pick me up and take me to their house in Wroughton where I spent Christmas.

Sunday 29th December 1996 – The little cottage that the Village and District used for nurses, which was sold here some years back and has been extended and occupied by various people has now been opened again. The overgrown gardens have had the brushwood cut down, smoke has been coming out of the chimney and lights on in the bedrooms at night. Lots of these Cotswold houses have been bought for people to spend a week's holiday in "Country Cottages" for around £200. Will let you know in due course.

Wednesday 8th January 1997 – On the ITV News at 6.30pm Coln Church is shown with Rev Tony Ross and the writer Joanna Trollope on the footpath to the church – a tape recording of the bells was being played. Joanna Trollope is a great help to Coln Church. Mears and Stainbank, Whitechapel was shown who are repairing the bells which are the finest light eight in Gloucestershire. Mrs Mellor and Ms Burkes were also shown. It is said that the bells were rung for Trafalgar and also after

Waterloo and at the end of the South African War. They were also rung at the end of the Second War when I was at a dance at Coln Village Hall. We went outside to hear the bells ring. All bells were silent during the War only to be rung for invasion in 1940. Thank the Good Lord it never happened. Hope the £100,000 for the repair of the bells at the Church will come – there are people here now who are good at fundraising.

Saturday 11th January 1997 – Have seven cards for my 74th birthday. One from Mona when she got my bread and a bottle of orange squash from Fairford. The Hon Mrs Cherry Malet brought me a card, bottle of sherry and a lovely cyclamen plant. I am very pleased, she is a fine Lady. Ian and Elaine bring me cards and a good stew – will have tomorrow. Chris and Bob Morley send me cards, also Mrs Susan MacKenzie brings me a card and a lovely cake. The best birthday I have had in years.

Wednesday 15th January 1997 – Go with Ian and Elaine to Cheltenham in their car and buy a Falcon smoking pipe at Tobacco World in the Arcade off the spiral car park. You cannot buy these pipes locally any more. I stepped on mine and broke it. I had not seen this Arcade before, yet have marched many times with the Brass Band down the promenade years ago. I am very pleased buying the new Falcon Pipe.

Thursday 16th January 1997 – Stay in bed late where it is warm then get up have some porridge and a pot of tea. Light fire. Have two herrings for tea I bought yesterday, watch TV. Princess Diana has been to Angola, saw the children with their legs blown off with landmines, she is supporting the Red Cross against countries using landmines and the tragedies they produce.

Wednesday 29th January 1997 – Catch Tesco bus and do my shopping. As we go out of Coln St Aldwyns, along the Aldsworth Road past the Dean Farm turning, I always look on the left hand side at the place where the Knoll Barn used to stand. It was pulled down by the late Earl St Aldwyn. We used to go in 1940 when I was 17 to look for the German paratroopers – you could see over a wide area. At dawn and just before sundown, a Church Army van was there for us to get in if it was wet. I used to go with Fred Wall of Dean Row, met him at Coln St Aldwyns Post Office where the telephone is. This building was put up after the War in stone, as the late Earl would not have a red kiosk. I remember well meeting Fred just before dawn there and walking to the Knoll Barn. It was surrounded by a Cotswold wall – all I can see today is some bushes. We used to have a rifle and five rounds of ammunition. When dawn had come, we used to come home and go to work. This type of action was also done at the top of Hatherop Castle Tower.

Wednesday 12th February 1997 – Watch a good program on the Aristocracy 1945–1970. How the Labour Government under Mr Attlee taxed them 80% and heavy death duties which many of them paid because they died before the time ran out. How we lost 400 country homes, at one time two a week pulled down. Then the National Trust told the government we were losing too many houses which were all National Heritage. Then it stopped. Some like Longleat, which I went to in 1949 on the back of Hutching's motorbike, brought in lions to entertain the public. It would have been a pity if such a house was pulled down. It was the gentry's money that paid for the Welfare State but whatever happens our gentry will be the gentry – a class on their own, marrying into peerage stock very resilient. I agreed like most people this should happen but not now – state ownership was not successful. My mother, though having no money, did not agree with the extent of the taxing of the rich. As Mr Morrison our MP said after five years of the Socialists: "The cry has been 'soak the rich' – well the rich have been well and truly soaked". I have not voted socialist since. When I was a boy the ex-servicemen used to go to Hatherop Castle and have a good dinner with Commander Cadogan including my father who had a marvellous time.

Wednesday 19th February 1997 – See a good program in the evening on the changing times for the aristocracy – how one family sold their house after a thousand years of history to a miner who was going to keep it going.

Saturday 1st March 1997 – A national outcry about shortage of drinking water in the future. The old Artesian borehole pipes still pour out the water that flows into the Coln River.

Thursday 6th March 1997 – Go to Mrs Malet for bread and cheese lunch for Lady Worsley's lunches in aid of Southern India. See Mrs Susan Vicary who said her son did buy the old nurse's cottage next to Maulden House but sold it to a friend of his and is doing it up.

Monday 17th March 1997 – Walk down to Mrs K Winfield's Lodge to see about starting my toy Bowman's steam engine which I gave her late husband but she was out.

Friday 21st March 1997 – Walk down Coln Street to Mrs Kathleen Winfield's Lodge. See Mrs Winfield and we go to the garden shed and find the Bowman Steam Engine. We were going to start it up but the boiler filler safety valve is missing so we could not do anything. She will try and get one from a model shop in Cirencester then we will have another go at getting the model going. My father bought it for me when we came back from a holiday at Sturminster Newton with my mother's mother. Of course there was no paid holiday then – he paid 16s 6d for it from Matthew's shop in Cricklade Street. My father used his last pound note and told me not to tell my mother. I never did. It was good to see the old engine of 1935 again.

Thursday 10th April 1997 – Mr Gerald Hartshorn takes me in his car to Mr Fred Murray's funeral at Quenington church at 1.30pm. Fred was a Hurricane pilot in World War II. I played a lot of cricket with Fred in the 50s and 60s for Williamstrip Cricket Club. We had some fine times, cricket local and Gloucester and Cheltenham, stopping at the Five Mile public house on the Gloucester Road on our return. We had some wonderful games of cricket, all going together and coming back together. My father used to hit the ball into the Ampney Brook. They used to come home on the trolley with the horse after a night at the Crown Inn. Lots of people at Fred's funeral – Peter Cook, Chris Moaby, Gerald and myself of the old team – lots gone now. Mrs Rose Bailey was there. She used to go and visit Fred I believe after he lost his wife twelve months ago. A good send off for Fred Murray, a big built man who loved life.

Thursday 17th April 1997 – Have heard our landlord Sir Thomas Bazley has died – the great supporter of the Liberal Party.

Sir Thomas Bazley at the Bledisloe Cup Presentation in 1951. From left: Earl Bathurst, Jack Sainsbury, Sorrel Taylor, Mervyn Bayliss, Sir Thomas Bazley.

Saturday 19th April 1997 – Catch bus for Cirencester at bus shelter at 8.45am. The only service bus to Cirencester for country shoppers in the week as so many people have their own cars now. A busy morning, buy towels at Rackams and a white Common Prayer Book at Smiths and a silver owl brooch for my friend John Iles grand daughter's wedding and his great granddaughter on May 3rd 1997 at Cirencester Registary Office.

Monday 21st April 1997 – Mr Gerald Hartshorn picks me up in his car and also Mr Mervyn Bayliss of the Piece Bungalows, both of them workmen on the Hatherop Estate, and we drive to St Andrew's Church at Eastleach for Sir Thomas Bazley's funeral. Together with Mr Squires and Mr Tornay, the Smith-Woolley Estate agent, we walk to the church and sign our name in a book. Mr Arkell is there and others and we sit in the pews near the tower. The Reverend Robert Hughes took the service. I remember when his father, an author, courted his mother Miss Frances Bazley when she was in charge of us Wolf cubs and had our meetings in the lofts at the stables at Hatherop Castle. We ran all over Hatherop Castle grounds, any mess on the lawns or paths was soon cleared up by the gardeners. Some poems were read by the family and we sung 'For the Beauty of the Earth' and 'O God our Help in Ages Past'. I put a pound in the collection plate by the main door at the end of the service which was for the homeless and St Andrew's Church Building Fund. Saw Lady Henriette Abel Smith and Christopher Cadogen's daughter [*Catherine Cadogan*] outside after the service.

Thursday 24th April 1997 – Meet Reg Mustow of Coln St Aldwyns whose wife has a broken hip and cannot get about – he does all the cooking and cleaning. Reg said his brother Jesse has his legs bad and cannot get around. He farmed at Perrott's Brook till he retired. He is my age and captained Williamstrip Cricket Club for many years. Saw Bill Smith of Quenington who hurt his foot some time back and he can now drive his mini car again. Walk home, see three workmen repairing the roof of the old turbine and battery house for the Hatherop Castle. Mr Chaundy and Reg Butler from Hill-Upton's of Oxford used to lodge with mother when I was a boy at 45 Hatherop when they serviced the electric lights of Hatherop Castle. Mervyn Bayliss lodged with us at the same time he worked on the Hatherop Estate. They were great days for us all with the Independent Co-op at Coln St Aldwyns bringing all the bread, groceries, fish, coal, boots and clothes. Mr Manley and his daughter Miss Manley who saw to the boot and clothes section were the right people for the job. It was never the same when they left.

Sunday 27th April 1997 – Mr Cecil Voaden rings me up to say he will bring one of the new Fairford Silver Band jackets of the new set bought by Fairford Band for £100 apiece – military style, green with gold braid and one middle button. A very smart jacket.

Friday 2nd May 1997 – Get suit out get ready for the wedding of Sharon Belcher (Bert and Wendy Belcher's daughter) to Brian Large at Cirencester Registry Office tomorrow. Miss Janet Hobbs wrapped my gift of two bath towels complete with a blue ribbon and wrapper. I happen to have some fancy paper so it is a great job.

Saturday 3rd May 1997 – Mona comes to get my bread money and looks me over complete with pink carnation. The taxi calls at 11 o'clock and takes me to Cirencester Registry Office at the old Cirencester Hospital in an upstairs room – quite a ceremony and a lot of us there. Mr and Mrs John Iles from Wroughton whose granddaughter was getting married. The Registrar was a lady. I gave Natalie, the bride's daughter, a silver owl to pin to her dress for the wedding. A coach then took them to the Bell Hotel, Malmesbury. I went with the taxi and we had a good lunch, plenty of everything.

The wedding of Sharon Belcher to Brian Large. Brian and Sharon are centre with Natalie. Wendy and Bert Belcher are behind them in the middle and to the left. Reuben Sims is in the front, 2nd from the left with John and Rachel Iles behind him to the right.

John and Rachel Iles.

Sunday 4th May 1997 – Watched the TV. The Conservative Party was well and truly beaten in the election. The Socialists have a greater majority than 1945. So will have to see what changes will come around. The Tories were squabbling amongst themselves and the electorate went off them. They will have to start afresh as Mr Major has resigned.

Wednesday 14th May 1997 – 3.30am very short of breath. Come downstairs to use smelling salts. I understand now what people mean when they say they are short of breath, everything you go to do is all effort huff and puff. I had never experienced it before. I sweat violently, slowed me up – job to get up the stairs to bathroom. Sat down in armchair then at 9am ring the Fairford Surgery. Dr Griffiths will come to see me at 12 noon. I have never had a time like this before. A long morning in my armchair gasping for breath. The doctor comes at 12 noon and gives me some tablets for the liquid on my lungs. Elaine the lady next door saw the doctor, so Ian Patheyjohns and her went to the corner chemist and got my tablets. The other 2 pills helped my breath. Ian and his lady friend are good to me. Go to bed at 10.30pm not interested in anything on the TV. Have a better night – could breath.

May 15th 1997 – Ian throws gravel at bedroom window to get me up. I come down, he does my fire and I have more pills, indigestion better.

Tuesday 20th May 1997 – Mona drives me to Coln Stores to get my pension and buy stamps for fuel. Can only walk a short distance. The Rev Tony Ross calls to see me – Sally Worsley had told him I was ill. Manage to walk out and fill my bird bath in the evening. Have a good steak and kidney pie with Ian and Elaine in the evening. Watch the film of Victoria and Albert and then to bed. Cannot breathe laid down in bed get up at 4am and have another of these chest pills then go back to bed but still cannot breathe when I lay down so get up and write this at 5.30am in the living room.

Wednesday 21st May 1997 – Ring surgery and doctor will call after morning surgery. Doctor comes, gives me stronger tablets but said I must go into hospital. He gets hold of Elaine, my next door neighbour, and with Ian driving they take me to Cirencester Memorial Hospital where I am examined and put on a course of pills. I am very ill. Stay in hospital till 14th July. Looked after well – plenty of visitors. Elaine and Ian visited me every night, did my washing and looked after my house. They were a blessing to me.

July 14th 1997 – A fine morning, I am driven home by car with my belongings to start life anew. My home is spotless, my green house and flowers superb everything was lovely. Elaine and Ian were there to welcome me – how nice to be back at my own home. I was free. Stacks of mail over two months to sort out. Go to bed late and sleep in my well sprung bed – what a wonderful night.

July 15th 1997 – Walk round all my flowers and admire them. Mona came in but I did not want anything from Coln. She has been a good girl coming to see me in Cirencester.

Tuesday 22nd July 1997 – The ambulance calls for me at 9.30am to go to Cirencester Hospital for a check-up. We pick up other old people on the way. We get to the hospital and go to a different department with another batch of nurses who made me sit down and have a cup of tea. The patients were there with their sticks, one man was in his eighties. We had pop music blaring at us in the ambulance, all the way there and all the way back. I strolled round the small garden which has been created. Then we had lunch then another long wait till I saw the Doctor and Sister in a room having previously given my name and all my private conditions to another nurse in another room. It costs a hundred million a day to run our hospitals. The Doctor says I have had a stroke, must keep off the fats. Have a job to eat my food, cough a lot when I start eating. He says my muscles are gone in my throat and I have to wait until that rights itself. The Sister present says give up sausages, butter, no fried rashers and eggs at most once a week. Eat chicken and scrambled eggs. Have skimmed milk, eat more fruit, no sugar because I am diabetic. In the main I lose all the lovely things of life to live.

Saturday 26th July 1997 – Sally Worsley came and saw me – she has just come back from Russia. We had a good chat and she said "was I fit for a church service?" I said no, my throat and nose is not up to that. Will now have a scrambled egg tea.

Tuesday 29th July 1997 – The Cirencester Hospital Ambulance staff come to pick me up for the rehabilitation centre where we had tea or coffee and had lunch at 12 noon and then was received by the Doctor and Sister. They said I had made good progress from the stroke and would have me in, in six weeks time.

Thursday 31st July 1997 – The Rev Ross came at 11am and gave me Holy Communion. The first time I have had it at home.

Saturday 2nd Aug 1997 – Frank Blackwell cycled up from Fairford in the afternoon – we talked about electric scooters. I am thinking of buying one but am waiting till all my applications have come through.

Saturday 9th Aug 1997 – Walk to post box with a letter and see the new village seat put opposite the school in memory of Sir Thomas Bazley being chairman of the Parish Council for 60 years. The Silver Jubilee seat in memory of George V and Queen Mary (when we had a mug given to us in the old Reading Room and sports in the evening in the Grandage) has been taken away.

Wednesday 13th Aug 1997 – Mr Mervyn Bayliss came in the afternoon and told me the Service for the burial of Sir Thomas Bazley's ashes went off well. The Rev Ross gave a good address and there was a lunch after the service. Half of his ashes were buried under a tree at Eastleach Downs Farm and half by the side of his brother's grave in the churchyard family plot.

Tuesday 19th Aug 1997 – Have a visit from Sunrise and Medical – the electric scooter specialists. They show me the scooters they make and I tried a three-wheel scooter up Hatherop Hill with the operator standing on the side in one place to show the power. I decided I would buy a second hand one at £2,000 plus £49 insurance. They will contact me again about a fortnight's time. Hope I have done the right thing.

Sunday 31st Aug 1997 – Diana, Princess of Wales has been killed with others in a car driving at 12 o'clock last night in Paris. Great shock everywhere, she was so good with ordinary people and campaigned for control of land mines, went to Bosnia and other places and saw those crippled with land mines. Her brother spoke on TV from South Africa. She was thirty-six years old. TV full of Diana's accident all day long.

Friday 5th Sept 1997 – Stay in all day and watch the funeral of Diana Princess of Wales on TV – a very moving service in Westminster Abbey. Thousands of mourners out for two or three nights. Lovely singing with the choir boys, a good soprano singer and Elton John sang his song 'Candle in the Wind'. So different to our military state funerals. For the first time the Union Jack flew at half-mast at Buckingham Palace. The crowds were glad when the Queen came back from Balmoral – she spoke to the nation about Diana at six o'clock and that put the crowds in a better mood yesterday.

Tuesday 23rd Sept 1997 – A man with a van drives a scooter to me here at Golden Row. He has come from Sunrise Medical Ltd, Wollaston, West Midlands. I have been in consultation with them and have got this demonstration model come. If I get on with it I shall buy it – the price £2,000. Ian and Elaine come and we have a good look at it and I drive it around. It is in good condition so I buy it. It fits just right in the shed.

Wednesday 24th Sept 1997 – Drive scooter to Coln St Aldwyns with some letters to post. Ian walks with me as I ride scooter on pavement. Come home – lovely up the hill.

Monday 29th Sept 1997 – Drive scooter to Coln Stores and draw pension. Drive into Hatherop Castle Gardens – buy two hyacinth bulbs and an earthenware pot. See some of my friends and they have a good laugh with my 'scoota'.

Friday 17th Oct 1997 – Elaine takes me to Fairford Surgery behind the Eight Bells public house to see Dr Knight. I told him I was short of breath, he tested my heart, have to have more pills – my heart is weak.

Sunday 2nd November 1997 – I have not made a church service since I have been in Cirencester Hospital with heart trouble. Will try later now I have this electric scooter to get up the church path.

Reuben with his mobility scooter.

Thursday 27th November 1997 – Journey to Coln Stores in the afternoon to get Standard – see a thank you notice from the Miller family on the death of Reg Adams, husband of Ciss Miller who was a love child – cousin of my Uncle Jim Sims wife, Minnie Miller of Poulton. My Uncle Sims loaned them the money to buy the little house in Poulton. I suppose it will now be sold.

Friday 19th December 1997 – Fall over after turning off TV. Bruise my nose but sleep alright.

Saturday 20th December 1997 – Mona gets my bread and looks at my bruised nose but I said I feel alright.

Monday 22nd December 1997 – Ian and Elaine take me to the hospital with my bruised nose and lovely black eyes. The nurse said keep it dry and it will come right. Rev Ross comes for cottage Communion – says "What have you been doing?"

Wednesday 24th December 1997 – Christine Morley brings me a lovely tart – she makes wonderful pastry.

Thursday 25th December 1997 – Have a lovely Christmas at home. Ian and Elaine bring me in a wonderful lunch of turkey, carrots, Brussels sprouts, baked potatoes and stuffing. Have a good sleep in the chair afterwards.

Monday 29th December 1997 – See Bill Smith of Quenington at the Coln Stores – he drove his car to the stores for his pension then lost his keys. Bill is 86 years old – has a job getting up the steps to the shop. Found his keys outside so all is well but I must keep out of his way in that car!

Sunday 4th January 1998 – See film on TV – The Battle of Britain. I remember each day in the newspaper, The News Chronicle, on the front page it used to say how many Nazi planes were shot down. Lovely boys in the RAF – they stopped the invasion of this country. Sandbags and poles across all roads into villages. What good that would have done I don't know.

Sunday 11th January 1998 – Visit from Miss Hobbs with card and present. Have my birthday cards for 75 years in the window. Hon Mrs Cherry Malet brings a lovely red cyclamen and a bottle of ginger wine. At night Ian and Elaine came in – they had brought me a good cooked tea with peas, potatoes, roast lamb and gravy. I brought out a bottle of wine which I get from the wine club.

Saturday 24th January 1998 – Bill Brindle comes with a recorder and wireless set on his back – a heavy thing. He bought it for £15 – a real bargain. We place it on my electric organ and have the wireless with two speakers going and the tapes of a brass band.

Dennis Bartlett.

Sunday 25th January 1998 – Brother Dennis Bartlett together with his wife in their posh diesel car picked me up and drive to the Spotted Cow at Marston Meysey for a RAOB lunch. A long room at the Spotted Cow just right for twenty-one Buffs and their wives. Soup, beef, apple pie and ice cream. Did not want anything else today.

Monday 2nd February 1998 – Ted Peare of Lechlade came to see me and brought a newspaper that showed photographs of the Hanson plane that crashed into a German bomber and brought them both down out by Windrush. Ted can remember seeing the glow in the sky when they came out of Meysey Hampton public house one Sunday night. The Germans were buried with white crosses in Northleach churchyard with a plaque at Windrush. Now they wish to find the relatives of the Hanson pilot. We talked about the RAF plane that crashed into Homeleaze Farmhouse. Dennis Taylor, the farmhand, lived there then and the shock of the crash brought on his daughter's asthma.

Friday 13th February 1998 – Miss Hobbs rings me to tell me that Mrs Sorrel Taylor, who was private secretary to Sir Thomas Bazley, has died aged 97 years. She lived in old Ted Griffiths' house which she named the

Hatherop Fete Committee c. 1950 with Sorrel Taylor middle front row. Back row from left: Reuben Sims, Wynn ?, Kath Brindle, Dorothy Pollard, Annie Barnett, Dorothy Westall, Fanny Mustow, unknown, Mrs Sainsbury, Mrs Taylor of Homeleaze Farm, Jack Sainsbury, Keith Sainsbury, Robin Lowe, Desmond Westall, Basil Brooks. Sitting from left: unknown, Nurse Wearing, Rita Westall, Gillian Sainsbury, Sorrel Taylor, unknown, Derek Hartshorn, Vic Cox.

Quest House. Mrs George Mustow used to look after the house for her and it had a water flush lavatory when we tenants had soil buckets. My mother did not like going to the Reading Room every six months to pay rent to Mrs Taylor – she was very dominating and always of a superior complex. She left the Quest and lived with Mrs Money in her extension but she could not get on with Mrs Money so when the council bungalows near the Piece were being built, I think Sir Thomas Bazley helped her get the first one.

Friday 6th March 1998 – Had a rough night last night – lots of coughing, very short of breath. Come down about 4.30am and blow the Paediatric Volumatic – helps my breath. Listen to the radio 6am news. Do not want any Shredded Wheat. It takes me until 12 noon until I can walk around.

Wednesday 11th March 1998 – Picked up by a party from Coln St Aldwyns and driven to Appleton to the Whites Bell Foundry Shop which they say has been there 200 years. [*Whites of Appleton Ltd is the oldest continuously trading Bellhanging Company in the United Kingdom. It was founded in 1824 by Alfred White who became interested in the workings of bells following his instruction in the art of campanology in 1818 when the three bells at Appleton Church were recast into a Ring of six by Thomas Mears.*] See the Coln St Aldwyns church bells all re-hung in a new cast iron frame. Also the 1625 Five Minute Bell has been attended to. It is quite an impressive sight to see the new wood

Canon Tony Ross visiting the Coln St Aldwyns bells at Whites of Appleton Bell Foundry.

wheels, new sliders and new ball bearings. They are all ready now to have the frame cemented into the church tower. The bells have been tuned – I have never seen a sight like it and I never will again. I was so pleased to see the wheels in their cast iron frame painted blue. In about a fortnight the frame will be cemented in the tower. I will not be going up there but young John Reeves is training young people to ring the Hatherop bells so they will be right for Coln Church.

Friday 20th March 1998 – Not well, have a bad night – no sleep, lungs bad. Elaine came in – phoned for an appointment with the doctor in Fairford. We go down in her car. Dr Benjy gives me more tablets for my lungs.

Saturday 21st March 1998 – Have a better night. John and Rachel Iles call in the afternoon – they bring me some lovely tulips. Elaine and Ian bring me a cooked chicken from Tesco.

Friday 10th April 1998 – Drive scooter to Coln Stores. On the TV it said an agreement has been made with the politicians in Northern Ireland – a very historic occasion as so much trouble and deaths in the last thirty years.

Tuesday 14th April 1998 – The Rev Tony Ross draws up with his car at 11am. We hold Communion in my living room. He told me that he is going with 28 other parishioners to Israel tomorrow for a week. We talked about how, at the Roman Catholic Arundel, lots of communicants take their wafer in their hands like we do. We also cross ourselves like they do. The Rev Cowmeadow brought that sign to our parishes. Lots of things are being changed with our churches which is good.

Wednesday 22ndApril 1998 – Not very well. I had a bad night with my breath. I have been watching the airliners flying over Sharringtons. They tell me there was a lot of information about the first airship and the first plane on a door in the Hatherop Estate Gardens but it was cut up by Mr Doug Staples who worked in the castle.

Thursday 23rd April 1998 – Catch the Tesco Kingsmeadow bus. Do shopping at Tesco – buy some begonia plants. See Stan and Rose Bailey – have a pot of tea with them in the coffee shop. When we come out to get our bus it is raining well and quite cold for the ladies with their young children. At home I light the fire and have a sleep after I have put away my shopping. It is a wet evening.

This is the last entry in Reuben's diaries. He died of diabetes and heart disease on 18th May 1998 in Cirencester Hospital.

Reuben in Fairford Silver Band Uniform 1947.

Index

Numbers in ***bold italics*** denote photographs